4/08

SNIPERS, SHILLS, & SHARKS

SNIPERS, **S**HILLS, & **S**HARKS

eBay and Human Behavior

Ken Steiglitz

PRINCETON UNIVERSITY PRESS

PRINCETON AND OXFORD

Library of Congress Cataloging-in-Publication Data
Steiglitz, Kenneth, 1939–
Snipers, shills, and sharks : eBay and human behavior / Ken Steiglitz.
p. cm.
Includes bibliographical references and index.
ISBN-13: 978-0-691-12713-2 (alk. paper)
ISBN-10: 0-691-12713-1 (alk. paper)
1. Internet auctions. 2. Game theory. I. Title.
HF5478.S73 2007
381′.177015193—dc28   2006050389

British Library Cataloging-in-Publication Data is available

This book has been composed in Minion Typeface
Printed on acid-free paper. ∞
pup.princeton.edu

Printed in the United States of America

10 9 8 7 6 5 4 3 2 1

To San

CONTENTS

* Note: Sections providing mathematical background are indicated with an asterisk.
Skim these sections if you don't need the review.

PREFACE

THIS BOOK is about the way buyers and sellers behave in auctions, especially internet auctions like eBay. We'll discuss the empirical evidence showing how they *do* behave, the theory of how they *should* behave, and the continuing work towards understanding the very interesting differences. It is designed for two kinds of readers: the general reader, whom I picture as an active eBayer; and the student in an undergraduate course designed to cover the basic strategic ideas of auction theory and practice. No previous work in economics is required, and I've arranged it so the mathematics is optional. Read on.

To the General Reader

I was first drawn to the study of auctions by my addiction to ancient coin collecting. In the 1980s and early 1990s ancient coins were available to the collector of small means largely through mail-bid sales, usually run by entrepreneurs who were collectors themselves, and who distributed simple, often mimeographed and unillustrated catalogs every few months or so. In their wisdom, the dealers ran the sales as what are now called Vickrey auctions, that is, sealed-bid, second-price auctions. When eBay arrived, it opened up an astonishing supply of low-priced and interesting items from around the globe, and attracted a corresponding clientele of collectors, some experienced and some new to the field. A second addiction—eBay—joined my collecting habit, and, at the same time, I naturally became interested in auctions from a professional point of view as a computer scientist.

The buyer and seller behavior I observed was fascinating, and often puzzling. Some bidders bid early and often, some got in bidding wars, and some bid at the last second. Some sellers set opening bids of $0.01, some set enormous opening bids, some used inexplicable combinations of opening bids, secret reserves, and buy-it-now prices. The variety of behavior seemed endless. What forces were at play here, and how can the best thinking of economists help us understand them? These questions led me naturally to start a course on auctions, and this book grew from my course notes.

I was determined to keep the focus on observed behavior and the practical questions that arise constantly on eBay, and to combat a tendency to dwell on the mathematics. I therefore decided to write the main text with no mathematics at all; it contains, literally, no equations. However, I also wanted to give the general reader the option of working through the mathematical theory when it suited her. So for those who have some freshman calculus, I set down the elements of the most basic theory in three appendices. This gave me the luxury of invoking important results whenever I needed them, quite informally, but with the authentic mathematics close at hand for those who want to follow it, either on first reading or later. In the same way, I summarize the important results from the work in laboratory experiments with auctions in a fourth appendix, and refer to it at various points when it bears on behavioral questions. On the other hand, I discuss in the main text the recent and exciting empirical work based on eBay itself.

Most of all, I hope this book contributes to the reader's enjoyment of the auction as a living, evolving institution, adapting to diverse environments: the tense uptown auction room, the friendly charity bazaar, the high-speed flower market, and, of course, the internet. Especially the internet, where the fierce and finely tuned eBay has enriched the lives of many people, from the thrifty small-timer turning some attic congestion into cash, to the full-time businessperson, to the eBayer so close to my heart, the obsessed collector.

To Students and Course Instructors

As mentioned above, this book can serve as a text for an introductory course in auctions. It emphasizes the importance of behavior, and uses the lively and familiar venue of eBay for its motivation and examples. What are these millions of people doing and thinking as they buy and sell the dizzying array of items every day on eBay?

The main text has no formal mathematics at all, no equations, no theorems, no proofs, and the main results of auction theory are stated and used in intuitive form. To see what the theory is like "under the hood," the appendix contains three chapters that cover the main results of auction theory and prove them. The scope is limited to the optimal auctions of Riley and Samuelson for symmetric bidders with independent private values, and the corresponding generalization to asymmetric bidders by Myerson. The generalization of Milgrom and Weber to affiliated values is described briefly, as well as the very pretty application of Bulow and Klemperer showing that one extra bidder is worth more than arbitrary negotiating power. The elegant treatment of the theory by Krishna (2002) is a perfect source for more mathematical depth and breadth of coverage when needed.

The background of the clientele will determine how much of this mathematical theory can be covered in detail, but I've found that the main ideas can be introduced naturally on an intuitive level, and the mathematics introduced gradually over a semester. When the students have a good working knowledge of freshman calculus, it should be possible to cover all of appendices A–C. This will provide an introduction to most of the central ideas of auction theory: dominance, strategic equivalence, private values, equilibrium bidding, bid shading, revenue equivalence, risk aversion, common values, affiliated values, the winner's curse, and the linkage principle.

A fourth appendix summarizes the literature in controlled laboratory experiments. When published field experiments are used, they are described in the main text. I also include the results of some of my own classroom experiments, anecdotally, for concreteness.

Synopsis

The first chapter gives a brief history of auctions in general, drawing on my own particular mania, ancient coins, for some examples of pre-eBay mail-bid sales. I then introduce the four standard auction forms, English, Vickrey, Dutch, and first-price, as well as the ideas of dominance and strategic equivalence.

Chapter 2 shows how eBay can be considered the logical result of mail-bid sales moving to the internet.

Chapter 3 is a survey of eBay behavior observed, with plots showing actual bidding histories for real items on eBay. Commonly observed strategies are identified and discussed, but with only passing reference to the theory.

Chapter 4 poses the question: What if eBay were first-price? This is the most common question a newcomer asks, and leads to showing how the independent private value theory works in prescribing bid shading, and also introduces the concepts of equilibrium and revenue equivalence. I argue informally that eBay is second-price instead of first-price for a good reason: the first-price format discourages early bidding more, and early bidding is both profitable for the seller and fun for the buyer. Attracting bidders and bids is paramount.

Chapter 5 examines the seller's problem in choosing reserves, both open and secret. This brings in, in a natural way, the linkage principle, and Milgrom and Weber's principle of full disclosure. Once again, I argue that bidder entry is critical.

In chapter 6, I return to the central problem faced by the buyer: how much to bid. I first examine critically the basic scaffolding of auction theory: the idealizations of fixed (if uncertain or interdependent) valuations, equilibrium behavior, and the ideal actor, *Homo economicus*. I then give several important examples of overbidding and out-of-equilibrium behavior in the empirical literature, including the winner's curse, overbidding in the experimental laboratory, and empirical failures of revenue equivalence. Two model adjustments are then introduced that are aimed at reconciling this behavior with theory: risk aversion and spite. I then draw some general lessons for eBay buyers and sellers. The chapter concludes with some discussion of price wars, frenzies, and bubbles, important and little understood phenomena in a broad range of markets beyond eBay.

In chapter 7, the last, we look at the seamy side of auctions. We now see cheaters taking advantage of the fact that competition plays such an important role in determining price. Bidders can decrease competition by colluding; sellers can increase competition by using shills. I finish with some discussion of other kinds of cheating and near-cheating, like knowingly selling fakes, withholding information, or misrepresenting items.

The appendices can stand alone as an introduction to basic auction theory, together with a summary of published empirical work in the laboratory. When a topic in the main text is repeated here, it will be treated more mathematically. You can think of chapters 1–3, chapters 4–7, and appendices A–D as three progressive stages leading from anecdotal description to the auction literature.

ACKNOWLEDGMENTS

IN PUTTING TOGETHER this book I accumulated debts to many individuals. Above all, I want to thank John Morgan, Haas School of Business, Berkeley, who helped me get started learning something of auction theory, pointed me to the really classic papers, and cotaught an early version of a course based on this material. He taught me, among many other things, that running economics experiments in class is at the same time sobering and fun.

For help of all sorts, I also thank Andrew Appel, Orley Ashenfelter, Peter Bogucki, Dan Clark, David Dobkin, Edith Elkind, Jack Gelfand, Kathryn Graddy, George Reis, Frank S. Robinson, Amit Sahai, Bob Sedgewick, Bonnie Steiglitz, Sandy Steiglitz, Glen Weyl, and Fengzhou Zheng.

Finally, a warm thanks to Peter Dougherty at the Princeton University Press for his early encouragement and advice, and, for their expert care, editor Tim Sullivan, production editor Debbie Tegarden, and copy editor and cellist extraordinaire Jodi Beder.

SNIPERS, SHILLS, & SHARKS

English and Vickrey Auctions

*I describe a bit of the history of auctions, the two pairs
of standard auction forms, and the ideas of dominance
and strategic equivalence.*

1.1 Auctions

IT IS HARD to imagine modern civilization without buying and selling,
which make possible the division of labor and its consequent wealth
(Smith, 1776). For many common and relatively inexpensive commodities, the usual and convenient practice at the retail level, in the West
anyway, is simply for the seller to post a take-it-or-leave-it price, and
for the prospective buyer to choose what to buy and where to buy it,
perhaps shopping for favorable prices. I haven't tried haggling over
price at a Wal-Mart, but I can't imagine it would get me very far.
For some big-ticket items, however, like houses and cars, haggling and
counteroffers are expected, even in polite society, and bargaining can be
extended over many rounds. In some cultures, haggling is the rule for
almost all purchases.

A third possibility, our subject here, is the auction, where many
prospective buyers compete for the opportunity to purchase items,
either simultaneously, or over an extended period of time. The main
attraction of the auction is that it can be used to sell things with
more or less uncertain market value, like a tractor in a farmer's estate,
a manufacturer's overrun of shampoo, or the final working copy of
Beethoven's score for his Ninth Symphony (see fig. 1.1). It thus promises
to fetch as high a price as possible for the seller, while at the same
time offering to the buyer the prospect of buying items at bargain
prices, or perhaps buying items that would be difficult to buy in any
other way. When there is one seller, the auction is sometimes qualified
as a *single* or *one-sided* auction, to distinguish it from a *double* or
two-sided auction, where there are many sellers (and by implication

1

Figure 1.1 Sotheby's auctioneer Roger Griffiths (left), conducting the auction of the working manuscript of Beethoven's Ninth Symphony (right), which realized £2.1 million ($3.4 million) in London, Thursday May 22, 2003. (AP/Wide World Photos, Edmond Terakopian photographer)

multiple items) as well as many buyers. A familiar example of the latter is a stock exchange.

The kind of sale where many sellers compete for the business of one buyer is called a *reverse auction*. In many respects the reverse auction is equivalent to the usual auction, with one seller and many buyers. This situation arises, for example, when we ask competing painters for bids to paint our house. We will concentrate almost entirely on auctions with one seller and many buyers, the usual kind of single auction.

The seller in an auction is faced with many choices. He[1] usually sets the rules, and he must therefore decide what kind of auction to hold. For

---

[1] I will adopt the convention, common in the auction literature, that the first mentioned and subsequent odd-numbered buyers are female, and even-numbered buyers are male; for contrast, the first (and usually only) seller will be male. Or at least I will try to do so when it isn't confusing or distracting.

example, does the bidder indicate her bid in a public venue by raising a numbered paddle in assent to bids solicited orally by an auctioneer (an *English* auction); does she submit her bid privately to a *sealed-bid* auction in which the winner pays her bid; or the next-highest bid; or does the seller announce descending prices and sell to the first buyer signaling that she is willing to buy (a *Dutch*[2] auction)? The seller must also then decide on any reserves, minimum opening bids, commissions, minimum bidding increments (ticks), time limits, and so on. Usually the seller's goal is to maximize his revenue, but other considerations may enter the picture, especially those that might affect reputation and future sales. For example, he may be faced with the problem of deciding on the order in which to place several similar items on the block. He might even be interested in who wins what item.

The bidder is faced with different questions, the most obvious of which are how much to bid and when. There are also what we might call "externalities" involving other bidders and future sales. Will there be other opportunities to buy a similar item? Is resale of the item a consideration? Does it matter to the bidder which rival might win and what he might pay? Typically these questions are complex and involve the interaction of different parties' strategies.

Auctions have been widely used in recent times on a large scale for selling such things as bonds, electromagnetic spectrum, oil and timber rights, and surplus commodities, usually involving businesses and the government, but not the average consumer. However, the widespread use of the internet, and especially eBay, has greatly increased the participation of the general public. This growing interest in auctions has attracted the attention of economists, of course, but more recently has also interested computer scientists, who see the auction not only as a means of trade, but with a somewhat different coloring as an algorithm for allocating resources, especially on the internet. The rapidly growing literature is trying to provide useful answers to the kinds of questions raised above: What kinds of auctions are best for which

---

[2] Caution! Throughout the auction literature a Dutch auction is exactly this, a descending clock auction, and we will stick to this usage. But on eBay, the term means a sale where multiple copies of an item are available, something utterly different. I have no idea why eBay chose to commandeer the term, but their usage sometimes confuses students, and might even change the standard terminology.

applications? How should bidders choose their bidding strategies? How do bidders actually behave in real auctions? How do auctions compare to alternative mechanisms? Researchers usually put the study of all these questions under the general rubric of "auction theory," even though it often involves the examination of empirical and experimental evidence as well as strictly mathematical theory.

Auction theory proper began with the extraordinarily insightful paper of Vickrey in 1961. As groundbreaking and influential as this paper is, it doesn't require any advanced mathematics—all that is really needed is freshman calculus. In fact, much of Vickrey's paper can be appreciated with no mathematics at all, and you might enjoy reading such a classic. It took a while for economists to digest Vickrey's ideas, and the field of auction theory didn't really flower until the 1980s, a surprisingly late date in the history of science in general. It seems that the whole field had to wait for the development of game theory in the 1950s, and especially the remarkably powerful concept of the *Nash equilibrium*. This work has led to the construction of a mathematical framework within which human behavior is neatly characterized, and which serves at least as a starting point for the study of real behavior.

While the development of auction theory has been a long time coming compared with the physical sciences, the development of *experimental* economics has been even slower. Theory does not play the same role in understanding auctions as, say, physics does in predicting the trajectory of a planet. In the latter situation, we can gather enough data—the position of Mars at different times, say—to predict with great precision, using Newton's laws of motion, where it will be at future times. If Jupiter or an asteroid affects the orbit of Mars, well, we can take that into account also, achieving greater and greater precision in our predictions. On the other hand, we can expect no such convergent exactitude in auction theory, which is, after all, a social science. The situation is further complicated by the fact that some participants in auctions read books about auction theory.[3] Despite the difficulties, an active segment of the research community, in admirable scientific

---

[3] The self-referential nature of auction theory (and all social sciences like economics) is always a problem, but also makes life more interesting.

style, gathers data and studies its reconciliation with current theory. Generally, we can classify this empirical literature into three categories:

- Laboratory experiments, in which experimental subjects are enlisted to participate in more or less realistic auctions;
- Passive collection of real data from real auctions, greatly facilitated by the internet;
- Field experiments, in which the investigator sells or buys real items in a real auction.

Despite the relatively late arrival of auction theory as a scientific discipline, auctions themselves have existed for at least a couple of thousand years, and we begin with a bit of their history.

1.2 A Brief History

I will rely on Cassady's 1967 book, *Auctions and Auctioneering*, for our early history. He traveled the world studying auctions, especially those for fish, which need to be marketed and distributed quickly and regularly. His book, although not quantitative or mathematical at all, is a valuable compendium of sharply and carefully observed details of the auction process, from all angles, and across many cultures, as it existed before the internet. It still makes enlightening reading.

Auctions were conducted at least as early as 500 B.C., when women were sold in ancient Babylon—on condition that they be wed.[4] By Roman times, auctions were evidently well established, being conducted in their own special building (the *atrium auctionarium*). There isn't much known about exactly how these auctions were conducted, but as Cassady points out, the fact that the word "auction" is derived from the Latin word *auctus*, an increase, suggests that these were ascending-price auctions, which, when conducted openly with a congregation of bidders, are now called *English* auctions.

One infamous auction during Roman times is described by Edward Gibbon in his *Decline and Fall of the Roman Empire* (1776). When the

---

[4] With this condition, undesirable women were sold in return for payment of dowries, to the lowest bidder, thus providing an early example of a *reverse* auction (see question 2).

Figure 1.2 Bronze sestertius of Didius Julianus, high bidder for the Roman Empire in 193 A.D. (Classical Numismatic Group, Inc.)

Praetorian Guard killed the Roman emperor Pertinax on March 28, 193 A.D., they sold the Roman Empire itself to the highest bidder, the wealthy senator Didius Julianus, who "rose at once to the sum of six thousand two hundred and fifty drachms, or upwards of two hundred pounds sterling" per man (Gibbon, 1776).[5] The new emperor lasted only two months, but did manage to strike some very handsome coins (see fig. 1.2 and question 3).

Auction houses were common in England in the late 1600s, selling paintings and ships, for example, although it is not necessarily the case that these were conducted as "English" auctions. The firms of Sotheby's and Christie's, now well known as prestigious auction houses, were

---

[5] An example of "jump bidding" in the second century, about which, more below.

founded in 1744 and 1766, respectively. The institution of auctions naturally migrated to America, where Cassady reports that they were often used to unload leftover inventory, and were usually regarded as discreditable proceedings. This spectrum of auction ware, ranging from the dregs to the most coveted items, continues to his day. Perhaps the most well known—and odious—early auctions in America entailed the sale of slaves. Here, it seems that some form of the familiar English auction was used.

Auctions of fruits and vegetables became established in the Netherlands around 1880, and grew to a vast system of markets for horticultural goods, associated today especially with tulips, mainly because of the phenomenon of "tulipmania" reported so vividly by Charles Mackay (1841).[6] About the same time, the selling of fish by auction became important in Germany. What is critical here is the fact that fish must be sold fast!

Ancient coins,[7] stamps, and similar collectible items and *objets d'art* were sold by regularly established auction houses by the late 1800s, and the important sales were usually accompanied by nicely produced and illustrated catalogs, many of which are still used as references today. Glossy auction catalogs began to include invitations for bidding by mail, to allow potential buyers to compete even if they could not attend the sale or send a representative. The rules here are often vague, but seem to suggest that the auctioneer will treat the mail bid as a limit, and bid for the mail bidder at appropriate points in the sale.[8] No later than the 1870s (Lucking-Reiley, 2000b), auctions developed that were conducted entirely by mail, and the rules for these were often spelled out in some detail, although ambiguity in stating the exact rules for auctions is always a potential problem for the bidders (and perhaps a profitable strategy for sellers). We will discuss mail-bid sales more later on; they fall in the category of *sealed-bid* auctions— that is, auctions in which each bidder's bid is submitted to the seller privately.

---

[6] We'll return this classic example of a price bubble in chapter 6.

[7] I will often draw on ancient coins for examples of collectibles commonly sold by auction.

[8] Cassady (1967, pp. 152ff) discusses this practice in some detail, calling the bids for absentees "book bids."

This brings us to the present day. The internet is spectacularly well suited for conducting auctions, because it allows an enormous number of potential bidders and sellers to be put in fast communication at very small cost. It was therefore inevitable that internet auctions became important—but it was not so easy to see that one auction site (eBay of course) would come to dominate all others by a wide margin.[9] In retrospect, it seems obvious that an early capture of market share is self-reenforcing. Once a venue is established that attracts buyers who know and trust the process, it attracts sellers, then more buyers, and on it goes. At this point, eBay seems to have a lock on many of the important auction markets, especially collectibles. The rules of eBay and how they are especially suited to the internet environment will be one of our recurring themes.

1.3 English Auctions

Consider now the most common kind of auction before the internet, the *English* auction. An auctioneer stands on a raised dais and asks for bids (figs. 1.1 and 1.3),[10] "What am I offered for this important van Gogh portrait?" "One million, one million, do I hear one million and one hundred thousand?" The requests for bids are interspersed with patter praising the virtues of the item in more or less colorful terms. When no one is willing to meet the next requested level, we hear the inevitable, "Going, going, . . . gone!" and the gavel falls to signal the close of the sale.[11] How are we to think of this process in quantitative terms? How can we decide what constitutes a good strategy for buyers or sellers?

It turns out that our intuition usually serves us well when bidding in an English auction. Consider the thought processes involved during the bidding. Somehow we have in mind, either explicitly or more or

---

[9] Japan and China, however, are significant exceptions. See question 5.

[10] Bids in an English auction can be indicated to the auctioneer in many ways, such as raising a paddle, raising a hand, or just nodding. Sometimes bids come in the form of prearranged signals that can be so complex that the auctioneer loses track of who is bidding what. Cassady (1967) has an amusing and instructive discussion of complicated and confused signaling and why bidders may be anxious to hide their identity.

[11] Thus, the final price achieved at auction is sometimes called the "hammer" price.

Figure 1.3 "Christie's Auction Room," drawn and engraved by A. Pugin and T. Rowlandson, aquatint by J. Bluck, from *The Microcosm of London*, R. Ackermann, London, 1808. Compare this with figure 1.1. Very little has changed in this kind of auction for at least two hundred years. (Christie's Images Ltd.)

less vaguely, the highest amount we might be willing to pay for the item. We call this our *value*, or, sometimes, interchangeably, *valuation*. If the bidding level is below our valuation and we are not the highest bidder, we bid up a small amount from the current level. Usually, there is a minimum increment demanded by the auctioneer, to speed up the process. We stop either when the competition drops out when our own bid is the highest, or when the bidding level exceeds our valuation. Simply put, we bid up, gradually, to the most we are willing to pay, and no higher. We call such a strategy *truthful* or *sincere* bidding because we drop out at our true value.

So much for the rational story, but there are already important problems with this picture of human behavior. This model assumes, first of all, that we are certain of our valuation to begin with, and that we don't change it during the bidding. We call this the *private-value* assumption. The model also assumes that we care only about getting the item as cheaply as possible, without regard to who else might win it. These assumptions are not necessarily true. In practice, we may have only a vague idea of what our valuation might be, and even if we do have a specific value in mind, we may be very prone to change it as we see how the bidding goes. We may also be anxious to keep the item out of the hands of certain rival bidders. A perfect example of the last motive is provided by a *Seinfeld* [12] episode in which the character Elaine is asked by her boss to act as an agent to bid on a set of golf clubs once owned by President John F. Kennedy. She is given explicit instructions not to bid more than $10,000, which is therefore her valuation. But she gets in a bidding war with an irritating acquaintance, and runs the bidding up to $20,000.

1.4 Variations on the English Theme

There are actually several ways in which an English auction can be conducted, as pointed out by Milgrom and Weber (1982). Up to now I have been blurring the distinctions, but now it is important that I describe in detail the two main variations of English auctions as they occur in practice, and a third version that is a simple and clear abstraction widely adopted in the theoretical literature. The seemingly minor differences in rules can mean big differences in bidding behavior.

- *The ascending-price English auction.* We have already described the usual picture, in which the auctioneer orally solicits bids in small increments from the bidders, who indicate their willingness to meet a price with a wave of a paddle, or a nod of the head, or some other, perhaps very subtle, signal. What is important in this model is, first, that bidders can hide their identity by using such subtle bidding moves. Second, *jump bids*—bids above the level being solicited by the auctioneer—are not allowed.

---

[12] For those visiting from another planet, a popular TV sitcom which aired first-run from 1989 to 1998, but which is often shown as a syndicated rerun. This particular episode is titled "The Bottle Deposit," and was first aired May 2, 1996 (season 7).

- *The English outcry auction.* An alternative is the English outcry auction, in which bidders call out their bids, or at least are allowed to do so, destroying any possibility of anonymity. Note that this allows *jump bidding*, the real difference between the outcry and ascending-price English auctions. In some English auctions, such as those you might find at local flea markets, for example, jump bidding is not explicitly forbidden, but is just not customary. These outcry auctions thus become ascending-price English auctions de facto. What matters in English auctions in general, and in many other kinds of auctions, are the kinds of signals that bidders can send to competitors with their bidding.

- *The Japanese button auction.* A third version of the English auction is described by Cassady (1967) as being used in Japan. In this variation, the current price level is displayed to the bidders on an ascending electronic clock. Each buyer has a button, and keeps her finger on it until a level is reached at which she wishes to drop out, at which point she (irrevocably) releases her button. At any given time, there are two important pieces of information available to bidders: the current price level, and the fact that the clock is still moving and there are therefore two or more bidders still pressing their buttons. When only one bidder is left pressing a button, the price clock stops and the auction is over. Milgrom and Weber (1982) in fact reserve the term "English auction" for this kind of auction, but with this additional assumption: Bidders are aware of who drops out, and when, and therefore know at any time exactly how many bidders are active. We will call Milgrom and Weber's model the *Japanese button auction.*[13] This form of English auction is very popular among theorists, who like it, I suspect, because

[13] Do not confuse this with the "Japanese simultaneous-bidding system," which is also described by Cassady, but which is quite different. In this latter kind of auction, used in the Greater Tokyo fish markets, at least when Cassady was writing in 1967, all bids are made simultaneously using hand signals. According to Cassady (p. 64), "The bidding starts as soon as the auctioneer gives the signal, and the highest bidder, as determined by the auctioneer, is awarded the lot." Complications arise when bidders try to raise their bids after seeing those of others, and Cassady discusses some of the action: "The confusion calls to mind the frenzied trading by brokers in the stock market, except that there is only one auctioneer in the simultaneous-bidding system."

it enables them to make certain precise mathematical statements and prove certain theorems. But in actual fact it is not very common, at least in the West, and the information about the number of active bidders is usually not accessible.[14]

You can also use another, equivalent picture: an auctioneer calls out ascending prices with small increments and bidders indicate their willingness to pay the current price by keeping their hands raised. When any bidder lowers her hand it means she is no longer interested, and the item is sold to the last bidder with her hand raised, at the price at which the next-to-last bidder dropped out (Krishna, 2002). Everyone can see everyone else's hands, and changing your mind (reentry) is not allowed.

Throughout this book I'll indicate, when it matters, which model we are using for an English auction. As I've mentioned, economists especially like the Japanese button auction because the model allows them to prove things that are not generally true for the other forms. This is not an altogether corrupt activity: it gives us a chance to develop insight and intuition by developing the theory, and is not dangerous or deceptive unless we forget our assumptions, or, for that matter, the usual gap between theory and real behavior in the first place. We'll next consider bidding strategies in the Japanese button version of the English auction, and see how the model, while somewhat unrealistic, enables us to introduce some very important ideas.

1.5 Truthful Bidding Is Dominant in (Japanese Button) English Auctions

Now return to the theoretical setting in which we accept completely the model in which bidders have a definite valuation for the item under auction—have private values. In this world the very simple and intuitively clear strategy just described in section 1.3—bidding gradually up to your value but no higher—is optimal in a very important way: it is at least as good as any other strategy, *no matter how other bidders bid.*

[14] It is certainly true that the number of potential competitors for an item on eBay is both interesting to the bidder, and unknown.

To see this, we first need to be clear about the criterion for judging strategies. Define your *surplus* as the difference between your valuation and the price you pay: valuation minus price. For example, if you place a value of $100 on a coin and you manage to buy it, when the smoke clears, at $75, you have earned a surplus of $25. Ordinarily, we might say that your goal is to get the coin "as cheaply as possible." But now we will use terminology that is a bit more formal: we assume that your goal is to choose a strategy that *maximizes your surplus.*

We can now say something precise and important about the strategy of truthful bidding in the button auction. Continuing with the example, if you stop bidding (by taking your finger off your button) when the current price is less than $100, you can only miss an opportunity to gain some positive surplus. Keeping your finger on your button keeps alive the chance of gaining surplus, and as much surplus as possible. On the other hand, if you stay in the auction past $100, you risk winning and paying more than your value, thereby earning a negative surplus— that is, losing surplus. Thus, the strategy of truthful bidding, which in this kind of auction means taking your finger off your button precisely at the point when the bidding reaches your value, is no worse than any alternative. In such cases we say that the strategy is *dominant.* The qualified term "weakly dominant" is sometimes used, because there is no guarantee that the strategy is always *strictly* better than any alternative. When we can find a dominant strategy, we have effectively answered the most important question about an auction.

Be sure you understand the argument in the preceding paragraph with crystal clarity. It is one of the most important and beautiful ideas in auction theory. Vickrey introduced it in his famous 1961 paper in connection with sealed-bid auctions, which we will discuss in the next section. But first I should explain why sincere bidding is *not* a dominant strategy in the English outcry or ascending-price auctions.

Remember that a strategy is (weakly) dominant if no strategy is better, regardless of how rival bidders bid. Well, in the Japanese button version of the English auction, there is no way that the actions of a rival can affect the fact that dropping out short of your value or staying in past your value can only decrease surplus. Our rival is constrained by the rules, as you are, of either acquiescing to the current bid level by keeping his finger on his button, or releasing it irrevocably. The imaginary price clock goes up smoothly (ignoring the bidding increments, which we assume are tiny), and no matter when your rivals do or don't drop out, you should simply stay in the bidding until your value is reached, and then drop out yourself.

But now suppose you are in an English *outcry* auction, where jump bids are allowed. You attach a value of $1000 to the item. Suppose now that a rival bidder is a bit crazy, and hates the prices between $100 and $200. He adopts the strategy of jump bidding to $10,000 if there are bids in this range. If you follow the bidding up to some price between $100 and $200, you will trigger this weird response, and miss the opportunity to buy the item. So what should you do? Clearly, you should jump-bid past this range when you get to it, preserving the opportunity to buy below your $1000 valuation. Such a jump is not consistent with the prescription of gradual increments in sincere bidding, and thus sincere bidding is not dominant in the outcry auction. This argument does require your rival to behave in a daffy way, but remember that dominance is a very strong notion: your strategy of sincere bidding must be bulletproof; it must be at least as good as any other strategy regardless of what your rivals do, daffy or not.

In the ascending-price English auction, your early actions can still send signals to other bidders. For example, in the early bidding you can either sit on your hands or bid. These variations in behavior, while more subtle than jump bidding, can still, conceivably, affect the behavior of rival bidders, as in the outcry auction with jump bids. The same reasoning as in the jump-bidding case shows that sincere bidding in the ascending-price version of the English auction is also not dominant.

1.6 Sealed-Bid Second-Price (Vickrey) Auctions

Now let's return to the mail-bid sales mentioned earlier.[15] Suppose we want to auction off an item, say a coin illustrated in a catalog, by mail. How might we emulate the conditions of an English auction?

---

[15] The term "sale" is often used instead of "auction" when bids are collected solely by mail. The reason seems traceable to the fact that "auctions" are subject to legal regulation and require licensing of the auctioneer (Lucking-Reiley, 2000b).

Well, when does the bidding stop in an English auction? Assuming that bidders are bidding sincerely, this happens precisely when no one is willing to pay more than the current high bid, which means that the high bidder wins the item, at a price equal to the *second-highest* valuation among the bidders. Based on this observation—a key point in Vickrey's 1961 paper—we can emulate an English auction as a sealed-bid sale, say a mail-bid sale, in the following way. Bidders independently mail in their bids to the seller. The seller then awards the item to the highest bidder, *who pays the second-highest bid.* This second-highest bid is conventionally called the *second price,* and such auctions are called *second-price* auctions. We will use the term *second-price sealed-bid auction* (or, interchangeably, *Vickrey auction*) to mean the simplest possible implementation of the form, with no conditions, reserves, or embellishments: bidders submit sealed bids, and the seller awards the item.[16]

How, then, should you behave in this emulation of an English auction? It should come as no surprise that you should emulate truthful bidding: you should submit a bid *exactly equal* to your value. The argument is the same as that for truthful bidding in the English auction: If you submit a bid less than your value, you can only miss an opportunity to pick up some surplus; and if you submit a bid greater than your value, you risk losing surplus in the case when you win and the second-highest bidder has also bid above your value. Thus, truthful bidding is a dominant strategy in the Vickrey auction as well as the Japanese button auction—optimal regardless of others' strategies. As Vickrey also points out, a great advantage of second-price auctions follows from the fact that a bidder need only know her value to decide how to bid; there is no calculation necessary, no incentive to bid other than truthfully.

In practice, the winner of a second-price auction is usually required to pay a bit more than the second-highest bid, by a small amount that represents the tick, the increment in bidding that would take place were the sale conducted orally as an English auction. Mail-bid sales often

---

[16] Lucking-Reiley's (2000b) history of stamp auctions shows that Vickrey was not the first to think of the form, although this is not to downplay Vickrey's important role in essentially beginning the game-theoretic analysis of auctions.

use a fixed value for the tick of 5–10%, although a sliding scale is also used.

As mentioned before, conventional English floor auctions often invite book bids—bids submitted by mail or privately in advance of the actual floor auction. Such a mechanism represents a marriage of English and Vickrey auctions. Here is an example of "Instructions for Mail Bidders" from the catalog of a prestigious sale of ancient coins by Numismatic Fine Arts, Inc.:

> Bid what you feel the lot is worth to you. Your bids will be executed by Numismatic Fine Arts, Incorporated. The lots will be awarded to the highest bidder at a price based on an increment of 5% over the next highest bid. Thus, even if your mail bid is 40% higher than the next highest bid, you will buy the lot for only 5% over the underbidder.[17]

This advice closely foreshadows eBay's advice for what they call "proxy bidding" (as we will see in section 3.2), reflecting eBay's natural ancestry.

1.7 Mail-Bid Auctions

From my own experience, second-price mail-bid sales of ancient coins were common at least from the 1970s to the advent of the internet and eBay.[18] Lucking-Reiley (2000b) traces mail-bid sales for stamps back to the 1870s, and reports that the earliest second-price mail-bid stamp sale he was able to find was run in 1893. These sales had the advantage of reaching a very select clientele with a large number of items at one time. In the case of ancient coins, as many as several hundred could be included in one list, often with photographs. In fact, the length of the lists was often determined by the breakpoints in the postal rates. Such a business could be very labor intensive, involving

---

[17] Auction II, March 25–26, 1976, Beverly Hills, CA. This is an example of the well-documented and beautifully produced auction catalogs that are of lasting value to the general art and antique community.

[18] I thank the Reverend Daniel C. Clark for some history of mail-bid sales of ancient coins.

research, photography, list preparation and production, mailing of the lists, processing of payments, and mailing of the items. Except for a few professional dealers, specializing in high-end material, the enterprise was often a labor of love. But mail-bid auctions served to bring together very narrow segments of collector populations with corresponding dealers, and were good examples of nearly ideal Vickrey auctions. They also anticipate eBay, which is, intentionally or not, a very logical development as an adaptation of the mail-bid sale to the real-time environment of the internet. We will pick this thread up in the next chapter, but we conclude this chapter with a quick discussion of the relationship between English and Vickrey auctions, and between their two natural first-price counterparts.

1.8 Weak Strategic Equivalence of (Japanese Button) English and Vickrey Auctions

The Japanese button English and Vickrey auctions are equivalent in the following sense. If we adopt the private-value model (where every bidder is certain of her value), then truthful bidding is dominant in both forms. That is, it is a dominant strategy for a bidder to remain in the bidding up to, but not past, her value in the English auction, and to submit her true value in the Vickrey auction. It is clear that the outcomes of the two forms will then be identical; the same bidder will win the object and pay the same price, and therefore the revenue to the seller will also be the same. In this sense, and in this sense only, we can say that the Japanese button English and Vickrey forms are equivalent, but the statement must be qualified by saying they are *weakly strategically equivalent*.

The reason for the qualification "weakly" is this. Information becomes available to the bidders during the conduct of the English auction, information that is never available to the bidders in a Vickrey auction. In particular, in the Japanese button auction, bidders know when rival bidders drop out. English bidders can incorporate such newly arriving information into their strategies, while the Vickrey bidders cannot. Thus, the two kinds of auctions can easily lead to different outcomes in practice, and are strategically equivalent only in the weak sense described here.

This is far from just a technical point. In practice, bidders may very well behave quite differently in an English auction, typically getting carried away in a war, as Elaine did in the Seinfeld auction of John F. Kennedy's golf clubs. It's also quite possible that they become intimidated by a jump bid, which is its psychological purpose. For example, in the Seinfeld auction, the auctioneer got only the bids he asked for—up to the point when Elaine owned the high bid of $6500. The auctioneer then called, "Do I hear $6600? The president's own golf clubs. Leisure life at Camelot. . . . $6500 going once . . . ," at which point Elaine's nemesis, Sue Ellen Mishky, raised her paddle and orally bid $8000. This jump bid, in this fictitious but very plausible scenario, did the very opposite of intimidating Elaine. Gibbon's description of Didius Julianus rising "at once to the sum of . . . " suggests that Didius's bid was also a jump bid, perhaps the earliest ever recorded. We will return to jump bidding when we discuss eBay strategies in chapter 3.

1.9 The Four Standard Auctions and Why They Are Two Pairs

In the *first-price* auction, the highest sealed bid takes the prize, and the winner pays her full bid, not the second-highest. The open, dynamic form of the first-price auction is the *Dutch* or *descending-price* auction, which we have already mentioned in passing. In the Dutch auction, the price starts higher than anyone is willing to pay (a judgement that must be made by the auctioneer), and is then decreased until it reaches a price that someone *is* willing to pay. This can be implemented orally, by successively calling out lower and lower prices; or mechanically, by a descending analog or digital "price clock," as shown in figure 1.4. Today the winner indicates her intention to buy on an electronic keyboard, but Cassady (1967, p. 32) reports that bidders in a seventeenth-century version indicated their intention to buy by yelling "mine," and that the auction method was called "mineing."

It may not be obvious at first blush, but the first-price and Dutch forms are even more closely related than the Vickrey and English. In fact, they are *strategically equivalent* in the *strong sense*, meaning that a bidder in the two forms has at corresponding points in the sale

Figure 1.4 Sale of cut flowers by Dutch clock in Aalsmeer, Holland, 2003. The present market (Bloemenveiling Aalsmeer, or BVA), according to its web site (http://www.vba.nl/), sells more than 20 million flowers and plants and turns over 6 million euros a day, all in 5 halls with 13 clocks. The web site provides some good detail about the Dutch auction rules: "Auctioning at the VBA goes according to the system of 'Dutch Auction.' This means that the clocks run from the highest to the lowest price, which is always per unit—that is, per single flower or plant. When this process takes place, the buyer sees the lights around the clock's edge run back from 100 to 1. If a buyer notices a product he wants to buy at a price which agrees with him, he quickly pushes the button and the clock stops at the desired price. If the number of the buyer appears on the clock face, it means that the buyer was the first to stop the clock and therefore he is the buyer. At the same time he tells the auctioneer, using his headset with microphone, how much of the consignment he wants to buy (the auctioneer determines the minimum amount). The remainder of the consignment is put up for auctioning again. . . . Per clock, some 1,500 transactions can be processed per hour." (Jerrold Patz, www.patz.com)

exactly the same decisions to make, and exactly the same information on which to base those decisions. In this case, a bidder, knowing her value and nothing else, must choose one number, her bid—and that is her only decision. In the first-price auction, she submits this number as a sealed bid. In the Dutch auction, she must wait until the price clock descends to this number and then buy; if the item is sold before the clock reaches her intended bid, then, well, there is nothing left to think about and no further choices to make—the auction is over.

The strong strategic equivalence between first-price and Dutch is a *logical* equivalence, but not a *psychological* equivalence. In a first-price auction, time is not a significant factor, while in a Dutch auction, time, dictating the descent of the price clock, must be the focus of the bidder's attention. An anxious or impatient Dutch bidder may jump the gun and overpay, or a cold-blooded bidder may dare to stare the clock down past her calculated bid and, on the average, risk losing surplus. A first-price bidder is not subject to these psychological pressures in the cool abstraction of a sealed-bid auction. There is good experimental evidence to support the view that people do, in fact, behave differently in the two settings, despite the logical equivalence.[19] It may be surprising that laboratory experiments yield higher prices in the first-price auction, conflicting with the argument that Dutch bidders may lack patience. Field experiments do, however, yield higher bidding in the Dutch format, as we will discuss further in chapter 6. These puzzles and paradoxes of behavior come up all the time, which is one reason auctions are so interesting.

Think of it this way: Writing longhand with pencil and paper is strongly strategically equivalent to typing on a computer keyboard. At any point, the writer must choose the next letter, number, or punctuation mark, and that is the only decision the writer must make. But the psychological settings of the two situations are different, and so may be the practical results.

To summarize, the four standard kinds of auctions form two pairs: (second-price)-English, and (first-price)-Dutch, with stronger kinship in the latter case than in the former.

---

[19] See appendix D for a brief review of auction experiments in the laboratory.

1.10 Disincentives to Truthful Bidding

The equivalence between English and Vickrey auctions, already qualified as weak, is even shakier than suggested above by the example of Elaine's frenzy. In a Vickrey auction, the bidder is called upon to reveal her true valuation, and there are two important reasons why she may be reluctant to do so (Rothkopf, Teisberg, and Kahn, 1990; Rothkopf and Harstad, 1995). First, the bid-taker may cheat by inserting a fictitious bid between the actual second-highest and the highest, thus increasing his revenue and decreasing the surplus of the winning bidder. Second, the information about the bidder's actual valuation may be useful to the seller in future interactions with the buyer. For example, suppose a bidder wins a mail-bid sale and her bid is $200 for an Alexandrian coin that sells for the second-highest bid of $20. This suggests to the seller that he may be able to extract a much higher price for a similar coin the next time he might offer one, and he will accordingly set a high reserve on it.[20] It may even happen that an unusually high bid attracts the attention of the bid-taker before the auction is over, who might then study the item more closely, and, if he finds it to be a "sleeper" (that is, a valuable item that has previously gone unnoticed), withdraw it from the sale (Lucking-Reiley, 2000b). If for these or other reasons the bidder is worried about revealing her true valuation, the general effect is for her to adjust her strategy by bidding less, thus lowering the expected[21] profit of the seller. These practical considerations—the possibility that the bid-taker may cheat or use the information later—are not intrinsic to the mathematical model, and are examples of what auction theorists call "externalities."

Notice, however, that in an English auction the bidder is *not* called on to reveal her true value; she just matches the second-highest bidder until he drops out. This argument is used by Rothkopf et al. (1990)

---

[20] More about reserves later.

[21] I'll use the term "expected" in this way throughout the book and you can think of "expected profit," for example, as meaning intuitively the "average profit over many auctions." See section A.3 for a technical definition of expected value.

and Rothkopf and Harstad (1995) to explain what they consider to be the rarity of Vickrey auctions in practice, at least in markets for noncollectibles. We should point out however, that bid-taker cheating is not only possible, but not at all uncommon in English auctions as well, as evidenced by the generous stock of terminology. The two standard ways are the use of confederates, or *shills*; and recognizing phantom bids, called *trotting, running, lift-lining, taking bids off the wall,* or *from the chandelier,* or *from the order book* (Cassady, 1967; Ashenfelter and Graddy, 2002).[22] By the way, according to Cassady, if an auctioneer has one legitimate bid and invents another, it's called "one-legged" trotting, and when he has no legitimate bids and invents two, it's called "two-legged" trotting.

We turn next to eBay, an auction form that we will argue is the logical extension of the English and Vickrey auctions to the internet. We will see that eBay plays the role of a trusted third party, and in this way eliminates some of the problems described above that mitigate against truthful bidding. But the use of shills by sellers is endemic to eBay, and we will discuss them in due course.

1.11 Questions

1. Find examples of auctions in film, TV, or literature. For each example, determine, if possible, the exact form of the auction, and evaluate how realistically you think the participants behave.

2. We mentioned that in ancient Babylon, undesirable women were sold to the buyer who would accept the lowest dowry. Explain why this can be considered a reverse auction, which is usually thought of as an auction with one buyer and many sellers.

3. Estimate how much Didius Julianus paid for the Roman Empire in current United States dollars. Ed Finn did some scholarly research for

---

[22] For a discussion of the way the conventional patter of auctioneers is reflected online in eBay, see J. Boyd's "Virtual orality: How eBay controls auctions without an auctioneer's voice" (2001).

my class in 2002, and estimated the cost to be $3.75 billion. I like his comment on Didius's fate:

> In terms of auctions, however, this story reveals an important real-life rule. While individuals may be able to name a monetary private value for anything, certain items do not operate under the laws of economic logic. Auctions rely on the concept of possession, which does not apply well to intangibles like love or the Roman Empire. The imperial throne was not the Praetorians' to sell, and Didius was certainly incapable of owning it.

4. I notice that eBay recently added a sales mode called "Best Offer." The item description invites the potential buyer to submit an offer, with the following warning:

> Make this offer your Best Offer. You can only make 1 offer on this item.

and the following agreement in a click-through box:

> I understand that my Best Offer price, including any Additional Terms I have specified is binding. If the seller accepts the offer, I am obligated to purchase the Item. I also understand that the Additional Terms I add as a part of my Best Offer may be reviewed by eBay in an effort to prevent fraudulent activity.

Does this form of auction correspond exactly to one of the four standard forms discussed in this chapter? If not, what form is it closest to, and what are the differences? When might a seller choose this form? What kind of "fraudulent activity" do you think eBay is worried about? How do you think you should bid in such an auction, assuming you know your value?

5. eBay is the dominant online auction in most of the world, but Japan and China are important exceptions. Yahoo! dominates eBay in Japan, and Taobao is fighting it out with eBay in China. Try to explain the reasons for the success of Yahoo! and Taobao in penetrating these internet auction markets by studying their business histories and practices, rules, rate structures, feedback reputation systems, and interfaces. To what extent can their relative success be attributed to cultural differences? For several relevant papers in a recent conference, see the *Proceedings of the 7th International Conference on Electronic Commerce*, ACM International Conference Proceeding Series, ACM Press; vol. 113, Xi'an, China, August 15–17, 2005.

From Vickrey to eBay

eBay can be thought of as the refined evolutionary product
of the English auction with absentee bidders, the mail-bid sale.

2.1 eBay as an Evolutionary Product of Vickrey: The California Auction

IT IS FAIR to say that for most people eBay defines what an internet auction is. In this chapter, we will take a look at how the particular mechanism of eBay got the way it is, with its time limit, its posted second price, and its second-price payment rule. We will argue that it results from the natural evolution of the mail-bid sale. It may all seem obvious in retrospect, but only in retrospect.

How would you run a mail-bid auction on the internet? This was a natural question to ask in the early days of internet commerce, although it probably wasn't asked so explicitly or in just this way. The most important choices that must be made are, first, what price the highest bidder will be required to pay, and, second, what information is posted about the current bidding level. The most obvious thing to do is to require that the highest bidder pay her bid (a *first-price*, as opposed to a second-price, auction), and to post the highest price bid so far. This is in analogy with the English outcry auction. It makes perfect sense if all the bidders are logged on at the same time and follow the bidding action, *and the auction ends only when no further bids are received*.[1] It can be considered a real-time, online English auction, which we've seen is weakly equivalent to the Vickrey auction.

In practice, however, we would like bidders to be able to submit bids at their leisure over an extended period of time, say a week, as in a

---

[1] This last proviso is crucial; we will reexamine the first-price online auction with a deadline later on, in chapter 4.

mail-bid sale. Such an auction would then need to have a specific starting and closing time. Suppose now that a bidder bids only once, logs off, goes about her other business, and just waits until the auction closes. In that case, if we ask the highest bidder to pay her bid, it no longer makes sense for her to bid sincerely. If she wins the auction, she will pay her valuation, and receive absolutely no surplus. This is exactly the situation in a *first-price*, as opposed to a second-price, sealed-bid auction. The right strategy for a bidder under these circumstances is to bid *less* than her valuation, so that if she wins, she does get a positive surplus. Just how much less is a nontrivial strategic choice, and this is a topic that we will discuss in chapter 4; we needn't worry about it now. The important conclusion to draw is that running a first-price internet auction over an extended period of time is not a good way to emulate the usual English outcry auction, or its close cousin, the Vickrey auction.

It therefore seems as if it might be a good idea to run a non-real-time internet auction as a *second-price* auction. What strategy should a bidder adopt under this rule? Is bidding truthfully dominant? The answer to these questions depends on our second design decision, the posted price level. Let us see what happens if we make the most obvious choice, posting the highest bid so far (the first price), even though the winner will pay the second price. This causes problems. Consider an example where an item worth roughly $50 is put up for auction, the first bid on it is $1, and the next bid is $100. The current posted bid will be $100, but the high bidder, who bid $100, will pay only $1 if he wins. This is a disaster from the point of view of the seller, because there is now no incentive on the part of any other bidders to bid more than the $100, and the item will sell for $1.

Suppose instead that we post the *second-highest* bid received so far at any particular time, the price that the actual highest bidder would pay. Then in the example above, the posted price will be $1, and prospective bidders will see only that; the $100 will be hidden from other bidders. A new bidder might very well enter a new bid of, say, $50, bringing the second price up to that level. This leads us to the idea of posting the *second price* instead of the first price, and this is the essence of eBay's mechanism: a dynamic second-price auction, with posted second price. There are already auctions called English, Dutch, and Japanese, so we'll call this generic form, without all the details and frills of eBay, a *California* auction, to distinguish it from the particular internet instantiation of an eBay auction. We will thus use the term to mean any sealed-bid, second-price auction that allows continuous bidding, and that has a deadline and a dynamically posted second price.

eBay describes the California auction mechanism in a different, more picturesque way. They ask the bidder to imagine that when she submits a bid, an agent is created who bids on her behalf, matching any bid between the posted (second-highest) and the actual, hidden bid submitted, up to the point when the competing bid exceeds the highest bid. These automatic bids are called *proxy* bids. It is easy to see, however, that this description, while more vivid and perhaps easier to grasp for some, is completely equivalent to the dynamic second-price-posted, second-price-paid mechanism described above, the California auction.[2]

Notice that the California auction (and hence eBay) shares the advantage of the English over the Vickrey auction of allowing the bidder to keep her true value secret in the event that she wins the auction—provided the bid-taker is honest (recall the discussion of disincentives to truthful bidding in section 1.10). This is a great benefit of using a trusted third party, and represents an important part of the value that eBay provides to bidders.

eBay as a product of the evolution English $\rightarrow$ Vickrey $\rightarrow$ eBay deals very effectively with the specter of bid-taker cheating that can dissuade the bidder from truthful bidding in both English and Vickrey auctions. There is no good reason to suspect that eBay is not honest in its calculations, and, besides, the bid amounts are listed after each sale, and the bids and arithmetic are subject to the scrutiny of all the participants. This is not to say that there aren't many other problems of deceit and cheating on eBay, but the creation of phantom bids by eBay isn't one of them. On the other hand, in the real world, with real bidders, this does not imply that truthful bidding at any time in the sale of an item

---

[2] One can go too far in accepting eBay's concrete description of the second-price mechanism as bidding by a proxy. I thank George Reis for relating the story of his friend who went through great pains to bid at the very last split second, so as not to give her rival's proxy bidder a chance to respond.

is an optimal, or even a good strategy. The dynamic but non-real-time nature of the bidding and the fixed deadline really complicate the issue of eBay strategy. In the next chapter we will examine the buyer's bidding strategy on eBay in some detail.

2.2 Other Online Auction Rules

There is no doubt that at this point eBay has captured the lion's share of the online auction market, at least for general items and collectibles. But there has always been competition beating on the door, most notably from Amazon and Yahoo!. It is interesting therefore to compare the auction rules of Amazon and Yahoo! with those of eBay. We should not infer, however, that the differences in rules account solely, or even in large part, for the differences in market share, since many other factors come into play in determining business success.

Searching for the details of the auction mechanisms at the three sites reveals that it is not so easy to find a precise statement of all the rules in one place for any of the three. The impression I get is that the sites want to encourage bidders to jump in without intimidating them first with technical details. That aside, my conclusion is that by far the most important difference in rules between eBay and both Amazon and Yahoo! is that Amazon and Yahoo! allow for the automatic extension of the ending time of an auction if bids occur near the one originally posted.

This mechanism at the Amazon site is called "Going, Going, Gone," and is described as follows:[3]

GOING, GOING, GONE

We know that bidding can get hot and heavy near the end of many auctions. Our Going, Going, Gone feature ensures that you always have an opportunity to challenge last-second bids.

Here's how it works: Whenever a bid is cast in the last 10 minutes of an auction, the auction is automatically extended for an additional 10 minutes from the time of the latest bid. This ensures that an auction can't close until 10 minutes have passed with no further bids.

---

[3] Amazon home page, January 2004.

The bottom line? If you're attentive at the end of an auction, you'll always have the opportunity to challenge a new bidder.

The corresponding rule at Yahoo! is a little less clear:[4]

AUTO EXTENSION
If you select this option the auction closing time can be automatically extended for 5 minutes if a bid is placed within the last 5 minutes of the auction.

Presumably, this means the same thing as the Amazon rule, but with an extension of five minutes instead of ten.

It is natural to expect that this difference in ending rules will result in less late bidding on Amazon than on eBay. Ockenfels and Roth (2006; Roth and Ockenfels, 2002), confirmed this expectation using real data from the respective sites. They also found that the effect is more pronounced in the antique category than in the computer category. This supports the idea that when bidders on eBay wait until the last few seconds of a sale, they may do so in order to avoid revealing expert information—such expert information is more important when buying one-of-a-kind antiques than standardized and widely reviewed computers.

Less clear than the effect of the extendible deadline on bidding times is the effect on the prices realized for comparable items. This is often the bottom line for auction theorists, who often like to consider expected revenue as an important criterion for goodness of an auction mechanism, evidently viewing things from the seller's point of view. This is not the only criterion, however. Efficiency—the idea that the bidder who places the highest value on an item receives it—is often an alternative, and sometimes conflicting, requirement.

I once asked a friend at Amazon why this deadline extension was incorporated in the rules, and he explained that Amazon had plenty of buyers and wanted to attract sellers, and that this feature is more attractive to sellers than to buyers. Offhand, it does seem that the Amazon ending rule may very well be less attractive to buyers than the eBay rule; it certainly does remove some of the sporting element for the kind of bidder who derives some excitement from the game.

[4] Yahoo! home page, January 2004.

29

The response of my friend at Amazon is very interesting from the perspective of auction theory, even the basic parts we have discussed so far. We have argued that if bidders *really* know their values (have private values), truthful bidding is a dominant strategy in both the Vickrey and Japanese button English auctions. If we think of both eBay and the extended-deadline auctions at Amazon as versions of these forms, and use this result as a guide, we might expect the extended deadline to have little effect on the final price. But as we've discussed, there are important differences in real bidding behavior between the English and Vickrey auctions because bidders receive information during the bidding that can affect their psychology and their estimates of value. The same considerations enter the picture in internet auctions. Information is posted during the auction, in the form of next-highest bids, and if we give up the private-value assumption, we must also give up the simple arguments leading to the dominance of truthful bidding and the equality of revenue that would follow if bidders really could and did bid truthfully.

This problem of choosing closing rules in online auctions is complicated by the fact that buyers ordinarily participate in many auctions over time, and can learn to adapt their behavior to the rules. I return to this topic, with more fire power, in question 3 of chapter 6.

2.3 eBay $\neq$ Vickrey

I was once at a cocktail party with lots of economists (really), and I mentioned my interest in eBay. Their response (to be fair, several years ago) was that it was simply a Vickrey auction, case closed. I hope that by now you disagree. Here's a list of seventeen ways in which eBay differs from the *ideal* Vickrey (sealed-bid, second-price) auction, as described in section 1.6. Can you think of more? (See question 1.)

1. There is a definite, fixed deadline for bids.
2. At any time a price representing the current second-highest bid is posted. This price is a tick above the second-highest bid, provided that the highest and second-highest bids are at least a tick apart. In the rare cases when the highest and

second-highest bids are closer than a tick apart, the posted price is simply the highest bid.

3. A new bid must be at least a tick above the posted price for it to be accepted.
4. Bidders may bid many times.
5. eBay implements the rules as a trusted third party.
6. The highest bid at any time is hidden from the *seller* (a consequence of the previous item).
7. There is a minimum starting bid (an open reserve).
8. There is a possible secret reserve.
9. The seller can cancel the sale before the scheduled ending time, but not if there are 12 hours or less remaining in the sale and there is a winning bid.
10. It is possible for bidders to send email to the seller (legal and facilitated by eBay).
11. It is possible for the seller to send email to bidders (legal and facilitated by eBay).
12. It is possible for bidders to send email to each other (legal and facilitated by eBay).
13. Sales are implicitly iterated with reputation feedback, which is publicly posted (buyers and sellers rate each other +1, −1, or neutral, and can leave a short text comment).
14. The seller can reject a bid.
15. The bidder can retract a bid under some circumstances.
16. Bidders in practice have different information because of equipment quality, most notably, in the display of photos.
17. Bidders in practice have different speed and reliability of bidding because of equipment.

eBay has thus adapted the second-price auction to the internet in many ways. As we've discussed in this chapter, this tuning shows a deep respect for the shortcomings of the straight Vickrey sale as it was previously incarnated as a mail-bid sale. Most important, the psychological setting of the English outcry auction has been, to some extent, preserved, and the use of a trusted third party encourages bidders to reveal their true values.

2.4 Summary

We've seen that in many ways eBay represents a logical adaptation of preceding auction types, especially the mail-bid sale, to the interactive environment of the internet.

We've also seen that the details can matter a great deal in determining how bidders and sellers behave, and therefore how auctions work. A good example of this is the choice of whether the closing time is fixed or extendible (Ockenfels and Roth, 2006; Roth and Ockenfels, 2002).

The rest of this book is aimed at understanding this complex inter-action between rules and behavior in auctions, using eBay as our main vehicle. eBay is, after all, by far the most widely used and well-known auction institution in the history of civilization. We'll draw on many resources to help us: the main results from the mathematical theory of auctions, controlled experiments in the economic laboratory, and field experiments, which collect data from real auctions with real bidders buying things they really want with their own money.

2.5 Questions

1. Can you add to the list in section 2.3 of differences between the ideal Vickrey auction and eBay?

2. The list of differences in section 2.3 ignores the problem of exactly what is posted when there is a secret reserve that has not been met. Fill in the missing details.

3. Can you ascertain the actual bid of the current high bidder during an eBay sale? If you think you can, explain when it is possible. Similarly, see if you can explain whether and when it is possible to ascertain the actual bid of the winner after a sale is over.

4. Yahoo! offers another option for the seller that represents a departure from eBay rules:[5]

---

[5] Yahoo! home page, January 2004.

ALLOW EARLY CLOSE

You can use this option to close your auction before the posted closing time if you are satisfied with the current "High Bid," and wish to sell the item to the current High Bidder as soon as possible. Select this option if you would like to enable "Early Close."

Discuss the effect you think this has on bidder and seller behavior. Using the same kind of reasoning we used in discussing extending the closing time, do you think it tends to make Yahoo! auctions more or less attractive to bidders than eBay auctions?

eBay Strategies Observed

We spy on some eBay bidding behavior and argue that the common and nasty bidding strategy of sniping on eBay is good, if not optimal.

3.1 Some Bidding Histories

A GOOD WAY to get a feeling for the decisions faced by buyers on eBay, and auctions in general, is to take a look at some real examples of bidding histories for different kinds of items. All the examples graphed in this chapter are taken from actual eBay sales, with the bidder IDs hidden, of course, and labeled 1, 2, 3, . . . , in time order of bid. The item descriptions are somewhat disguised also.

3.1.1 Start and End Clustering, Snipers

Figure 3.1 shows the history of a ten-day auction for a Greek bronze coin. The bids are shown as large dots, with dollar amounts on the vertical axis, and time in hours on the horizontal axis. The second-highest bid at any time is shown as a dashed line.

The six different bidders are identified with the numbers 1 through 6. Bidder 1 bids shortly after the sale begins (actually, about 3 hours after the starting time), and she bids $9.00, which is also the opening bid for this sale. Bidder 1 makes no further bid, so she is betting that no one else will bid, and goes on to other things. She will be notified in email from eBay when she is outbid, but she will ignore these notifications. Evidently, she is hoping that by bidding very low, she may get a bargain if the item is overlooked—a long shot. Some bidders may also use this device of an early low bid as a placeholder, to make a record of interesting items to come back to later.

About 12 hours later, bidder 2 bids $21.00 and becomes the high bidder, but the displayed price is $9.50, a tick above the second-highest

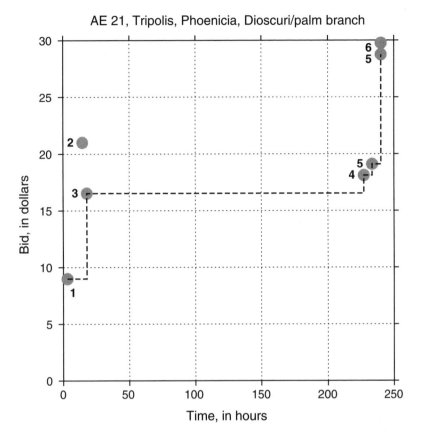

Figure 3.1 Bid history illustrating the typical clustering of bids near the start and end times of a sale, and sniping. The large dots represent bids, the numbers next to them identify the bidders, and the dashed line shows the second-highest bid at any time.

bid of $9.00. About 3 hours later, bidder 3 bids $16.52, which raises the displayed price to $17.02, while bidder 2 remains the highest bidder, with his bid of $21.00. Notice that as we plot the bids recorded by eBay in chronological order, the bid amounts are not necessarily ascending, simply because, as in this example, a bid may raise the price that is currently second-highest but not highest.

In this example, bids cluster near the start and end of the sale, and this pattern is typical of many eBay sales. For one thing, buyers sometimes examine the list of newly listed items, and may enter early bids to bookmark them for themselves, even if their bids are not high enough to be serious candidates to win the item. Or, early bidders may adopt the simplistic view, promoted by eBay, that one should bid sincerely and rely on the "proxy" system to meet potential competition: "Enter the highest amount you'd be willing to pay for the item. eBay will automatically raise your bid only as much as is needed for you to remain the high bidder."[1] The bids at the end tend to be last-minute—or more often last-second—bids, by bidders who want to prevent rivals from having the time to respond to their bids. Such bidders are called *snipers*, about which more below. In this example there is really just one sniper, bidding 8 seconds before the ending time of the sale. The second-to-final bid was actually received 56 seconds before the ending time, much too much time for any respectable sniper, and ample time for the bid to be posted and answered (assuming normal internet traffic).

Do not make the mistake of assuming that the plotted final price was actually the high bid of the winner. In this case, the final price is $29.75, a tick above the next-highest bid of $28.75, but quite possibly well below the winner's actual bid.[2]

3.1.2 A Bidding War

Figure 3.2 shows the bid history for a real floor fight between bidders 2 and 3. After an inconsequential early bid by bidder 1, bidders 2 and 3 are evidently treating the auction as if it is an English outcry auction, with 3 answering 2, sometimes with multiple sequential bids. Bidder 3 tries to snipe when bidder 2 is in the lead, and gets her last bid in 25 seconds before the end, probably late enough so there is no time to respond when it is unsuccessful. Actually, bidder 3's snipe is at $75, which ties bidder 2, and 2 takes the coin because a tie is resolved by awarding the item to the earliest bidder. It might be relevant to point out that according to their feedback profiles,[3] bidders 2 and 3 are relatively inexperienced, with ratings of 11 and 6, respectively.[4] Of course, it is

[1] eBay home page, March 2004.
[2] But see question 3 in the previous chapter.
[3] Note, however, that these individuals could have other eBay IDs.
[4] We use feedback ratings as indicators of experience, which is reasonable because negative feedback is relatively rare. The data analyst's jargon is that feedback ratings "are *proxies* for the number of transactions" (Roth and Ockenfels, 2002).

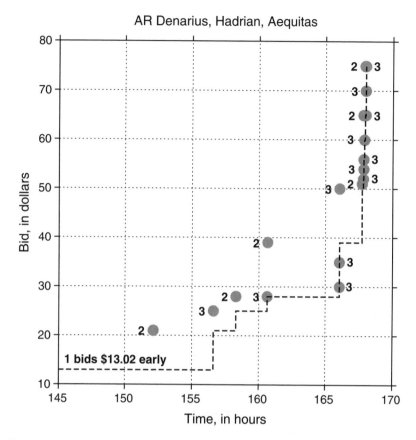

Figure 3.2 Bid history illustrating a bidding war in the style of an English auction. Note that the time scale shows only the last day or so of the sale.

impossible to say what would have happened if bidder 2, say, had waited till the final few seconds and sniped. Given, however, that the last few bidding levels were going up by even $5 increments ($60, $65, $70, and $75), it seems likely that bidder 2 could have benefited quite a bit by avoiding the war with bidder 3 altogether and sniping with a single bid.

This is one of many examples I've seen that suggest that some bidders do in fact misunderstand the rules of eBay, or have not even attempted to find out what they are. People I consider very intelligent have told me they have bought a few things from time to time on eBay, and it has turned out that they thought the posted price was highest, not second highest!

37

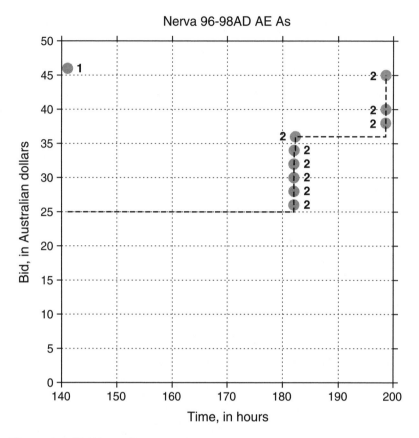

Figure 3.3 Bid history illustrating the potential downside to early bidding. Notice that after the first bid, the bidding sits at the minimum opening bid of $25 until a second bid is received.

3.1.3 *An Early Bidder and Her Fate*

Figure 3.3 shows a rather extreme (but nonetheless real) example of what can happen to an early bidder who treats eBay as she would a Vickrey auction. Bidder 1 places her only bid very early and never bids again, apparently following eBay's advice to "Enter the highest amount you'd be willing to pay for the item." Bidder 2 places nine subsequent bids, none of them exceeding 1's bid, but creeping up on it, and establishing the final price of $46. (Notice once more that we don't know what bidder 1 actually bid, but only that it was at or above the final bid of bidder 2.) As in the previous example, and as usual in these kinds of situations, it is impossible to say what bidder 2 would have done without the information provided by 1's early bid. But as he bid, he continued to receive messages from eBay telling him that he was "outbid" by another bidder. It seems a fair bet that bidder 2 would not have had the impetus to raise his bid repeatedly had bidder 1 waited to snipe.

3.2 "Enter Your Maximum, Then Sit Back and Watch!"

In view of the maneuvering we've just seen, eBay's guidance in the matter of bidding strategy is disconcertingly naïve:

PROXY BIDDING

Enter your maximum, then sit back and watch!

eBay uses a helpful bidding system (called proxy bidding) to make bidding on auctions more convenient and less time-consuming for buyers.

Here's how it works:

When you place a bid, you enter the maximum amount you'd be willing to pay for the item. Your maximum amount is kept confidential from other bidders and the seller.

The eBay system compares your bid to those of the other bidders. The system places bids on your behalf, using only as much of your bid as is necessary to maintain your high bid position (or to meet the reserve price). The system will bid up to your maximum amount.

If another bidder has a higher maximum, you'll be outbid.

BUT, if no other bidder has a higher maximum, you win the item. And you could pay significantly less than your maximum price!

This means you don't have to keep coming back to re-bid every time another bid is placed.[5]

In other words, eBay would have bidders behave as if they were participating in a Vickrey auction, bidding truthfully with private values, and, moreover, early.

---

[5] eBay home page, November 2003.

We have already pointed out that we cannot expect ideal, truthful bidding in an environment like the internet, where bidders may be unsure of their values, may receive information during the course of the auction—and may even be unsure of the rules. In fact, we have not even defined truthful bidding precisely in the general setting of a California auction. Even if a bidder is certain of her value, she can bid it early, submit lower bids first, or snipe. As we see next, uncertainty about values in a dynamic setting makes life very interesting, and quite plausibly provides an incentive to snipe.

3.3 Good Reasons to Snipe

It is easy to think of reasons why we may find it difficult to assign a definite value to an item on the auction block. On eBay, we may have only a blurry photo or an unreliable description to go on. In fact, even the reliability of the seller to deliver may be quite uncertain, and this will be reflected in the value we attach to winning the auction. It may also be that the item needs to be researched, and that process can take many hours of work if the item is a rare or obscure collectible. Or, if we intend to resell the item, there is always uncertainty about what price it will fetch on resale. As a practical matter, we can never be completely certain what value to attach to either a collectible or a commodity item.

Uncertainty about one's value plays a very important role in studying strategies in auctions, not so much because of the doubt connected with the true value of an item to oneself, but because it means, generally, that other bidders may have information that is potentially useful to you in estimating your own particular value. As a rule, the more they reveal of their information, and the less you reveal of your own, the better off you are.

A very useful mathematical model for the situation where bidders may be uncertain about their valuations is the *common-value* or *mineral-rights* model (Milgrom and Weber, 1982; Krishna, 2002).[6] The latter name is motivated by the situation where the right to drill for oil,

---

[6] Krishna (2002) makes a distinction between "common-value auctions" and "mineral-rights auctions," but Milgrom and Weber (1982) do not, and neither will we.

say, is being auctioned off, and, while there is some definite amount of payoff that a driller will earn, bidders have only their own estimates of that payoff. We can think of each bidder receiving a *signal*, which is composed of the "true" value, the same for all bidders, plus a corrupting random element, the *noise*. The key point in the common-value model is that the bidders' values are *interdependent*. That is, the bidders' values are statistically interrelated, and a bidder's early bid can reveal information that is useful to the other bidders. This is a very concrete argument for sniping on eBay in the common-value situation: Bidding early gives away information that may be of use to other bidders.

In the standard auction literature, common-value auctions are very often associated with the "winner's curse," which is the term applied to the persistent tendency for the winning bidder to discover, after the auction, that she has overestimated the common value. We will return to this important trap and the reason for it in section 6.4.[7]

In a context somewhat different from the common-value model, in which everyone is uncertain about the "real" value of an item, it may be that a known expert, perhaps a dealer, recognizes a prized rarity while ordinary collectors do not.[8] It would clearly be foolhardy for the expert to play her hand early and draw more attention to the item than necessary. eBay does reveal bidders' IDs,[9] and a dealer who does not take care to use an unrecognizable ID for bidding may well be spotted as a dealer by another bidder. Since the dealer usually intends to resell the item at a profit, the ordinary collector might in this way obtain rarities at what amounts to wholesale rather than retail prices. In such a situation, we might say that the dealer should snipe to protect the value of her special knowledge.

There is good theoretical support for the idea that private information is valuable, and should be kept secret as much as possible. In an

---

[7] See Thaler's book entitled *The Winner's Curse* (1994) for a chapter on the winner's curse—hence the title. This is a collection of articles about our central theme in studying auctions: the differences between how people ought to behave according to economic theory, and the way they actually do.

[8] We say in this situation that the bidders are *asymmetrically informed*, in contrast to situations when bidders all have the same information, when we say they are *symmetrically informed*.

[9] Unless the seller chooses to keep them private, which raises suspicions of all kinds.

important paper, Engelbrecht-Wiggans, Milgrom, and Weber (1983) consider the situation when one bidder in a sealed-bid sale has proprietary information, and the others do not. To take a specific example, suppose only two bidders are competing for a tract of oil-bearing land in a first-price sealed-bid sale. Let us also assume that bidder 1 owns a neighboring tract, and because of this knows the value of the land to himself with complete certainty; but bidder 2 is completely in the dark. That is, bidder 2's signal tells him nothing about the value of the tract that he didn't know before he received his signal. This is a very extreme example of a common-value model with asymmetrically informed bidders, but it proves a point. It turns out that in this situation, there is a way for bidder 1 to choose her bid so that, no matter what bidder 2 bids, bidder 1 earns a positive surplus, and bidder 2 can do no better than break even. That is, even if bidder 2 responds optimally, he winds up with no average surplus at all.[10]

There is another specific reason to withhold bidding until very late in an auction: it is possible for other bidders on eBay, by searching "by bidder," to see what you are currently bidding on, a practice known as "shadowing." If you regularly spend time searching the listings looking for attractive items and potential bargains, and if you bid early, you are inviting other bidders to take advantage, not only of your expertise, but of your time.

Here is yet another, perhaps less obvious advantage of sniping. It often happens that in a flurry of, literally, last-minute bids, your bid is rejected by eBay because it was received after other last-minute bids had raised the minimum allowable price above your bid. In this case your bid goes unrecorded, and your interest in the item is not revealed to others. This strategic reasoning has implications beyond the particular auction in question. (See question 4.)

The reasons given in this section to bid at the last moment can be summarized in this general, heuristic, argument: If you bid early, you reveal information unnecessarily, and that works against you when you

---

[10] This turns out to be an *equilibrium* bidding strategy for the two bidders. Actually, Engelbrecht-Wiggans et al. (1983) describe equilibrium bidding strategies for any number of bidders when one of them is perfectly informed, and the others are completely uninformed. More about the important idea of equilibrium strategy in chapter 4.

are trying to snap up a valuable item as cheaply as possible. Many eBay bidders seem to agree with this general principle, and there is empirical evidence that more experienced bidders are more likely to bid late. This is confirmed by Roth and Ockenfels (2002), who studied bid timing empirically for antiques and computers; and Wilcox (2000), who observed sales of handheld power drills, men's neckties, desk-top staplers, and Rookwood Pottery vases. Both of these studies also find that the correlation of late bidding with bidder experience is greater for the items likely to have a common-value component: antiques in Roth and Ockenfels (2002), and pottery and neckties in Wilcox (2000). It would be a little bit misleading, however, to claim that this heuristic argument for late bidding is completely conclusive. There are situations when revealing information early can help coordinate a kind of implicit collusion, and we will return to this possibility in section 3.4.2.

3.4 Other (Generally Good) Reasons to Snipe

There have been some recent papers that argue that there are other reasons behind sniping, besides uncertainty about values and the desire to hide information. We summarize this work next.

3.4.1 Bidding Wars, Response to Incremental Bidding

Bidding early may ignite a bidding war, as in the example in section 3.1.2, and this is yet another reason to snipe. We can think of a bidding war as a manifestation of bidders being influenced by observing the posted second prices, and reconsidering their values. In this sense a bidding war is a symptom of uncertainty about values, although one could also argue that some bidding wars are more akin to irrational frenzies.

Or, as mentioned before, a bidding war can come about because bidders simply misunderstand the rules and bid as if the auction is some form of English auction, with or without jump bidding. If this happens to be the case, then it is certainly best to withhold one's bid until the final seconds, to make a response bid impossible. As Roth and Ockenfels

(2002) put it, sniping is a best response to naïve incremental-bidding strategies.[11]

3.4.2 Implicit Collusion

Ockenfels and Roth (2006) are very much concerned with the possibility that sniping carries with it a significant risk of missing the deadline because of unpredictable network delays. My own experience is that this is not really a problem, perhaps because I have reliable internet service, and because it is easy to estimate delays due to traffic by pinging the auction site in the few minutes before closing. I've missed a closing or two, but none I really cared about, and certainly no more than one in a hundred. But the argument of Ockenfels and Roth is interesting, even if their premise is a bit strained.

To take a concrete and highly simplified example, suppose there are only two bidders, that each misses the deadline when sniping with probability 1/2, and that each decides to bid truthfully, once, either early, or by sniping. Suppose also that they both have a private value of \$21 for an item, and suppose that the starting bid for the item is \$1. If they both snipe, the only way a bidder gets any surplus is if she snipes in time and her rival doesn't. This occurs, on the average, one time out of four, and therefore each bidder's expected surplus is \$20/4 = \$5.

Suppose now that bidder 1 bids early, so that her bid is sure to arrive. If bidder 2 still snipes, he never wins any surplus, but bidder 1 wins more. However, if bidder 2 responds by also bidding early, neither bidder wins any surplus at all. Thus, there is mutual advantage in both players sniping, and this can be thought of as implicit collusion between the bidders.[12]

As mentioned at the beginning of this section, this model depends critically on a significant probability of missing the deadline, and in my experience this is not a driving factor in determining bidding behavior

---

[11] It may also be that incremental bids come from a shill; more about that in chapter 7.

[12] This simple model is actually an example of the iterated Prisoner's Dilemma (Axelrod, 1984). If the players are making a habit of cooperating by sniping, then one of them can benefit by a surprise early bid. But her rival may then retaliate in the future by also bidding early, and so on.

on eBay. Roth and Ockenfels (2002) report the results of a survey: The median response indicated a 10% chance of missing a snipe because of network delay, and another 10% chance of missing a snipe because of unforeseen personal delays. My own experience is more on the order of 1%, but I'm a fanatic.

Roth and Ockenfels (2002) also report that "more than 90% of the responders to our survey never use sniping software." They refer here to web services that can supply you with automatic sniping, such as eSnipe.com, in case you plan to be living your life when a particular sale closes. The use of such services entails a certain risk, of course, because they require you to supply your eBay password. There is also the possibility that the services may be less clever at adapting to unexpected network delay than you are, and a spike in traffic may cause you to miss the deadline. For example, from eSnipe's web page: "Monday, August 11, 2003: eSnipe missed 5% of its bids on Sunday, August 10, far above the usual less than one percent it usually misses, due to problems with a database server." This 1% is what I would expect from the sudden network delays that I have experienced, and makes the incentives for their proposed coordinating strategy rather weak.

3.4.3 *Nonstrategic Reasons to Bid Late*

Some reasons to bid late, if not in the last few seconds, stem from what Roth and Ockenfels (2002) call *nonstrategic* reasons. That is, a bidder may choose to bid late for reasons other than consideration of what her rivals will do. They cite the following reasonable hypotheses, all of which tend to favor later rather than earlier bidding, but none of which really leads to bidding at the last possible second:

- Bidders naturally tend to procrastinate.
- Soon-to-expire auctions are displayed first in some lists presented by eBay.
- Bidders naturally want to delay decisions.
- Bidders naturally avoid "hanging" bids.
- Bidders' willingness to pay tends to increase over time (perhaps because of the so-called "endowment effect").

Roughly speaking, the endowment effect states that people tend to attach a higher value to an object if they own it than if they don't. For example, in a classic experiment (Knetsch and Sinden, 1984), subjects were given either lottery tickets or $2 cash. Few subjects with lottery tickets were willing to sell them for $2, and few subjects with the cash were willing to buy lottery tickets for $2. Somehow, subjects who owned lottery tickets put a higher value on them than those who did not. Watching an item on eBay for a week and contemplating its ownership might have a similar effect. I think it does for me (see question 3).[13]

3.5 Some (Questionable) Reasons to Bid Early

3.5.1 Uncertain Values and the Cost of Discovery

Rasmusen (2006) analyzes two-bidder California auctions (among other types) in which one bidder is uncertain about her value, and where the key feature is that she can learn her true value at a certain cost, both in money and time. He shows that in certain situations, early bidding can be advantageous to both bidders because it can be used to facilitate what amounts to collusion between them. Here's how it works.

Suppose bidder 1 is uncertain about her value, but can pay a price c to find it out exactly, and suppose that bidder 2 knows his value with certainty. Further, suppose that the bidders have values that can be high or low, according to some probability distributions. Then it turns out that the following strategic plan has the property that if one bidder chooses to follow it, the other can do no better than to follow it also.[14]

Bidder 1 starts by bidding some carefully chosen small amount, early in the auction. If bidder 2 has a high value, he meets that bid, also early in the auction; and in any event, he waits to snipe with his true value. If bidder 1 sees the posted second price rise, she knows that

---

[13] For another famous paper testing the endowment effect, see Kahneman, Knetsch, and Thaler (1990). See also the chapter on the endowment effect in Thaler (1994).

[14] In other words, Rasmusen shows that this pair of strategies is an equilibrium. We also described an equilibrium in section 3.3, and, once again, we promise the reader that this central idea will be discussed in more detail in chapter 4.

bidder 2 has bid early, and when that happens she pays the cost of discovering her actual value. This can be interpreted as bidder 2 signaling to 1 in order to provoke her to discover her value when his value is high.

Rasmusen shows that if the cost of value discovery is in the right range, and if the level of the early bid is chosen appropriately, this implicit pact is mutually beneficial: Bidder 1 saves some cost (on the average) of bidding a blind estimate of her value, because she is warned to invest in value discovery when bidder 2's value is high; and bidder 2 consequently pays a lower final price (on the average). This is a good story, and an interesting example of a game-theoretic setting for an auction problem, but the argument hinges on the idea that there is a significant cost associated with discovering one's value.

Rasmusen's strategic plan can be interpreted as a kind of implicit collusion, similar in spirit to the one of Ockenfels and Roth (2006) described above. In the latter situation the risk of missing a snipe was important; here the cost of value discovery is important. In both situations, the two bidders are coordinating their activities to their mutual benefit via signals. The next subsection is devoted to yet another example of this theme.

3.5.2 Scaring Away Competition

It might be that early high bids "scare off" some competition, at least when there are two or more bidders doing the early bidding, so the posted second price actually increases. This would make sense in situations when a competitor is likely to revise his value upward during late bidding (say in a bidding war), but would simply stop watching the auction if high prices appear early. My own intuition is that the price-increasing effect of early bidding is usually much stronger than the intimidation effect, but to my knowledge there has been no empirical research that bears directly on this behavioral question.

The argument that early bidding scares away competition in second-price mail-bid sales is made by Frank S. Robinson, a well-known coin dealer. However, he has an incentive to convince bidders of this, because he wants to avoid being swamped with last-minute email bids. If you believe that sniping is best for bidders, then he has another incentive, namely higher realized prices.[15] Robinson's rules do deviate from those of a California auction. If you phone or email him and make a bid before closing, he will not only tell you where you stand, but will tell you how high you need to go to be accepted as new high bidder, thus revealing something about the actual current high bid. He also distributes email, a day or so before closing, with a list of "lots going cheaply." Thus, his format is somewhere between a mail-bid sale as I've described it and an English auction.

In contrast to Robinson, Dan Clark, who also runs mail-bid sales for ancient coins, is scrupulous about preserving the sealed-bid nature of his format. Here's what he says in his standard rules:

> We do not reveal the high bid to anyone unless the bidder clearly indicates he or she is finished bidding, or has become the highest bidder. This maintains an auction quality to our sales, in our opinion.[16]

The Reverend Clark thus runs his mail-bid sale as a good approximation of a Vickrey auction, but evidently will reveal to a bidder the fact that she owns the current highest bid. He's been conducting his sales the same way for many years, and in this respect he anticipated eBay.

Early and high bidding on eBay to scare away competition plays a role analogous to jump bidding in an English auction, which we mentioned in chapter 1. But it is not the same thing. The fact that the posted price on eBay is the second-highest bid means that the current highest bid is not visible, and therefore its magnitude cannot intimidate anyone. Thus, as mentioned above, early bidding is most intimidating when there are two or more bidders engaging in it. The highest bidder can, however, raise her own bid on eBay, and *the fact that she has* will be registered, but without an increase in the posted price—except in the special situation when the highest bid was less than a bidding increment (tick) above the next highest bid from competing bidders.[17]

[15] See question 2. By the way, Frank is an honest and knowledgeable dealer, and for those interested in ancient coins, I recommend his charming book, *Confessions of a Numismatic Fanatic* (1992).

[16] His mail-bid sale of March 16, 2005.

[17] Or was a tie: eBay home page, February 2006.

I interrupt to note that this latter case is, in fact, the subject of a lawsuit against eBay. Here's an excerpt from the Reuters new article:

> eBay is being sued by a Pennsylvania man who charges that it illegally forces up prices when certain high bidders raise their maximum bid to guard against last-minute offers, an attorney for the plaintiffs said on Wednesday.
>
> In a proposed class-action lawsuit filed Feb. 17 in Santa Clara County Superior Court, lead plaintiff Glenn Block claims that eBay raised his bid from $111 to $112.50 after he responded to an email from [the] auction site that said he was the highest bidder for an item.
>
> The email warned that he could be outbid if he did not increase his maximum.
>
> Block alleged that he could have won the auction at $111, and accused eBay of forcing him to overpay by $1.50.
>
> "Based on what we know about what's being alleged, it appears the plaintiff completely misunderstands the functionality of the eBay bidding system," eBay spokesman Hani Durzy said. He said the company had not yet seen the lawsuit.
>
> Durzy told Reuters that eBay only notifies winning bidders that they could be outbid when they have hit their preset maximum bid. Increasing a maximum bid is voluntary.
>
> eBay automatically increases bids only when the maximum has been hit and when the prior top bid was between bidding increments. For example, bidding increments on items priced between $100 and $249.99 is [sic] $2.50. Block, however, raised his bid increment by $1.50.
>
> Durzy says eBay discloses such information on its web site.[18]

At first glance, this may seem trivial, but multiply the $1.50 and similar fractions of increments by the number of times this might happen on eBay in a year.

To return to the strategic implications of raising one's own bid on eBay, it does send this signal to other bidders: "I'm the high bidder, and, furthermore, I care enough about this item to have raised my own bid."

---

[18] "eBay Sued in California over Bidding Practices," Reuters, February 23, 2005, by Lisa Baertlein.

This raise could, of course, be nominal, perhaps even the fraction of a tick just mentioned. But it could be substantial. I've seen this done many times myself, and it is, after all, a very inexpensive way to signal interest in an item. But, as in the case of jump bidding, this is a double-edged sword. It can intimidate rivals and cause them to drop out of the sale. But it can also spur them on to higher bidding, and perhaps spark a bidding war. I should also point out that such a strategy will be revealed in the bid history after the auction, and may be detected and discounted in future auctions by attentive rivals.

Avery's theoretical paper, "Strategic jump bidding in English auctions" (1998), is notable for pointing out the deficiencies of the Japanese button auction model, and analyzing jump-bidding strategies when the bidders' values are interdependent. He shows that bidders can lower average prices by signaling with jump bids, but as always, the theoretical results must be interpreted carefully. First, they assume that bidders find and follow equilibrium strategies—a questionable assumption in any discussion of human behavior, and one to which we return again and again. The fact that bidders are excitable and can get swept up in the emotion of bidding is not included in the mathematics.[19] Second, the mathematical setup requires that bidders know a lot about the population of bidders: how many there are, what the statistical distributions of values are, and how these are interrelated. Finally, of course, eBay allows only the extremely limited signal that the high bidder has raised her bid, nothing like the powerful signal exemplified by Sue Ellen Mishky's oral jump bid of $8000 against the high bid of $6500 that Elaine held for President Kennedy's golf clubs (chapter 1).[20]

3.5.3 Nonstrategic Reasons to Bid Early

The simplest reason to bid early, of course, is to avoid the problem of having to be online at the closing. This assumes the user, for one reason or another, chooses not to use an automatic sniping service.

[19] Bulow and Klemperer do model in rational terms what appear to be frenzied, or at least unpredictable, price patterns in their interesting paper, "Rational frenzies and crashes" (1994).
[20] Avery (1998) gives some real-life examples of dramatic jump bidding in company takeover wars.

The problem of being there at closing can sometimes be especially troublesome for bidders who are in time zones far removed from the usual active bidder population. Sellers generally choose closing times when most prospective buyers are awake.

There may also be psychological rewards, hard to quantify, to be listed as the current high bidder. It can make a bidder feel as if she is somehow "winning" the auction, although if there are snipers out there, this is largely an illusion.[21]

Finally, a bidder may feel that it is underhanded, cowardly, or generally unethical to snipe. We will return to this aspect of life on eBay in chapter 7.

3.6 On Balance, Snipe

To summarize, at the ever-present risk of oversimplification, the two main strategic arguments in favor of sniping are:

- It preserves the secrecy of information that may be valuable to rival bidders;
- It avoids provoking a bidding war;

and the main strategic argument in favor of early bidding is:

- It can intimidate rivals and scare them off.

On balance, my vote goes to sniping, and the empirical evidence in Roth and Ockenfels (2002) and Wilcox (2000) shows that seasoned eBayers support me in my conclusion.

3.7 Seller Choices

We now return to the strategic choices faced by the seller, the most important of which are the opening bid, the possible use of a secret reserve, and the possible use of the buy-it-now option. I should point out that in the auction literature, as in Riley and Samuelson (1981)

---

[21] I for one tend to feel vulnerable and uneasy in those instances when, for one reason or another, I've bid early and been listed as the current high bidder on an item that has not yet closed.

for example, the opening bid is usually called, simply, the *reserve*, and I will sometimes use this terminology as well. If there's a danger of confusion, I'll call the opening bid the *open* reserve, to distinguish it from the secret reserve. Remember that the seller also chooses the time the auction starts, its duration (from a limited menu), the shipping charges, acceptable methods of payment, and the presentation on eBay's page, which includes the item's description, the seller's guarantee and return policies, and the quality of the photograph. There's a lot for the seller to think about.

The most obvious function of the opening bid and the secret reserve is to protect the seller from letting an item go too cheaply. eBay *forces* the seller to choose a minimum opening bid (which might be only $0.01), but the secret reserve is optional. However, the fact that a secret reserve exists, and whether it has been met, is posted on an item's eBay page. We should mention also that the premium extracted by eBay from the seller depends on these choices.

The optional buy-it-now price is a fixed price at which the item can be bought and the auction closed. The opportunity is open to buyers at any time during the sale, but *only until a bid above reserve has been received and posted*—yet another example of how eBay is fine-tuned to encourage early and competitive bidding. In the case that an acceptable bid is received, both the fact that the buy-it-now offer existed and the buy-it-now price disappear from the item's web page. Subsequent bidding levels might very well exceed the original fixed-price offer.

We will discuss below some intuitive observations about how the seller might make the choices just described. As usual, we will return to these questions later and try to answer them, as best we can, from the point of view of theory and empirical research.

In discussion like this, never forget that the buyer is almost always looking for a bargain, and often has larceny in her heart.

3.7.1 *Opening Bid*

The simplest choice for the seller is to forgo a secret reserve and the buy-it-now option, and to use only the (mandatory) opening bid. In this case we can break down the common strategies into three categories, which we might call *blowout*, *low-open*, and *high-open* sales.

BLOWOUT SALES: NO SECRET RESERVE, VERY LOW OPENING BID

When a seller chooses a very low (essentially zero) opening bid and no secret reserve, he is putting full reliance on the free-market, competitive nature of eBay. In the collectibles area of ancient coins, this strategy seems to be very popular with large-volume dealers who are acting essentially as wholesalers. Typically they offer little or no detailed information about their products, and I'm guessing they are outlets for consignments of large lots, perhaps even obtained under situations of borderline legality.[22]

The strategy is also popular with dealers who occasionally come across items outside their fields of expertise. They simply rely on the auction mechanism to price the article at something like its "market value."[23]

Both kinds of sellers using the blowout strategy attract bargain hunters and experts looking to cash in on their expertise. It makes for great sport, but one must be prepared to suffer regular setbacks. It would be foolhardy for a seller to offer too many potentially high-end items this way. Most of the sales of this nature, at least in my observations of the ancient coin market, are of relatively common items, or items in beat-up condition.

I should mention a somewhat subtle advantage to choosing low opening bids when selling: potential buyers can, and do, opt to list the results of eBay's search engine in order of increasing current price, so that items with low opening bids will tend to be listed early in the resulting list of hits. This effect is more likely to be important for more common items, where searches produce long hit lists.

NO SECRET RESERVE, MEDIUM OPENING BID

Choosing a reasonable, nontrivial opening bid is the middle road. The seller risks giving an item away for a relatively low price, perhaps what he paid for it, in return for the chance to attract bidders who will run

---

[22] For example, some countries forbid the export of some kinds of artifacts, and some material may travel through several countries before reaching market (see section 7.3).

[23] Quotes because I'm trying to be careful not to give the impression that an item can have an intrinsic price attached to it, independent of the sale mechanism and the set of potential buyers.

the price up. This strategy is very popular among the experienced and regular dealers I see in the ancient coin market. The low opening bid is a hedge against catastrophe, but reliable sellers, even those doing low volume, manage to attract good competition for decent items.

NO SECRET RESERVE, HIGH OPENING BID

As a third possibility, the seller may ask for a very high opening bid. This has the advantage of ensuring a high price, *if the item is sold.* But this strategy carries with it the disadvantage of discouraging bidders from bidding at all, and since bids below the opening are rejected, there will appear to be no interest in the item at all until a bidder meets the high opening bid. The seller has cut off the possibility of drawing bidders into a war, and it can often happen that bidders caught up in such war will ultimately bid above what might have seemed to them a prohibitively high price as an opening bid. I have seen this strategy used by sellers who want to extract unreasonably high prices for items that are highly touted. The seller will often relist the item many times, hoping to find the one buyer he needs to realize a high price.

3.7.2 Use of a Secret Reserve

We next consider the ways in which a secret reserve can be added to the cases above. Roughly speaking, only two such strategies are reasonable: either a moderate secret reserve that protects the seller against loss, while encouraging bidding with a low opening bid; or a very high secret reserve that essentially precludes sale, also while encouraging bidding with a low opening bid. We take each case up in turn.

MODERATE RESERVE, LOW OPENING BID

Adding a moderate secret reserve to a low opening bid has the advantage of encouraging early bids, with a second price that is visible to other potential bidders. This secret reserve almost plays the role of a shill bidder,[24] an agent of the seller, although the amount of the reserve must be fixed once and for all before the sale. Often, bidders will search up by small increments to find the reserve, as illustrated in figure 3.4.

---

[24] This was pointed out to me by John Morgan. We will return to the relationship between a shill bid and a reserve in section 7.1.

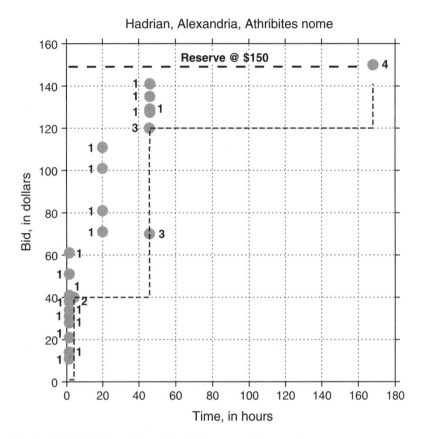

Figure 3.4 Bid history illustrating bidders searching up for a secret reserve.

In this case there is a reserve of $150 on the item, an ancient coin from Roman Alexandria. Bidders 1 and 3 give up a couple of days into the auction, falling short at $141. Bidder 4 then snipes and picks the coin up at the reserve, being the only bidder to meet it. If instead of a reserve the seller had simply used an opening bid of $150, lower bids would not have been accepted and it might well have seemed to bidders that there was no interest in the item.

VERY HIGH RESERVE, VERY LOW OPENING BID

There are dealers who may choose a low opening bid but a very high secret reserve for an item, considerably above what they might expect it to fetch. The motive is twofold. First, as in the case with only a very high opening bid, a dealer may just hit upon the bidder who attaches an unusually high value for the item, and this is a way to extract a high price for it.

Second, and probably the more common reason for choosing a really high secret reserve, is that the seller can in this way locate potential buyers, and then consummate the deal privately by email, thus cheating eBay of its commission (although he must still pay the listing fee). In effect, the dealer is using eBay to advertise his goods. This is forbidden by eBay rules, and is, of course unethical, but the rule is difficult to enforce.[25] Katkar and Lucking-Reiley (2000) described the practice in 2000, and conducted a survey of high bidders in auctions where the secret reserve was not met. They found that about half of the respondents had at some point been contacted by sellers, and about 30% had actually completed a transaction in this way at one time or another. It also sometimes happens that buyers contact sellers with offers after incomplete sales, so the practice of "dealing around eBay" may be even more prevalent than these numbers indicate.

Such carryings-on represent a loss of revenue to eBay that is not easy to gauge, but it is interesting to note that changes in eBay over the last few years have made it a bit more difficult for sellers to contact bidders privately after an unsuccessful sale. Warnings against the practice appear more prominently, email addresses are no longer public, email to bidders goes through eBay, and IDs are no longer allowed to be the same as email addresses.

3.7.3 *Use of the Buy-It-Now Option*

The seller on eBay also has the option of posting a buy-it-now price, which is an offer to sell immediately at the given price, until an acceptable bid is received (one that meets the opening bid, and secret reserve when it is present).[26] The buy-it-now option can be used in three ways.

---

[25] This mechanism is called a *gray market* in Ockenfels and Roth (2006) and Roth and Ockenfels (2002).

[26] The buy-it-now option was anticipated in mail-bid coin sales well before eBay, in auctions called "buy-or-bid" sales. Perhaps the most well known is run by Harlan J. Berk Ltd. in Chicago.

First, the buy-it-now price can be chosen just a bit above the opening bid, in which case the option is essentially a fixed-price sale. In fact, the buy-it-now price and opening bid can be identical and the item listed simply at a fixed price, a special option offered by eBay. This selling strategy makes sense when the seller has a pretty good idea of the "market value" of an item, or when he's fishing for a high price from an inexperienced buyer.

Second, the buy-it-now price can be set moderately high, in conjunction with a low opening bid. The idea here, once again, is to encourage early bidding. An interested bidder may meet the opening bid, just to remove the possibility that the item is snatched up at the buy-it-now price by another bidder. Here the seller must be careful to keep the opening bid attractive and the buy-it-now price credible. The buy-it-now option in this case is designed to create tension in the minds of the bidders.

Finally, the buy-it-now price can be quite high, with a relatively high opening bid as well. The idea here is to use the buy-it-now option to send a signal that an item has high value.

3.7.4 Other Seller Choices

The seller has other significant choices to make besides the opening price and a possible secret reserve or buy-it-now option. These are all interesting strategic choices, and are all worthy of some serious thought. I'll take up the strategic implications briefly in the sections below.

LENGTH OF SALE

A seller on eBay chooses the duration of the auction for each item, one of 3, 5, 7, or 10 days. There may be cases where a short fuse is an advantage, say if an item has great topical interest and you are assured of attracting many interested buyers; but generally speaking, the longer the better—up to a point. Ten days may be a bit long to hold the interest of a potential buyer, for some items, and by far the most common duration for the collectibles I see is one week. A one-week auction can have the advantage of closing at exactly the same time-of-day and day-of-week that the item is first posted,[27] and many sellers make it a point to post at about the same time each week. This sometimes has the effect of creating a community with common interests, all monitoring closing sales at around the same time each week, similar to specialized shopping districts in large cities, with clusters of sellers all offering items of the same general type.[28]

There is another reason why a longer auction duration may be a good idea for the seller. People tend to make investments of time and emotion in an item they are watching, and the longer the duration of the sale, the stronger this effect. The investment may be one of research time that is quite purposeful, or it may be only time spent contemplating potential ownership of a desirable item. We mentioned this attachment already in connection with the endowment effect.

Empirical evidence for these conclusions is given in Lucking-Reiley, Bryan, Prasad, and Reeves's 2000 study of U.S. cents on eBay. They find statistically significant higher prices realized by comparable coins in 7- and 10-day auctions than in 3- and 5-day auctions.

TIME OF CLOSING

Closely related to the choice of sale duration is the choice of just what time-of-day and day-of-week to close an auction. As noted before, the seller often needs to consider time zones, especially if he expects an international clientele. Lucking-Reiley et al. (2000) do include a bar chart of closing time-of-day, and, as you might expect, closings peak in the U.S. evening, with the most auctions closing during the 6 P.M. hour, U.S. Pacific time. To my knowledge there has not yet been a study of the effect of closing time-of-day on realized prices (see question 7).

It is common lore among eBayers that sellers will realize higher prices by choosing closings on the weekend—the so-called "weekend effect." Lucking-Reiley et al. (2000) found no statistically significant weekend effect in their study of U.S. cents. But so far as I know, there has also not been a study of this effect across different categories of items (see question 7).

---

[27] The exact hour and minute can be chosen by the seller.

[28] This effect is very noticeable in large cities like New York, where there is, for example, a cut-flower district, a diamond center, a used musical instrument district, and so on.

My own intuition is that the best timing of auction closings is closely tied to factors like the category and price level of the item, and the average age of prospective buyers. For example, I suspect that the prices fetched by commodity items are more sensitive to such timing issues than collectibles. A collector is much more likely to chase a rare autographed photograph of Maria Callas than the readily available, in-print CD of her 1953 *Tosca*.

METHOD OF PAYMENT

PayPal has been bought by eBay, and is usually preferred strongly by buyers for its speed and convenience. There are other online payment methods, including some that send money orders, but PayPal seems ideally adapted to eBay. It has the disadvantage of costing the seller money, however, and sellers seem very reluctant to pass this cost on to buyers explicitly by tacking on a surcharge for paying with PayPal. For various reasons, it may also be more difficult or less convenient for sellers in certain countries outside the United States to collect payments through PayPal, and such international sellers sometimes ask for personal or bank checks, money orders, or even cash sent by registered mail. Needless to say, asking for cash at least hints at some hanky-panky, and many buyers will shun dealers who do so. Overall, offering to collect via PayPal seems to be well worth the cost to the seller in attracting buyers, although I know of no published study yet (see question 7 of this chapter, and question 1 of chapter 5).

ITEM DESCRIPTION

The seller has important strategic choices in deciding how much time to invest in creating an attractive and informative description of an item. Certainly, a photo of some kind is considered essential. A photo is obviously important for collectibles like jewelry, coins, stamps, paintings, and so on, where the appearance and condition of an item is paramount, and items may be unique. But photos seem to be very important even for standard items, like new computers. People just want to see what they are buying (see question 7).

In the area of collectibles like ancient coins, the detail and accuracy of the description vary widely, depending on the seller's expertise, willingness to invest the time, and honesty. At one extreme is the expert dealer who provides an accurate and useful description of an item, and at the other extreme is the deceptive or uninformed seller who provides, typically, nothing but a photo. The former is the place to buy safely, but the latter provides the lure of the rare find or bargain. Needless to say, such gambling should be done with low stakes.

SHIPPING COSTS

Finally, the seller must decide exactly how the shipping and possible insurance costs for an item will be passed on to the buyer. On the one hand, buyers may fail to take account fully of the shipping costs when bidding.[29] They may even ignore them. This argues for charging the buyers higher shipping costs. On the other hand, a very low shipping cost, especially on items likely to go for low prices, can be very attractive to potential buyers. Psychologically, a buyer is not going to like the idea of paying a shipping fee of $5 on a coin that costs $8. The conclusion is that higher shipping costs will fetch higher total revenue, provided the shipping costs are perceived as a small fraction of the total.[30] There are theoretical arguments, based on the idea that bidders are perfectly rational, to the effect that the shipping costs don't matter, that bidders will discount them perfectly in their bids—but we know better than this by now. We'll take up one aspect of this theory in section 6.5.2, under the rubric of *revenue equivalence.*

3.8 The Next Three Chapters

I'll postpone drawing any further or firmer conclusions about bidding levels, or about good seller strategies, until we learn more about both auction theory and empirical evidence from the laboratory and the field. The next three chapters will provide this background and apply it to eBay. Chapter 4 will consider the question of why eBay is not a first-price auction; chapter 5 will then return to the many choices facing

---

[29] Much like the buyers in English auctions where there is a "hammer fee" or some such surcharge.

[30] This question has been investigated by Hossain and Morgan using field experiments on eBay (2003). For more on field experiments, which have become practical on a large scale only with the internet, see section 5.7.

the seller, including the setting of reserves; and chapter 6 will deal with the ultimate problem of how much to bid.

3.9 Questions

1. In his mail-bid sales of ancient coins, Frank Robinson will take bids by phone, and, if your phone bid is not high enough, he is willing to suggest a bid that will be high enough to make you high bidder. How would you expect this deviation in rules from eBay to affect the bidders' strategies and the seller's revenue?

2. Discuss the following claims made by Frank Robinson in his mail-bid sale:

> PLEASE BID EARLY! In my sales your best strategy is to enter early your top bid, to scare off competition. By waiting till the end you decrease your chances for success & increase the price you have to pay. Also, early bidding is a great help to me in managing the logistics of the sale, so I am highly grateful for early bids.
>
> —Frank S. Robinson
>
> UNRESERVED MAIL BID SALE #59
>
> CLOSING 11 PM, TUESDAY, MARCH 2, 2004

3. The endowment effect is usually framed in terms of a gap between "willingness to pay and compensation demanded," to quote from the title of Knetsch and Sinden (1984). Discuss the relationship between this effect and the idea that potential buyers in an auction may, through investment of time, develop an attachment to an item over the duration of an auction, and thus value it more highly with time.

4. (This is a mathematical problem that requires some probability theory.) Assume that a barrage of bids for a particular item arrives at eBay within the last few seconds of an auction. They will be processed sequentially, so some will be rejected because they will be below the current second-price at the moment they arrive. The more snipes in the barrage, the higher the fraction, on the average, that will be rejected. Make some reasonable assumptions about the distribution of the dollar amounts of the last-second bids, and their arrival times, and derive the expected number of accepted bids as the number of last-second bids in the final barrage grows.

WARNING

The next problems ask you to write "screenscrapers" for internet auctions. Whenever you write any program that interacts with a commercial site, you need to be absolutely sure that you will not interfere with the operation of the web site in any way. In particular, please read the rules posted by eBay about such interference, and be absolutely certain that you do not even *risk* violating the rules. For one thing, be sure to debug your programs on downloaded sample pages, rather than repeatedly pinging the site. Be extra careful to avoid runaway loops. In short, tread lightly and carefully!

5. (Programming project) Write a program that, given the item number of an eBay item that has been sold, creates a plot of the bidding history like the ones in this chapter. The abscissa should be time in hours, and the ordinate dollars (or alternate currency units if you want to get fancy). The graph should show the posted price at any point in the sale, and the amounts bid by the (anonymized) bidders, each identified by a unique number designating the order of the bidder's first bid. Extra points for getting the bidder labels neat; I edited them by hand.

Use any language you want. I used UNIX tools, mainly: wget or lynx to download web pages, sed, grep, gnuplot, and a C program. More modern UNIX aficionados may want to use Perl. Those at the other end of the spectrum (whatever spectrum that may be) may prefer Java. It's instructive to see how different schools of programmers will attack this problem with totally different kinds of tools. See Shmueli and Jank's "Visualizing online auctions" (2004) for many interesting and creative ways to display data collected from eBay auctions.

6. (Related programming projects) Once the previous project is done, it should be easy to produce a number of useful related tools. For example, it might be nice to have a program that tracks a given set of sales and reports current prices and the number of bids, and perhaps informs you by email of new bids. More interesting, but more prone to abuse, would be a program that "shadows" a particular bidder. Before plunging ahead, please reread the warning above, think about the ethics involved, and read the discussion in section 7.3.

7. (Related programming projects) There is no end to interesting projects that process the information available at internet auction sites. I'll just list a few further, more advanced suggestions.

- Write a program that reports only the *negative* feedback in the feedback history of an eBay bidder or seller. Positive feedback is often pro forma. It's the negative feedback that really counts (Lucking-Reiley et al., 2000), and the details often make it clear where the fault lies. But it can be very time-consuming to sift through pages to find it.
- Write a program that snipes at a predetermined time, like eSnipe. Needless to say, be very careful with a program that can spend your money!
- Write a program that tries to identify likely shill bidding.
- Write a program to measure how often negative feedback is reciprocated.
- Compile the prices realized for comparable items, and correlate with seller reputations (as represented by feedback).
- Repeat for closing time-of-day, keeping day-of-week fixed.
- Repeat for closing day-of-week, keeping time-of-day fixed.
- Repeat for accepting payment through PayPal.
- Repeat for posting a photo of the item for sale.

8. (Another programming project) Set up your own web site to conduct auctions and experiment with different rules. I suggest you restrict your population of potential bidders to those in your local community. For example, in a university community it may be easy to restrict bidding to those with university logins. Local auctions like these have three important advantages over wide-flung auction venues like eBay.

First, there is no problem with shipping. Items can be delivered in person. Second, there is much less of a problem with trust, since it will usually be possible to identify the people you sell to. Finally, it may be easier to find a market for items of specialized local interest—for example, tickets to local events or textbooks for particular courses.

9. Discuss the following argument: If sniping is good for buyers, lowering competition and prices, then sellers should try to discourage it by arranging auction closings at inconvenient, rather than convenient times.

What If eBay Were First-Price?

Early bidding on eBay seems to be exciting to bidders and profitable to sellers, and is key to its success. I argue that eBay would break if it were first-price, because early bidding would be punished more severely and obviously, and the "proxy bid" story would be destroyed. Along the way, we describe some useful theoretical ideas: independent private values, equilibrium bidding, bid shading, and revenue equivalence.

4.1 First-Price Is the More Natural Assumption

THE MOST confusing and most often misunderstood characteristic of eBay is that it is a second-price auction. I have run into quite a few people who have bought on eBay without fully understanding the rules, despite the fact that they are, in other respects, sophisticated computer users. One reason for this is the temptation to plunge in and bid without looking up the rules, a habit encouraged by the general internet culture of trial-and-error. Furthermore, the rules themselves are not stated on eBay's site as precisely as they might be, are not easy to find in one place, and are explained in terms of "proxy bidding," which I think, for some people, obscures the actual mechanism. And even if a buyer does understand the rules, it is all too easy, in an optimistic reverie, to forget the rules momentarily, and think of the posted price as the "price to beat." By far the most natural assumption is that the posted price is the current highest bid—despite the fact that even one bid will almost always show this to be utterly wrong.

In this chapter we return to a question raised in chapter 2: What if eBay were, in fact, run by posting and charging the highest instead of the second-highest current price? In particular, do we expect the prices realized to be, on the average, higher, lower, or the same as when second prices are posted? This is an interesting question from the point of view of all concerned: the buyers, the sellers, and the people in the business of designing auction sites (who collect their cut of the selling price), not to mention economists in general. And this question of economics turns out to be as difficult as any we are likely to encounter in studying auctions, for the familiar reason that it involves complex human behavior.

Suppose, then, that eBay is exactly the same as usual, except that the posted price reflects the current *highest* and not the second-highest bid. We've already pointed out that if we also assume that bidders sit at their terminals for the entire duration of the auction, and the auction ends when bidding stops—so that sniping is not possible—the situation becomes identical to an English outcry auction. In his case we can expect the price to stop ascending when it reaches the second-highest valuation of all the bidders, and the first-price version of eBay becomes, in theory, a Vickrey auction. But people do not (usually) sit in front of their computers for a week at a time, and we are assuming that online auctions terminate at definite, predetermined times, so this is, therefore, not a realistic model. If we suppose, at the other extreme, that all bidders snipe in every auction, the situation changes dramatically, and leads to all kinds of interesting questions that go to the heart of the theory of auctions.

4.2 The Sealed-Bid First-Price Auction

If all the bidders snipe in our first-price version of eBay, the situation is completely equivalent to a sealed-bid auction. There is no opportunity to observe others' bids, and no opportunity to change one's one and only bid. As we pointed out in chapter 2, in this situation there is good reason to bid less than one's valuation, for the simple reason that if one were to bid one's valuation and win, the realized surplus would be zero. We say in this situation that the bidder has an incentive to *shade* her bid—that is, bid less than her value. The next question then becomes: Just how much should one shade one's bid?

We can argue that in any given situation, there should be an "optimal" shade. On the one hand, if you shade a very small amount, you have a very good chance of winning—your bid is high. But if you do win, your surplus will be tiny. On the other hand, if you shade a lot, you decrease your chances of winning, even though your surplus is large when you do win. In fact, if you bid zero, shading the most you can, you will, generally, never win, and you can expect a surplus of zero. There should therefore be a "best" shade somewhere between the two extremes that balances these two effects, but how do we find it? This is one of the first problems ever considered in auction theory, and goes back at least to Vickrey's 1961 paper. To understand the simplest kind of answer, and how to interpret it, we need to examine the basic framework and assumptions of auction theory as it was codified in the years following Vickrey's work.

4.3 The Simplest of All Worlds

An economic theory works by inventing an idealized world and studying the consequences. No one, least of all the theoreticians, believes the model is 100% accurate. But to the extent that the model mirrors an aspect of reality that we are interested in, the analysis can give us important guidance in how we conduct our affairs when there may be little else to go on. The best and most valuable theoretical results in economics suggest principles that can help us recognize and think about a wide variety of situations. The idea of *bid shading* is one of these principles.

The simplest model that is used to understand bid shading in first-price sealed-bid auctions is called the independent private values (IPV) model. The world in this model is so idealized, and the assumptions of how people behave are so restrictive, that it's good at this point to list in detail all the model's pieces. We'll see that they fit together, by design, in an exceedingly elegant and productive way.

4.3.1 The Independent Private Values (IPV) Model

In general, a model that can make it possible to determine things like average price levels and the allocation of items must include assumptions of four sorts. It must tell us what the rules of the auction are (the *mechanism*). It must tell us how many bidders there are, and how their valuations are distributed. Trickiest and most troublesome, it must tell us how the bidders behave when they bid. Finally, we must know what the bidders themselves know about the model and the other bidders. In auctions, and in economics generally, information is usually valuable, and what the bidders know, especially about the values of rivals, can affect behavior in important ways.

The following, then, is a complete picture of a first-price sealed-bid auction, the starting point for all mathematical auction theory. Almost all theoretical models since Vickrey are expansions and elaborations of this basic theme.

THE IPV (FIRST-PRICE) MODEL (WITH UNIFORMLY DISTRIBUTED VALUES)

1. There is one, indivisible item for sale by one seller, and it is awarded to the bidder with the highest bid, who then pays exactly her bid (the *first price*).

2. There are n bidders, and each bidder has a value that is known to herself, and only herself (*private*). Furthermore, the values of any one bidder are randomly chosen so that all values between 0 and 1 are equally likely (*uniformly distributed*), and are statistically *independent* of those of any other bidders. A bit of terminology: when all bidders have the same distribution of values, as they do here, we say the bidders are *symmetric*.[1]

3. The bidders all follow the same strategy for arriving at their bids, given their values, and this strategy is to use the common *bidding function*, $b(v)$, assumed to be an increasing function of value v (see fig. 4.1). In addition—and here is the key notion that is really at the bottom of our behavioral assumptions in this model—we assume that there is a bidding function $b(v)$ that has the following special characteristic: If all bidders except you follow the bidding strategy $b(v)$, you can gain no surplus, on the average, by deviating from that

[1] Don't worry about the range being between 0 and 1. This is just to normalize values, and is conventional. For example, if you think in some situation that the range is really $0 to $100, simply multiply all the normalized values by $100.

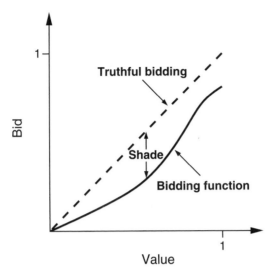

Figure 4.1 The bidding function *b(v)*, which tells you what to bid when your valuation is *v*. The *shade* is the difference between your bid and your actual value, and allows for surplus in first-price auctions.

same strategy. And we assume that each bidder *does*, in fact, follow the bidding strategy $b(v)$, given her value v. We say in this situation that the bidding strategy $b(v)$ is a *symmetric Nash equilibrium*.[2]

4. The bidders know all the conditions stipulated in the three items above, including the fact that all values are uniformly and independently distributed. The standard terminology for this in economics and game theory is that the preceding assumptions are *common knowledge*.

Any framework of this sort is generally called an IPV model, because of the key assumptions of independent and private values. To be more specific, it should really be called the "IPV model for first-price, sealed-bid auctions with symmetric bidders, uniformly distributed values, and a symmetric bidding function." This basic IPV setup can be, and is, applied to many other auction mechanisms, and with more general

[2] More properly a symmetric *Bayesian* Nash equilibrium, "Bayesian" because it uses not just surplus, but expected surplus. See appendix A.

distributions of valuations. But we are focusing on the first-price case, and, as we'll see, even this simple and somewhat fantastic scenario leads to conclusions that are interesting and instructive.

Of course, we can see immediately that the IPV model is unlikely to model exactly the bidders we usually see on eBay. We know that bidders are not symmetric, for example. It is safe to assume that the potential bidders for an item on eBay are a heterogeneous lot, often with a wide range of preferences and behavioral characteristics. They have different knowledge about the items for sale, different budgets, different ages, different personalities, and so on. Besides being asymmetric, real bidders do not have private values that are perfectly evenly spread and statistically independent. But the most intriguing and creative of the assumptions is that they follow an equilibrium strategy, an idea we next examine more closely.

The assumption of equilibrium behavior places extraordinary demands on the bidders in requiring them, not only to behave with surplus-maximizing rationality when all rivals are at an equilibrium, but, somehow, collectively, to find such a point in the first place. The popular picture is that bidders learn to do this, by trial and error, over the course of many auctions; but such a process is complex, and requires some considerable faith in both the intelligence and motivation of bidders, who on eBay are, after all, samples of a diverse sea of humanity. We know that bidders in any particular auction can vary greatly in their levels of experience, in their motivation to extract maximum surplus, in the time they have to analyze their bidding experiences, and in their ability to do so. The Nash equilibrium exercises an irresistible attraction to auction theorists, and economists in general, simply because it is in many cases all we have. John Nash cut the Gordian knot of understanding human behavior by reducing it to the mathematical problem of finding a certain function, from which all manner of delights follow, including predictions of bidding behavior, of expected revenue, and of the relative performance of different auction forms. This apparatus of value-model-plus-equilibrium is a well-oiled machine that has been lovingly constructed and perfected by truly dedicated and brilliant workers.

This said, the reader should expect my usual caveat: Mathematical theory is one thing, and human behavior another.

4.4 How to Shade

Return now to the original question, the reason for building this model in the first place: If your value is v in the IPV model, just how much should you bid? To keep it simple, suppose that you are facing only one rival bidder. That is, suppose $n = 2$.[3]

First, observe that if you accept the assumptions of the IPV model, then both you and your rival will use the same recipe, the function $b(v)$, to determine your bid from your valuation v. Not only that, but we also assume that $b(v)$ is an increasing function, so that the bidder with the larger valuation will submit the higher bid. Thus, the bidder with the higher valuation will always win the item. This property is important from the point of view of society in general, and auctions which ensure that the item always ends up in the hands of the person who values it the most are called *efficient*. It's not always easy to ensure efficiency, and people who design government auctions worry about it a great deal. We can, however, ignore the consideration in the self-absorbed world of eBay.

Now, here's a simple but important observation: If you were tele-pathic, and knew, somehow, what your rival's value actually is, you would know exactly how to bid. If his value happens to be above yours, you needn't bother to bid at all. He will outbid you. So assume you have the higher value. In this case you should bid just a tiny, negligible amount above his value, because if you were to bid lower than his value, it would allow him to outbid you and still earn a positive surplus.

You must take leap of faith here (which is what makes this argument heuristic), and in the absence of telepathic knowledge, bid the most reasonable *estimate* of what your rival's value is. That is, you should bid the expectation of your rival's value, *given that his value is less than*

---

[3] Unless otherwise noted, all the heuristic arguments and outright claims in this and succeeding chapters are backed up by the mathematics in appendices A–C, and I'll usually indicate exactly where. The equilibrium bidding function we're after here is derived in section A.8. The heuristic argument in this section is after McMillan (1992), although it is explicit in the theory, eq. A.52. McMillan's book treats auctions informally in the larger context of strategic decision making, and is highly recommended to managers and business people who want to see more real-world applications of strategic thinking and game theory.

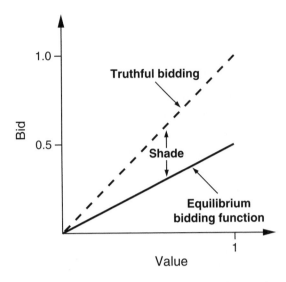

Figure 4.2 The equilibrium bidding function in a first-price auction with two bidders and uniformly distributed private values. Each bidder bids half her value.

yours.[4] This last proviso is absolutely crucial: When you win, it will be in those circumstances when you happen to have the highest valuation. The idea that the outcome of an auction is actually an informative event will play an important role in understanding the winner's curse, discussed later.

It is now not hard to see what to bid in a real first-price sealed-bid auction, where, of course, you do not know your rival's value. Imagine that you have won with the value v, which means that your rival's value must be somewhere between 0 and v. Given the assumption that values are initially distributed uniformly between 0 and 1, your rival's value must now be distributed uniformly between 0 and v, and the most reasonable estimate of it is $v/2$. So you should simply bid half your value, as illustrated in figure 4.2. It turns out that this simple argument works perfectly; this strategy is really an equilibrium (for a proof, see section A.2).

The same sort of reasoning can be applied when there are more than two bidders. Suppose, for example, that there are three bidders. Then if your value is v, you know that, if you win, your two rivals'

---

[4] In the language of probability theory, this is a *conditional* expectation.

valuations will be distributed uniformly and independently between 0 and v. It turns out that the expected value of the higher of the two is $(2/3) \cdot v$, which is also then your equilibrium bid. With four bidders, the equilibrium bid is $(3/4) \cdot v$, and so on. In general, if there are n bidders, the equilibrium bid is $(1 - 1/n) \cdot v$.[5]

This equilibrium bidding function confirms what we come to expect in auctions: Competition drives the price up. The larger n is, the larger the equilibrium bid. It also suggests that it drives the price up a great deal when there are few bidders. A bidder in the kind of auction discussed here pays, on the average, only 50% of her value when she has one competitor, but 90% when she has nine competitors. Sellers on eBay are usually acutely aware of this, of course, and often pay quite a bit extra to get items featured in the listings in one way or another. The importance of attracting just one extra bidder is analyzed theoretically in a well-known paper by Bulow and Klemperer (1996), and the result is proven in section C.7. More about this from the seller's perspective in the next chapter.

4.5 Revenue: The Bottom Line

Even more follows from the simple argument above. The equilibrium bid in our first-price auction is the expectation of the next-highest value, given that we win. The expected price paid by the winner, the seller's *expected revenue*, is therefore the expectation of the value next-below the winner's value—the expected second-highest value from among all the bidders. What revenue can the seller expect to receive in a second-price sealed-bid auction? It is not hard to see that this must also be the expected second-highest value from among the values of all the bidders—exactly the same price!

Thus, on the average, the two auction forms are what is called *revenue equivalent* (given all our assumptions, never forget that). Revenue equivalence is a very general principle in auction theory, and holds for a great many kinds of auctions, and for a variety of models for value distribution. Finding out just when revenue equivalence holds and when it breaks down has been one of the auction theorist's main jobs.

[5] The proof is in section A.7.

So far, it looks as if there is little in the theory to tell us how to choose between the first-price and second-price versions of eBay. But, we know that eBay is very successful, and that first-price internet auctions are actually very rare, and this situation cries for explanation. We look at the problem from a strategic point of view in the next section.

4.6 A First-Price eBay Would Discourage Early Bidding

I will argue that sniping becomes much more attractive to bidders in the first-price form of internet auction than in the second-price (California) version. Or, to put it more accurately, early bidding becomes much *less* attractive.

Suppose, for simplicity, that there are only two bidders, bidder 1 and bidder 2, and that they both snipe. Take the example where values are uniformly distributed between $0 and $100, bidder 1 happens to have a value of $80, and bidder 2 has a value of $70. If they both snipe and bid their equilibrium bids, they bid half their values: bidder 1 bids $40 and bidder 2 bids $35. Bidder 1, who values the item more, wins, gets it for $40, and earns a surplus of $80 − $40 = $40. Of course, bidder 2 would, after the fact, be happy to pay $41 for it, but we know that if he sniped correspondingly high in every auction against the equilibrium bidding strategy of bidder 1, he would, on the average, lose surplus.

Now, what would happen if bidder 1 decided to deviate from this state of affairs by bidding early? Could she benefit by doing so? Suppose, for example, that she submitted an early bid of $30, just to get the action started. We certainly see this kind of behavior all the time on eBay. This prompts bidder 2 to think, "I now know that bidder 1's value is at least $30. I should, therefore, in analogy with the argument in the usual case, snipe my best estimate of her value, *assuming that I win*, which is the midpoint between $30 and $70, or $50." Bidder 1's early bid has revealed some useful information to bidder 2, and bidder 2 has used the information to raise his bid. The result is catastrophic for bidder 1; she will still snipe the same $40 (there is no reason to change her initial best snipe), and bidder 2 will win the item for $50.

We can see that in general a sniper will never benefit by bidding early in addition to her snipe. By doing so she can only raise the rational snipe of her rival (or rivals, when there are more than two bidders). This can only decrease the chances of her winning the item when she snipes. Or, if she compensates for this effect by bidding higher, it can only result in her paying a higher price if she does win.

What has happened here is that bidder 1 has given away information by bidding early, and in this hypothetical first-price version of eBay, bidder 2 has made good use of it. The point is that in the real, second-price eBay, information in early bids remains at least partially hidden. It takes more than one early bidder to increase the posted current second-highest price above the minimum opening bid, and the current highest bid is, with rare exceptions, secret.

There is thus a much stronger disincentive against early bidding in the first-price online auction than in the real eBay. My feeling is that this is an important part of eBay's success. It's more fun to bid early, and the "proxy bid" story, which is just the second-price rule, is worded in a way that suggests there is no punishment for early bidding on eBay at all. This attracts buyers, and hence sellers—determining factors for the success of an auction house. On the other side of the ledger, the argument above suggests that revenues might be higher if eBay were first-price. But the key to eBay's success has been in attracting customers, and establishing what seems like a solid monopoly on the internet auction business. Of course, I argued earlier rather strongly that sniping in the real, second-price, eBay is also the best strategy. But there the punishments for early bidding are less directly felt, and the arguments against it are more subtle, and take us outside the standard IPV model.

And this is what the theory for the IPV assumption has to say about the choice between first-price and second-price formats: early bidding is potentially more damaging with the first-price payment rule because it may help others to shade more cleverly. At this point, there is little theory available for auctions with deadlines; that topic cries for attention.

4.7 First-Price Is More Work for the Bidder

Another argument against a first-price version of eBay is based on the fact that finding an equilibrium strategy is in general a lot more

difficult than discovering that bidding truthfully is a reasonable idea—
or even a dominant strategy, which we know it is when everyone
snipes on eBay and it reduces to a second-price auction. eBay even
supplies the explicit (and perhaps self-serving) suggestion to "Enter the
highest amount you'd be willing to pay." There are two ways this extra
difficulty in deciding strategy in first-price auctions can affect auction
behavior. First, just the extra work in trying to determine a good bid
may repel bidders relative to a second-price alternative. This would give
a second-price competitor an advantage in the all-important battle for
customers on the internet. Second, the bidders are simply less likely to
seek and find an equilibrium, and the bids themselves are likely to be
off equilibrium. In fact, there is good experimental evidence that non-
equilibrium bidding in a first-price auction will result in higher prices,
which would also tend to turn bidders away.[6]

4.8 Further Theory Disappoints

Most of the theoretical work outside the IPV model stems from a
very influential paper by Milgrom and Weber (1982), in which the
idea of *affiliated values* is used. This model includes the IPV model
as a very special case, but also covers the common-value or mineral-
rights model mentioned in chapter 3. The main outcome of this
research is summarized briefly in section C.2, but the upshot, in less
technical terms, is this: Suppose valuations of bidders are interrelated
in complicated ways and bidders are not certain of their own particular
valuations. Then when bidders are *symmetric*, we can say very generally
that the expected revenue from the English auction exceeds that of the
second-price auction, which exceeds that of the first-price auction. It
may be surprising to you that English auctions promise higher average
prices than second-price auctions, in light of the fact that they are
strategically equivalent. But remember that this strategic equivalence is
weak (section 1.8). Bidders can observe the bids of others during the
course of an English auction, and, when they are uncertain of their
values and know that the values of rivals are related to their own,

[6] See the summary of experimental laboratory work in appendix D.

they can, and will, adjust their bids to take that extra information into account. Of course, we also know from chapter 1 that first-price auctions are strategically equivalent to Dutch auctions in the *strong* sense, and from this it follows that the revenue from Dutch auctions should be the same as that from first-price auctions, regardless of how values are distributed.

It is a sad fact, however, that Milgrom and Weber's beautiful revenue-ranking result just cannot be applied with any conviction to an auction venue like eBay. In my experience, bidders really are a heterogeneous lot, with widely differing experience, knowledge, and willingness to spend money, so the assumption of symmetric bidders is simply not credible. And this is absolutely crucial, because when bidders are not symmetric, the revenue ranking between first- and second-price auctions can go either way (Krishna, 2002). Add to this the fact that eBay is neither an English nor a second-price auction, but rather a hybrid. Finally, remember that no one ever really knows how many bidders are participating in a given sale, whereas almost all the theoretical results assume that the number of bidders, as well as their value distributions, are common knowledge.

4.9 Conclusion

In this chapter we asked what eBay would be like if the bidders saw and paid the first instead of the second price. The insights we used for the argument in section 4.6 came from the simplest IPV model, and relied on the assumption that bidders in a first-price auction will at least tend to follow an equilibrium strategy based on their current knowledge of rivals' valuations. It is not really necessary that bidders find the equilibrium shading factor exactly; our argument depends only on the idea that when a bidder learns, from an early bid, that a rival's value is likely higher than she would have a right to assume before that early bid, she tends to increase her own bid. We conclude—and this part is necessarily a judgement call—that this kind of response would make sniping a more obvious strategy, destroy the "proxy bid" story that encourages bidders to bid early and truthfully, and change the character of eBay entirely.

We can summarize the argument more simply as follows: The driving force behind eBay, despite the prevalence of sniping, is the excitement and competition stimulated by early bidding. Otherwise, it might as well be run as an ideal second-price sealed-bid sale. Online, the second-price rule supplies much more incentive to bid early.

The general kind of argument in this chapter provides a good example of how auction theory is usually applied. Theory supplies us with handy mental constructs, like bid shading and equilibrium behavior, and we use these ideas as best we can in situations that usually do not match the model exactly. In the next chapter we will see what an ideal theory says about another important aspect of eBay—the seller's choices of open and secret reserve. Once again, we will look to the foundation of equilibrium strategy to guide our intuition. But there is recent empirical work that bears directly on these decisions, and we will also review that work in drawing our conclusions.

4.10 Questions

1. Suppose your are participating in a first-price, sealed-bid auction with independent, identically distributed private values, and you happen to know that the valuations are not distributed uniformly, but are biased towards the low side. That is, low values are more likely than high. Should you shade more or less than in the case of uniformly distributed values? Justify your answer.

2. You had planned to snipe in an eBay auction, but you are suddenly forced to bid early because of an unforeseen engagement. Let's say that you had originally planned to snipe with a bid of $100. When you bid early, should you bid more, less, or the same $100? Why? How might you determine the amount of the early bid?

The Signals That Sellers Send

We examine the seller's choice of opening bid and secret reserve.
What seems to matter most in the end is attracting
bidders—competition! More theoretical ideas: the linkage
principle, and Milgrom and Weber's principle of full disclosure
when values are correlated. We also describe the new genre of
empirical work using field experiments.

5.1 Reserves

So FAR we have concentrated on the strategies of bidders. Now it's
time to take a closer look at the choices faced by the seller, especially
what are probably the most important decisions presented to a seller
posting an item on eBay: What opening bid (reserve) should he choose,
should he use a secret reserve, and, if so, what secret reserve should he
choose?[1] Reserves, both open and secret, are a long tradition in auctions
in general, and their most obvious function is to enable the seller to
refuse a sale at too low a price. But as we'll see later in this chapter, there
is another very important, more strategic reason for an open reserve: in
many situations it can force prospective buyers to pay more than they
would with no reserve.

Here's an example, a real one that I observed on eBay, that illustrates
the seller's complicated array of options. A seller was offering a bronze
of Antinous.[2] Such coins are highly prized for their portraits of an

---

[1] Recall that in the auction literature, the minimum opening bid is usually called,
simply, the *reserve*, and I will sometimes follow that terminology. When there might be
confusion, I'll call the opening bid the *open* reserve.

[2] Companion of Hadrian described with varying degrees of frankness over the years
by numismatists and historians in general. Typical of the nineteenth century and

historically important personage, and are rare as well, so they command high prices, even in poor condition. The particular piece for sale was, in fact, worn, pitted and very much on the shaggy side, but still a prize for the humbler collector. The seller posted it first with an opening bid of $750, which I found very high, but I watched the item, hoping it would not sell and be reposted. It was, at $499, and I toyed with the idea of destroying my budget and bidding for it. Mentally, I included the price I would pay for authentication, since these items are among the most often faked. I decided against bidding, and watched the close. Only a single bidder appeared, who therefore paid the $499. Now, was the seller's strategy of posting a high reserve and then reposting with a lower one a good one? A deep question. You might argue that the buyer who was willing to pay $499 but not $750 was probably willing to pay more than $499, and that the reduction to $499 was therefore too large a cut. But you could also argue that the original post at $750 shaped the buyer's valuation and made the $499 seem like a bargain. Or was the seller's strategy of posting with a high opening bid and reducing it all wrong, and should he have started at $0.01, or maybe $100, to attract as many bidders as possible to drive up the price in competition?

There is yet another factor to consider when trying to extract a high price with a high reserve, either open or secret. If the item goes unsold, it places an upper bound on the price that it will eventually fetch if relisted, at least psychologically, and it may also confer on the unsold item something of a stigma. Ashenfelter and Graddy (2002) discuss the issue of whether the ultimate sale prices of such items, termed "burned," are in fact depressed, and conclude in their empirical study of the art market that it is difficult to sort out other factors, but that the evidence for the idea is "suggestive."

The choice of reserves is determined by the information that the seller has about an item, and how he wants to use it. This leads us to consideration of the price estimates that may be provided by the seller in any auction, and, more generally, to all the information in the catalog description or eBay posting.

---

the more austere present-day catalogs would be something like "handsome youth of Bithynia and favorite of Hadrian."

5.2 Price Estimates and Related Revelations

Auction catalogs for coins, and art objects in general, often provide estimates of market value, sometimes in the form of a low-high range. For example, Dan Clark gives price estimates in his mail-bid sales, and states in his auction rules that "Bids below 60% of our estimates are not accepted except in the 'Minimum Reserve' section (where $2.00 is the lowest bid allowed)."[3] He continues, "Some lots have reserves up to 90% of the estimate," thus giving us altogether an estimate, a minimum opening bid, and an upper bound on any possible secret reserve. This 60%-of-estimate formula is typical of many of the mail-bid sales I've seen. In any event, it is almost always the case that when a secret reserve exists, it is assumed to be below any published estimate. The situation may be complicated by the fact that the auctioneer sometimes provides a range of values for an estimate, rather than just one price; but in this case, as Ashenfelter and Graddy (2002) report in their study of art auctions, "The auction houses do commonly observe an unwritten rule of setting the secret reserve price at or below the low estimate."

The wording in the "Terms of Sale" is often noncommittal, and sometimes even slippery. Of course, it's natural for auction houses to try to leave for themselves as much discretion as possible in settling sales. For example, the beautiful catalog of Numismatic Fine Arts, Inc. for their Auction IV, March 24–25, 1977,[4] states in the "Terms of Sale":

> The prices printed on the enclosed sheet are estimates based on recent international market prices. These are not limits or reserves but are intended as a guide for bidders. The prices realized may be higher or lower than these valuations.

There are also "Instructions for Mail Bidders" in the same catalog:

> Please consult the enclosed list of estimates as you plan your bids. The bidding for each lot will be opened at approximately 60% of the estimated value. Please do not submit bids for a small fraction of

---

[3] His mail-bid sale of September 20, 2004.

[4] If your interest in a bronze of Antinous was stimulated by our mention above, you might be interested in lot 588 of this sale, a very nice medallion from Tarsos. Its estimated price was $1200, and it sold for $3600—and these were 1977 dollars.

the fair market price. We understand your desire to get a bargain, but we ask you to understand our obligation to protect the interests of our consignors.

I can't resist juxtaposing these chilly remarks with Frank Robinson's friendly note:[5] "Never fear 'insulting' me with cheap bids. I am insult-proof."

A further word about these price estimates, which we see can play an important role in determining the opening bids. Sometimes they are listed in the auction catalog itself, but often an auction house, especially a high-tone one like the one quoted above, will list the estimates on a separate sheet, I suppose so that they can be edited late in the preparation process. It might also be considered contaminating to have prices printed in the main catalog, which traditionally has a scholarly tone, and can serve as a reference for many years after the sale. The result is that the lists of estimates often get lost, and someone who likes to read a calculated profit motive into every business decision might suspect that some auction houses want the estimates to get separated from the catalog after the sale, perhaps because some selling prices may show the estimates to be embarrassingly inaccurate. A list of prices realized is usually printed after the sale, on a similar sheet, and mailed to bidders. These are lost even more often, and I feel lucky when I can get an old catalog with both the list of estimates and the list of prices realized tucked inside.

The question of whether the price estimates provided by the auction house or auctioneer accurately reflect the market is a very interesting one, and the same sort of question arises about opening bids and secret reserves on eBay. Do, or should, sellers send accurate price signals to prospective buyers? Is it in the interest of an auction house to inflate its estimates, or for an eBay seller to tout his wares extravagantly? This is a question that has been studied by economists using both theoretical and empirical methods. In my own experience, the answer depends critically on whether the auction house or seller is interested in building trust over many auctions with experienced buyers, or rather is interested in short-term gain by giving deceptively high estimates. Reputable auction

---

[5] Usual in his mail-bid sales, for example Mail Bid Sale #62, closed 11 P.M., February 22, 2005.

houses and private sellers do seem to me to provide more or less accurate estimates, perhaps with a slight upward bias. I think of these prices as "high retail," prices that buyers at a brick storefront might pay without haggling from a reputable dealer. A reserve of 60% of the estimate is in this case a tempting opening bid.

The situation on eBay is a little different from a traditional English auction with a catalog, because estimates are rarely given explicitly, and the price guidance is provided by the opening bid itself and the presence or absence of the secret reserve during the auction period. As we discussed before, in section 3.7, trusted, large-volume dealers with regular repeat buyers often have very low opening bids, sometimes even the minimum $0.01, but in any case well below normal levels. They depend on the functioning of a market of knowledgeable, competitive bidders to yield fair prices, and by setting the minimum opening bid, they minimize the eBay fee based on it. On the other hand, there are some eBay sellers who seem to use very high opening bids, with correspondingly high buy-it-now options, with the aim of misleading inexperienced buyers. Typically, they continue to re-post the same item over months with consistently high opening bids (running up an eBay bill), evidently waiting for the one newly arrived "sucker" to fall for the bait. Judging by the rarity of such sellers in the ancient coin category, I'm guessing they don't make out very well, at least in the more specialized collecting categories.

Providing price estimates is one way to transmit information to bidders, but we should not forget the item description itself, which plays a critical role in all auctions. As discussed in section 3.7.4, there is a wide spectrum of quality, detail, and fidelity in item descriptions on eBay, and the variation provides a fertile ground for strategic interaction between different kinds of sellers and buyers. As mentioned, the question of just what the seller should reveal to prospective buyers has come under the scrutiny of theorists, and we next discuss the one very famous result.

5.3 Virtue Rewarded, in Theory

Milgrom and Weber (1982) is invariably cited when discussing what a seller should reveal to prospective buyers. The assumption in that paper is that the seller has access to private, useful information about the item and that he must decide how to release this information to the bidders so as to maximize his revenue. The information can be statistical in nature, and therefore accurate only on the average, but it must correlate positively with the true values assigned to the item by the bidders.[6] Furthermore, and this is crucial, it is assumed that the seller is *credible*, which amounts to stipulating that the seller cannot deliberately send false signals. He could, at one extreme, adopt a policy of never reporting any of the information, or, at the other extreme, he could decide always to report the information accurately and completely. But he could also decide to report only the most favorable information, or to randomize his reporting policy. Any policy of information release is allowed, but outright fabrication is not an option. Milgrom and Weber's result is that the seller should choose the policy of complete revelation. As Milgrom and Weber put it, and as others almost invariably quote it, "Honesty is the best policy." But the generality of this injunction may be a bit overstated here, because the alternative is not to lie about the item, but just to withhold information about it. Milgrom and Weber's theory simply tells the seller how to use his information as profitably as possible, assuming that he is truthful and has earned the trust of the bidders.

The intuition behind the result is provided by the "linkage principle," which, loosely speaking, tells us that the more the price paid by the winning bidder is linked, statistically, to the valuations of other bidders, the higher the average price she is willing to pay. Where, on the one hand, the revenue equivalence principle[7] shows that the revenue of many auction forms is the same when valuations are IPV, the linkage principle shows that when bidder valuations are statistically linked, the auction forms are *not* revenue equivalent[8] Ashenfelter puts it well in his informative article about his firsthand experiences in auctions of fine wines and art (Ashenfelter, 1989): "The basic idea is that revealing information tends to remove uncertainty and make low

---

[6] Technically, the seller's private information is assumed to be *positively affiliated* with the bidders' information about their valuations. See section C.2.

[7] Discussed earlier in section 4.5.

[8] As we mentioned in section 4.8. See appendices A–C for much more about revenue equivalence.

bidders more aggressive; this puts upward pressure on the bidding of others, which is in the interest of the auctioneer." The whole process of price formation when the information of bidders is statistically linked can be thought of as one of information aggregation, in some sense the essential function of the auction institution, or, for that matter, any market.

By the way, Milgrom and Weber's paper does not take into account the cost to the seller of ascertaining this private information, such as the time or money for research, expert appraisals, or high-quality photos. This can be considerable, and a seller faces a trade-off in deciding how much to invest in describing an item. Clearly, it doesn't make much sense to spend $20 in time and eBay fees in posting a coin that will sell for $10. But the marginal expected return in revenue may well justify this cost for a $1000 coin. This is reflected in the premiums paid for displaying expensive items on eBay in the special "Featured Items" section, as well as the beautifully produced and well-researched printed catalogs for high-end items sold by the big auction houses.

It is also important to remember the framework of the results in Milgrom and Weber (1982), which is notable for handling the case when bidders' values are not independent, but are affiliated.[9] Besides assuming that the seller is credible, it is also assumed, critically, that the bidders are symmetric, and that bidder behavior is at equilibrium. As I've said before, I find it hard to accept the symmetric bidder model for eBay. And the evidence from laboratory and empirical tests shows that bidders do not always find or follow equilibrium behavior.[10] And always keep in mind the standard assumptions of most of the theory, that the number of bidders and their value distributions are known to everyone. It is even assumed that the seller's revelation policy is public knowledge.

Granting these reservations, there is still a lot to be said for an honest revelation policy, and honesty in general, on the part of the seller. There is, first of all, the not inconsiderable satisfaction of behaving

[9] See section C.2 for more on affiliated values.

[10] We will return to this problem repeatedly in future chapters. See also appendix D for a summary of the literature on laboratory experiments and experimental evidence that bidders may not follow equilibrium strategies.

morally. But the building of trust, plus the honest reporting of data about wares, also seems to be the most profitable policy in the long run from a practical point of view. My favorite auction sellers are those who describe faults scrupulously and provide honest price estimates, and I'm sure I am joined by most buyers in this view. Building customer loyalty is surely the way to build any successful business with repeat customers. The eBay dealers who violate this precept, as I've mentioned above, do not seem to make out well in the ancient coin world, although fly-by-night, dishonest sellers may do better in categories that are not likely to involve as much repeat business.

A conclusion similar to Milgrom and Weber's, supporting honest disclosure, is reached by Forsythe, Isaac, and Palfrey (1989) in a laboratory study of auctions in which sellers have information about item quality that they may or may not choose to reveal to the potential buyers. They mention as a motivation for their study the motion picture industry, where the exclusive distributor of a film auctions off the film rights to exhibitors. They report that "over 90% of the films distributed by the major American distributors are blind bid"—that is, auctioned off before the production of the film begins. Exhibitors have claimed that the blind-bid auctions are a way for distributors to earn excess profit from low-quality films. There have even been laws passed in some states against this blind-bidding practice, and distributors have threatened to stop location filming in those states. Their experiments with sealed-bid first-price auctions show that buyers learn not to be gullible, and to assume the worst; and that sellers learn to reveal all of their information. As they put it (p. 230), "even unsophisticated buyers need only a few observations . . . to learn that high quality items are not sold via a blind-bidding auction."

5.4 Art, Silver, and Jewelry Auctions: Empirical Observations of Seller Price Estimates

Ashenfelter (1989) gives the results of observing the pre-auction estimates and sale prices of impressionist paintings at auctions held by Sotheby's and Christie's in London and New York from 1980 to 1981. We show a reconstruction of his scatter plot in figure 5.1. The

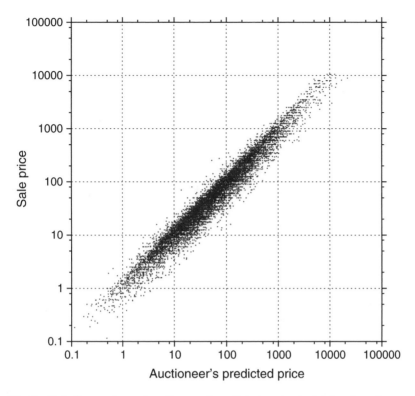

Figure 5.1 Comparison of auctioneers' predicted and actual sale price of impressionist and modern paintings, 1980–91, at auctions conducted in London and New York, at both Christie's and Sotheby's. Some 11,530 sales are shown. The prices are in thousands of dollars, only completed sales are shown, and the auctioneers' predicted prices are the averages of their high and low estimates. This figure is a reconstruction of the one in Ashenfelter (1989), using data kindly provided by Kathryn Graddy; the data was originally gathered by Orley Ashenfelter and Andrew Richardson, and reported by Richardson in his senior thesis (1992). For more on price estimates, including data for auction sales of contemporary art, see Beggs and Graddy (1997).

agreement is excellent, and in fact the percentage difference between sale and estimated price ranges from 1.5% for Sotheby's in London to 3.9% for Christie's in New York. Quite convincing.

In contrast, in the same field of fine paintings, Mei and Moses (2004, p. 1) find that "price estimates for expensive paintings have a consistent upward bias over a long period of thirty years." They also find that high estimates are associated with adverse returns on subsequent resale, and suggest that some buyers are credulous, and that the auction houses take advantage of their credulity—at variance with the Milgrom and Weber prescription for the honest and complete publication of estimates.

The more recent survey of Ashenfelter and Graddy (2002) finds general confirmation of the accuracy of price estimation in the art world, except for some systematic biases found by Beggs and Graddy (1997), which suggest, for example, that auction houses tend to underestimate the consumer demand for larger paintings. By the way, this unexpectedly high correlation of gross size with price seems to hold also for ancient coins, although I do not know of any systematic study of the question. All things being equal, the very large ancient coins seem to fetch much higher prices than do the smaller. Even moderately common and medium-sized coins are sometimes touted enthusiastically as "medallions," with the implication that they were produced for special reasons and not just for use as circulating cash.

The accuracy of pre-auction estimates by the house seems to vary with the field. Bauwens and Ginsburgh (2000) gathered data for auction sales of English silver coffee- and teapots in London, between 1976 and 1990, again by Christie's and Sotheby's. They found consistent but small biases, and found that Sotheby's overestimates low prices and underestimates high prices, while Christie's "tends to underestimate more systematically." Ashenfelter and Graddy (2002) also cite a study of price estimates in the jewelry field by Chanel, Gérard-Varet, and Vincent (1996), who also find undervaluation (except for some watches).

5.5 The Complexity of the Seller's Signaling

All this bears on eBay sales in very complicated ways. The eBay seller does not usually provide a price estimate, but he sends many signals to prospective bidders, including most obviously the opening bid, the presence or absence of a secret reserve, the secret reserve itself when it is discovered or lower-bounded by bidding, and possibly a buy-it-now price. The enthusiasm of the item description, and its detail and quality, also signal the seller's assumed regard for the item, and if he subscribes to the Milgrom and Weber theory, he will fashion the presentation to maintain credibility over many sales.

Consider this example of just how complicated the message encoding can be.[11] Here was a nice Jewish city coin of Sebaste, Samaria, offered by a professional dealer, who stated: "This coin is from a collection that I put together for myself." The starting bid was $9.99 (ridiculously low), tempered by the eBay notation "Reserve not met." There was also a buy-it-now offer at $500, which suggests that the secret reserve was, using a 60% rule-of-thumb, around $300, although this can only be a guess. The seller added that a similar, but larger (33mm vs. 29mm), version of this coin was valued, in somewhat better condition (Very Fine vs. Fine), at $1500. In the end the item went unsold. There were six bids by four different bidders, the highest of which, $156.44, did not reach the secret reserve. This is another example of bidders searching up in an attempt to find the reserve, as in section 3.7.2.

This item was then relisted soon after the unsuccessful sale, with an opening bid of $299 and a buy-it-now offer of $350, thus making it explicit that the seller was not going to let go of this item for a song. The first listing left open the possibility that the item would fetch as much as $500, and the second sale, given the bidding level of the first sale, almost amounted to a fixed price offer at $299. The second listing received no acceptable bids either. As far as I know, the coin went unsold, at least through the visible channel of eBay, which I've found is not an uncommon outcome when such games are played. But the story shows how expressive the seller's reserve language can be. It also illustrates how a narrowing range between the open reserve and a buy-it-now price can suggest a take-it-or-leave-it offer.

This dance is a far cry from a simple price estimate—an option always available to a seller—and seems to be designed to conceal the seller's true view of the item's market value. Evidently this dealer, along with many others, does not follow Milgrom and Weber's famous recommendation for full revelation. This presents somewhat of a puzzle, and Vincent (1995) gives a theoretical argument for keeping reserve prices secret despite the Milgrom and Weber principle of full

---

[11] A real example from eBay.

disclosure. Essentially he argues that a secret reserve encourages bidder participation, which then increases the linkage between price paid and the value of the purchased item.

This phenomenon of hiding the secret reserve is evidently widespread in non-eBay, English auctions; Ashenfelter (1989) reports that auction houses are very careful to conceal their secret reserves, and even whether they exist. He describes how this happens in outcry wine and art auctions as follows (p. 24):

> When the bidding stops, the item for sale is said to be "knocked down" or "hammered down." ... What is not so well understood is that the items knocked down have not necessarily been sold. Here is the reason. The seller will generally set a "reserve price," and if the bidding does not reach this level the item will go unsold. Auctioneers say that an unsold item has been "bought in."

The items that are bought in are purchased through "phantom bids" that the auctioneer takes "off the wall" or "from the chandelier." Cassady (1967) also describes the process as it occurred back in the 1960s, and the practice probably goes back a couple of millennia. Generally, it is considered ethical to take bids off the wall before the bidding has reached the secret reserve, and unethical—tantamount to using shills—when the bidding has passed that point. In some cases there may be laws regulating this sort of thing; we will return to the subject of shill bidding in chapter 7.

eBay posts, for all to see, the existence of the secret reserve and whether it has been met, which goes some way towards eliminating this kind of chicanery. There is always the possibility, however, that bids, either below or above the secret reserve, are from shills, agents of the seller. This practice may be quite widespread on eBay, judging from anecdotal evidence from my unidentified sources. It is, of course, against eBay's rules.

5.6 What Theory Has to Say about Reserves

We return to the main question of setting reserves on eBay, and here the basic independent private-value theory with symmetric bidders offers some very definite advice. Let's assume for the following discussion that there are three bidders altogether, and that their values are independently and identically distributed between $0 and $200.

5.6.1 The Tradeoff in Second-Price Auctions

Consider first the Vickrey auction (sealed-bid and second-price). Suppose, for simplicity, that the seller attaches no value whatsoever to the item for sale, he just wants to unload it, but he chooses an open reserve (minimum starting bid) of, say, $100.[12] It is a wonderful property of the second-price auction that it is still a weakly dominant strategy for each bidder to bid her true value. As long as a bidder is sure of the item's value to herself, there is nothing to be gained by bidding either above or below that value, by Vickrey's 1961 argument, even if there is a reserve.

Now, given that we know how the bidders will bid in equilibrium, it is easy to see that the reserve can cut both ways for the seller. If, on the one hand, all the bidders have values below the $100 reserve, there will be no sale, whereas there would have been one without the reserve. So the seller in this case loses some surplus. On the other hand, if the highest bidder bids, say, $120, and no other bidders meet the reserve, the seller will get the reserve price of $100 for the item. He therefore comes out way ahead, while the winning bidder comes away with less surplus. We'll see shortly what reserve the seller should choose to maximize his expected profit, but first, let's look at the first-price auction.

5.6.2 The Tradeoff in First-Price Auctions

Consider next, then, the effect of the $100 reserve in a first-price auction. The seller still strikes out if all the bidder values are below the reserve. He will miss a sale where he would have made one before,

---

[12] See section B.3 for the theory of how to set reserves in the case of independent private values and symmetric bidders, from Riley and Samuelson (1981), the second-most famous paper in auction theory (after Vickrey (1961), of course). The theory when the seller does attach a positive value to the item is not much different from the case when he does not.

assuming that some bidder has a value more than zero. Suppose, though, that as before the highest bidder has a value of $120. Without the reserve, her equilibrium bid would be, as we discussed in chapter 4, shaded down from her value by an amount that depends on the number of bidders. In our example, we know there are two other bidders. Then her equilibrium bid would be just $80, two-thirds of her value. But she is constrained to bid at least the reserve of $100; a bid of $80 would be rejected. She can, and will, earn some surplus by winning the item at $100, but again, the seller is able to extract a higher price because of the reserve.

5.6.3 *The Optimal Reserve*

We come now to one of the truly remarkable results in auction theory. For cases like this example, where bidders have independent and identically distributed private values, it turns out that

- The seller should choose a reserve strictly *above* his value. Thus, even if he values the item at zero, he should set a reserve above zero.
- The best choice of reserve for the seller does not depend on the number of bidders, and can be calculated in a straightforward way once we know how the values are distributed.
- The best choice of reserve is the same for a very wide class of auctions, including first- and second-price auctions.

In the simple case we like to use for examples, where the values are uniformly distributed, the optimal reserve is just one-half the maximum possible. The $100 reserve used above, when the maximum possible bidder value is $200, is therefore the best possible for the seller.

5.6.4 *The New Equilibrium*

In a first-price auction with a reserve, bidding two-thirds of one's value when there are three bidders is no longer an equilibrium strategy, and the new equilibrium is not quite as easy to calculate as before. But it's not that difficult either (using eq. B.20), and the result is shown

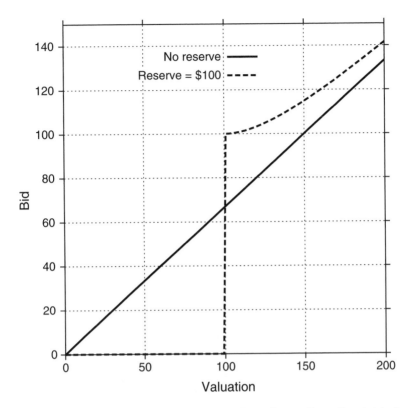

Figure 5.2 Equilibrium bidding functions in a first-price auction with a total of three bidders whose values are independently and uniformly distributed between $0 and $200. Shown is the equilibrium with no reserve, and with the optimal reserve of $100. Bidders with values above the reserve bid higher, in equilibrium, in the presence of the reserve.

in figure 5.2, along with the old two-thirds strategy. The equilibrium bid with the reserve is considerably higher than the old equilibrium, especially for values near (but above) $100, which reflects the situation described above. A bidder with the value of $120 might prefer to bid below the reserve if it were possible, but is forced to bid at least the $100 and settle for less surplus. Not only that. In equilibrium she will actually bid *above* the reserve, because the competition drives all the potential bids up. In fact, her equilibrium bid with a valuation of $120 is $103.15, quite a bit more than the no-reserve equilibrium of $80.

5.6.5 *Practical Implications*

The theory of how to set a reserve price optimally when bidders have independent private values is quite clear in its recommendation. As a seller, you should set an opening price above your value. In particular, you should set an appreciable opening price even when the item for sale is worthless to you. The reserve will force bidding up in general, and increase your expected return. Before we report some empirical work that puts this recommendation to the test, we should, as usual, examine the context of the theory, and decide whether we want to believe it applies to eBay, and auctions generally.

The IPV assumption, plus the assumption of symmetric bidders, should always give us pause. The resulting recommendation for the seller to set an opening bid above his value and independent of the number of bidders is not what is commonly observed. In many auction settings, including eBay, there is a strong tendency to use low reserves when the competition is high, which is tantamount to saying that the reserve decreases with the number of bidders. Besides this conflict with reality, the theoretical result can also be a bit troubling to economists, because the resulting auction is *inefficient*. That is, the item can end up in the hands of someone who does not value it most highly (the seller), and so this choice of reserve is, in some sense, not best for society as a whole.[13] While this may not matter when worrying about auctions of antique fountain pens on eBay, it may be very important when the government auctions off public goods, like radio spectrum.

These problems led Levin and Smith (1996) to consider the optimal choice of reserve when bidder information is either not private (taking the "P" out of IPV), or not statistically independent (taking the "I" out of IPV). Their results show that in these auction models, the seller's optimal starting bid converges to his true value as the number of bidders gets large—essentially negating the conclusion that it is independent of the number of bidders, and removing inefficiency. This theory is certainly much better at explaining many real-world auctions, where the bidders' information is very likely to be statistically correlated. For example, it explains the frequent eBay sales that start

---

[13] See section C.4.

at $0.01 with no secret reserve. As Levin and Smith (p. 1281) put it, "we may interpret advertisements for items that will be auctioned 'without reserve' simply as evidence that the seller anticipates 'sufficient competition' in the auction, rather than as an inexplicable departure from the IPV prediction."

The theoretical study of choosing the opening bid is a good example of how the IPV model can help us think about a problem, but it also illustrates the dangers of accepting conclusions without questioning the underlying assumptions. In this case I think it is important to refine the model so that it reflects the likely correlation of bidders' valuations and the stimulating effect of early bidding.

5.7 Field Experiments

We consider now the collection of data from authentic auctions, where bidders have sought out the sales and are competing to buy things they really care about. There is nothing new about collecting data from real auctions, of course. I've already mentioned such work in this chapter by Ashenfelter and Graddy (2002; Ashenfelter, 1989). But the internet has made it possible for the first time to collect sizable amounts of data, automatically, and with very little effort after the initial investment in programming. eBay, in particular, has a remarkably open policy for making the details of its transactions public. This has the beneficial effect of engendering trust, and at the same time, as a side effect, provides a cornucopia of information for the auction theorist-voyeur. The internet has not only facilitated the *passive* collection of real auction data, but has also made possible large-scale experiments in real auctions. These are called *field experiments*, in contrast with *field observations*.[14]

For field experiments we will rely especially on the work of David Lucking-Reiley,[15] who was one of the first to exploit the internet for this kind of work, beginning with markets that evolved spontaneously in

---

[14] There are, however, field experiments in economics that do not use the internet. For example, List and Lucking-Reiley (2000) sold sports cards at sports card shows, and (2002) solicited contributions for a university fund-raising campaign.

[15] By the way, David changed his name to David Reiley in August 2002.

newsgroups, and then on eBay. He and Katkar describe their experiences selling on the internet in vivid and entertaining detail in Lucking-Reiley (1999, 2000a) and Katkar and Lucking-Reiley (2000), and I strongly recommend these papers to the interested reader. Lucking-Reiley does a good job of summing up the role of experiments in the field relative to the laboratory in Lucking-Reiley (2000a, footnote, p. 9):

> In a field experiment, one cannot verify many of the underlying assumptions of the theory; instead one checks whether the predictions of the theory hold true in a messy, real-world environment.

The adjectives "messy" and "real-world" seem especially appropriate to me when considering eBay.

In contrast with field observations and field experiments, laboratory experiments recruit subjects to play a carefully controlled economic game (such as an auction), usually at a university, and sometimes in a classroom. I am guilty of running such experiments in my classes, and I'll give examples of how they go in chapter 6. This experimental laboratory work began in the early 1980s, and is a bit more mature than the experimental field work (which got a big boost recently from the internet), but is still growing fast. I summarize the generally accepted research results in this area in appendix D.

We next lay out in more detail the many important differences between auction work in the field and in the laboratory. Some differences represent, on the whole, plusses for the field, and some for the laboratory. Some cut both ways. Both approaches have something important to contribute; the more kinds of experiments and the more data the better.

ADVANTAGES OF THE LABORATORY

- *What is testable.* We can control much more in laboratory experiments than in field experiments, and, therefore, there are things that we can test in the laboratory that we just cannot test in the field, either by active experimentation or by passive collection. For example, we can design and run laboratory experiments with private-value auctions, because we can simply dictate to the participants what their values are insofar as their payoffs are concerned. But it is not possible to know with any precision the extent to which bidders know their values, or what the distribution of those values might be, in real auctions. Consequently we cannot run a "field experiment with private values," or a "field experiment with common values."

I should mention, however, a devilishly clever exception. Bapna, Jank, and Shmueli (2004) measure surplus in the field, on eBay, which sounds impossible. They accomplish this by running a (free) sniping service, Cniper,[16] thereby gaining access to the winner's actual bid. Or at least they measure something like surplus, since they must assume that bidders are following the dominant strategy of bidding their values. They report in their paper on the results of 5187 eBay auctions, and estimate from this a total accrued consumer surplus of $1.47 billion for the year 2003. Their experimental results confirm intuition and our analyses perfectly: Buyer surplus is "negatively influenced by seller experience, auction duration and competition, and positively influenced by bidder experience, bidder aggressiveness [lateness of sniping] and item price" (Bapna et al., 2004, p. i).

- *Number of bidders.* The investigator running a laboratory experiment has strict control over the number of participants (conventionally denoted in auction theory by n). In contrast, her counterpart observing a real internet auction has no way of knowing how many potential bidders are out there—logged on, staring at their screens, fingers poised to bid. It is even worse than that: As we mentioned in chapter 3, on eBay, a bidder will have her bid rejected whenever it is below the second-highest price at the moment it is received, and this can lock out any last-second snipers whose bids happen to fall to third position in the time interval between the decision to enter the bid and its arrival at eBay. It is therefore quite possible that some bidders will remain out of sight completely whenever there is a final flurry of snipes (see question 4 of chapter 3). Since almost all theoretical models start with a number of bidders n that is fixed and known to the bidders as well as the seller, the field observer has already run out of much of the directly applicable theory before she begins.

[16] http://www.cniper.com/.

- *Learning.* Laboratory experimenters quite commonly focus on bidder learning, by running several rounds of auctions with the same rules, and comparing behavior from round to round.[17] This is just about impossible to do on the internet, where, as just mentioned, we don't generally know who is out there.

ADVANTAGES OF THE FIELD

- *Sequential vs. simultaneous.* Most laboratory experiments, even if they are automated, auction items off one at a time. On the other hand, it is quite common even for a single seller working by hand to auction off several hundred items at one time.[18] As Lucking-Reiley points out (1999), this means two things: First, the field experimenter can very naturally create an auction environment that mirrors reality much more closely than the laboratory experimenter. And second, he can collect data on a much larger scale.
- *Number of bidders.* Establishing a fixed number of bidders was listed above as an advantage for the laboratory experimenter, in the sense that it makes it possible for her to manufacture the conditions necessary to test certain theory. But having an uncertain number of potential bidders, who can come and go on their own, can also be viewed as a plus for the field experimenter, because it more closely reflects reality.
- *V. Smith's parallelism.* Finally, we mention a central question, discussed early on by Vernon Smith (1982): Do people behave the same way in laboratory experiments as they do in real life? To the extent that they do not, field experiments certainly hold a clear edge over the laboratory.

We now take a close look at a field experiment that asks some of the same questions we have been discussing in this chapter.

---

[17] I've done this in class, repeating the same experiment at successive meetings. I always post all the results, and I suspect that the competitive element has a beneficial effect on both class attendance and attention, not to mention the effect of the cash payoffs.

[18] Frank Robinson's Mail Bid Sale #60 (closed 11 P.M., June 29, 2004), which was also posted on his web page and included photos of most coins, listed 691 lots.

5.8 A Field Comparison of Public vs. Secret Reserves on eBay

Katkar and Lucking-Reiley (2000) report on the results of a field experiment on eBay aimed at answering a key practical question raised earlier in this chapter: Is it a good idea for a seller to use a secret reserve? In April 2000 they auctioned off 50 matched pairs of relatively rare *Pokémon* cards, in top condition, with eBay listings that were identical except for the choices of minimum bid and secret reserve. One of each pair was auctioned off with a minimum bid of $0.05 and a secret reserve set at 30% of the card's book value, determined from a catalog; and the other member of the pair was auctioned off with the minimum bid at the same 30% of the card's book value, and no secret reserve. We'll call the two ways of selling "secret reserve" and "open reserve." To allow for the effects of time variations, they split the 50 pairs into two similar groups of 25 pairs. They sold one group of 25 using the secret reserve first and the open reserve second (a week later); and sold the second group with an open reserve first and secret reserve second.

I can summarize their main results under two main categories: the probability of a sale and the price realized for the card.[19]

1. The use of an open reserve significantly increased the chances of selling a card, 72% for the open reserve vs. 52% for the secret reserve.

2. Using an open reserve yielded a price $0.61 higher on average. The mean value of a card in these experiments was $7.19, so this represents an increase in revenue of 8.5%, not inconsiderable. This result does not take into account the fee charged by eBay for the secret reserve, so the open reserve wins even more convincingly.

---

[19] Katkar and Lucking-Reiley also measured the effects of whether a card was sold first with secret and second with open reserve, or vice versa, and they also measured the number of bids. See Katkar and Lucking-Reiley (2000) for good detail. By the way, eBay changed their reporting policy on bids since these experiments. At the time, multiple bids by the same bidder were reported as one bid, whereas now every bid by every bidder is reported. This is one reason we won't be discussing their results on the number of bids.

These results seem to show that using a secret reserve on eBay is bad idea, but Katkar and Lucking-Reiley emphasize the important qualification that their study used only relatively low-priced items. I have observed myself, in the ancient coin category, that secret reserves tend to be used only for high-priced items, usually in conjunction with low opening bids (recall the bidder strategy of searching up to find the secret reserve described in section 3.7.2). This conclusion is confirmed by empirical data in sales of mint and proof U.S. coins collected on eBay by Bajari and Hortaçsu (2002).

The question of just why secret reserves are used more frequently for expensive items deserves more research work. The secret reserve seems to have two opposing effects on attracting bidders, and we have argued before, and will argue again, that attracting bidders is a good idea. On the one hand, when used with a low opening bid, as mentioned above, it can attract bidders who are trying to discover it. On the other hand, it tends to repel bidders who are looking for bargains because it signals that the seller is, in fact, *not* going to give the item away cheaply. Then there is the more obvious advantage of providing a safety net for the seller. It seems reasonable that the disadvantage of repelling bidders outweighs the other considerations for low-priced items, but the need for a safety net wins when high stakes are involved. As I said, this is a good research problem.

It might even be that the two-stage strategy used by the dealer for the coin from Sebaste (section 5.5) is a good way to extract a high price for an expensive item with little risk. The study of multistage auctions is just beginning, and this is another promising research topic.

5.9 Lucking-Reiley's Magic Window in Time

Lucking-Reiley (2000a) tested the effects of opening bids in a first-price, sealed-bid auction, one of the four basic kinds of auctions discussed in chapter 1 and Vickrey (1961). The first draft of this paper goes back to 1995, pre-eBay, and he reports selling collectible trading cards for the game *Magic: the Gathering* on the internet. What is remarkable about this study is that it seized an opportunity for auction research that is likely never to be repeated in the history of civilization. The internet had proliferated to the point where there was a flourishing online marketplace for *Magic* cards. Lucking-Reiley reports that the newsgroup rec.games.deckmaster became overwhelmed with offers to buy and sell these cards, and soon spawned a second newsgroup devoted exclusively to trading them. He reports (p. 8) that "in the spring of 1995, the marketplace newsgroup had nearly 6,000 messages posted each week, making it the highest-volume newsgroup on the entire internet." And all this was happening about a half year before eBay came into existence on Labor Day, 1995.

The trading newsgroup was the auction experimentalist's heaven. There were already a variety of different auction formats being used by the sellers, and the experimenter could melt into the crowd, with the freedom to try almost any rules he could dream up. This venue had all the advantages of the field experiment mentioned above, but before eBay captured the internet auction market, and therefore without the straitjacket of its particular rules.

5.9.1 *Field Confirmation of Some First-Price Theory*

Lucking-Reiley ran first-price sealed-bid auctions of *Magic* cards in this marketplace newsgroup, and his results (2000a) confirm several important predictions of what he calls the "benchmark theoretical model"—which is the IPV theory of Riley and Samuelson (covered in appendix B) with symmetric bidders. In particular, he confirmed that holding all else fixed, using a nontrivial open reserve reduces the number of bidders; increases the chances that an item will go unsold; and increases the prices fetched by an item, conditional on its being sold. The first two of these predictions should be intuitively clear from our discussion in section 5.6.2 of how a reserve functions in first-price auctions.

The theory also predicts that the total revenue, without regard for cards being unsold, should also increase if the reserve is chosen appropriately. Lucking-Reiley's evidence overall is in the opposite direction, although it is difficult to say whether he set the reserve prices well. According to theory, the optimal setting depends on the particular distribution of bidder values, something that is just not knowable in these experiments.

The most important and interesting observation in this paper concerns the bidding level of the same bidder for the same card in two different auctions—one with essentially no reserve, and one with a nontrivial reserve. The theoretical equilibria for these two situations were discussed for the IPV symmetric benchmark case in section 5.6.4, and illustrated for uniform values in figure 5.2. Theory predicts that bidders will raise their bids when the reserve is introduced. This is exactly what Lucking-Reiley observed, confirming the fact that bidders in his auction behaved *strategically*, anticipating that other bidders would raise their bids also.

We ought to think about what this field experiment and its attendant theory might imply about second-price auctions, since eBay is more like those than like first-price auctions. As we noted above, when a reserve is introduced in a second-price auction, it is still a dominant strategy for a bidder to bid her value. The increase in expected revenue that is predicted comes about because the winning bidder is forced to pay the reserve when the second-highest bid is below the reserve. We should not, therefore, expect bidders to increase their bids in response to the reserve. This would make an interesting field experiment, but the time window for doing it on the internet on a reasonably large scale may have passed forever.

5.10 Flatness of Revenue vs. Reserve Curves

Lucking-Reiley (2000a) raises a very important point that is directly relevant, not only to first-price, but to second-price auctions, and to eBay as well. Return to the question of how the expected total revenue varies with the reserve. This is precisely what the seller is interested in, his bottom line. We mentioned above that the optimal reserve, in the benchmark Riley and Samuelson model, does not depend on the number of bidders. But we can go much further. For the broad class of auctions considered in Riley and Samuelson (1981), which includes the first- and second-price auctions, the entire curve of expected revenue vs. reserve does not depend on the rules of the auction![20] This is an example

---

[20] For a proof, see section B.3.

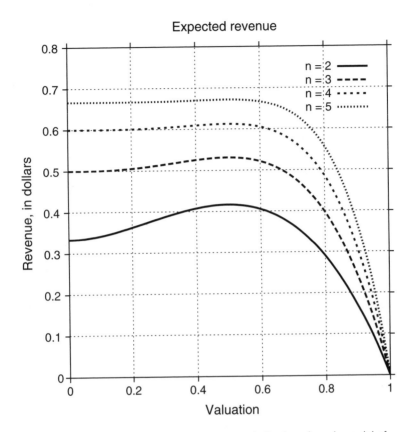

Figure 5.3 Expected revenue vs. open reserve in the benchmark model of Riley and Samuelson. Equation B.13 was used to calculate the curves, and the cases shown are for 2, 3, 4, and 5 bidders, and a uniform distribution of bidder values. After Lucking-Reiley (2000a).

of revenue equivalence, which we mentioned in section 4.5. The curve does, however, depend on the bidders' value distributions.

Let us see, then, what this curve really looks like for some reasonable value distribution, say our favorite for the purposes of illustration, the uniform distribution.[21] Figure 5.3 shows the curve, which, remember, applies to both the first- and second-price auctions, and almost any other auction form for the IPV, symmetric-bidder model. The figure shows four cases, for 2, 3, 4, and 5 bidders. As expected, the peak

[21] We can calculate the curve easily using eq. B.13.

expected revenue occurs at the point when the reserve is exactly 0.5, independent of the number of bidders.[22]

The point is that the revenue curve becomes amazingly flat as the number of bidders increases, even to just 4 or 5. In fact, the variation in revenue when the reserve is varied between 0 and about 0.6 is barely noticeable, and the fact that the peak occurs at 0.5 for 5 bidders, say, requires a magnifying glass. From a practical point of view, the conclusion is that in this theoretical setting, any reserve between 0 and about 0.6 will yield about the same average total revenue. This holds for second-price auctions as well as first-price auctions.

Because of the flatness of the revenue curve, and also because there are so many other factors that do matter, like the bidders' value distributions, we are forced to conclude that this particular theory is not much help in choosing the reserve. The fact that this effect is so general, being independent of auction form in Riley and Samuelson's wide class, is a sign that the conclusion might apply also to eBay. It's only a small leap of reasoning.

5.11 The Importance of the Extra Bidder

I have already mentioned the elegant 1996 paper of Bulow and Klemperer, when discussing the effect of the number of bidders on equilibrium bidding strategies in section 4.4. Their theoretical result is quite general, and bears directly on the importance of competition. To put it simply, they prove this: It is better to attract one more bidder to an ordinary auction with no reserve, than to allow any negotiation whatsoever, including the setting of an optimal reserve, with the original number of bidders.[23] The fact that any conceivable wheeling and dealing is trumped by getting one more bidder in an ordinary auction, without even bothering with a reserve, is quite remarkable.

---

[22] Don't forget that we usually use valuations normalized to the range between 0 and 1, so this value of 0.5 represents a reserve halfway between the lowest and highest possible bidder valuation.

[23] Their result does require that the bidders be symmetric. See section C.7 for details and a proof.

5.12 Extracting Some Advice for the eBay Seller

We started this chapter with questions about the seller's choices on eBay, especially his opening bid and possible use of a secret reserve. After looking at both the theory and the empirical evidence, what conclusions can we draw?

As we just saw, there is a worrisome lack of the detailed information we need to support a theory with any conviction. Not only is eBay not in Riley and Samuelson's class of sealed-bid auctions, we don't know the number of bidders, or much about the nature of their value distributions. Add to this the fact that in the benchmark theory the expected revenue is remarkably insensitive to the choice of reserve price. The general puzzle of choosing the reserve in practice is summed up by Lucking-Reiley (2000a, footnote, p. 22):

> After spending months observing this market environment and running auctions myself, it is hard for me to imagine how any auctioneer in a real-world environment could ever have enough information to choose precisely the optimal reserve price.

But I am not so discouraged, and I believe we can come to some definite recommendations based on the evidence in this chapter. Let's review it.

- Reserves, both open and secret, together with item descriptions, are important signals to bidders. Milgrom and Weber's (1982) quite general result shows it is best for the seller to reveal his information honestly and fully. This *encourages bidders to bid*, because they have less uncertainty about their value estimates. The model assumes that the seller has tread the righteous path and earned the trust of bidders, so that his information is credible. The prediction is borne out by observations of real auctions.
- The IPV benchmark theory recommends that the seller choose a significant reserve, more, in fact than the item is worth to himself, which excludes low-value bidders from entry and drives up expected prices. But there are two factors that tend to qualify this advice. First, the expected revenue in this model is remarkably insensitive to the choice of reserve. Second, when values of bidders

are correlated, the results of Levin and Smith (1996) show that as the number of bidders grows, the best choice of reserve approaches the true value to the seller.

- In their field experiment, Katkar and Lucking-Reiley (2000) matched the secret reserve against an equal open reserve on eBay. They concluded that the open reserve both increases the chances of selling an item and raises the price realized, relative to an equal secret reserve. However, this result seems to hold only for lower-priced items (Katkar and Lucking-Reiley, 2000; Bajari and Hortaçsu, 2002), and the secret reserve can be a useful way to limit risk for higher-priced items.

- The field experiment of Lucking-Reiley (2000a) matches first-price internet auctions with and without reserves. His results are opposite to the predictions of the benchmark theory, and show that the introduction of a reserve actually lowered average revenue. He suggests that the difficulty in setting the reserve optimally may explain the result, but I tend to think a no-reserve auction raises revenue because it *attracts more bidders*. Even bargain hunters grazing with very low bids may attract the attention of other bidders, who may turn out to be more serious.

- The theoretical result of Bulow and Klemperer (1996) shows that, for symmetric bidders and a wide class of auctions, *attracting just one more bidder* is more effective in raising revenue than allowing even the most elaborate negotiations, including the setting of an optimal reserve.

The evidence points overwhelmingly in one direction: The seller should set reserves to attract as many bidders as possible. He should use relatively low open reserves, and no secret reserves, except, perhaps, for high-priced items. The conclusion is not surprising. Competition is all important in getting top prices.

The qualification about using secret reserves only for expensive items is important. In fact, Bajari and Hortaçsu (2002) find in their field study that secret reserves *are* used on eBay more frequently for high-priced items. It seems that when a seller is selling a valuable item, he must buy some insurance, and the best way of doing this might be to use a secret reserve, but in conjunction with an enticing opening price to attract bidders. We also observed a more complex strategy, for the relatively high-quality Samarian coin, in which the seller used secret reserves, different opening bids, and different buy-it-now offers in two successive auctions. Such complex maneuvers belong to the province of multistage game theory, and might be interesting to students looking for research topics.

The theory and the empirical evidence, then, both point consistently to a simple recipe for sellers, which I will risk stating explicitly. The overriding principle is to attract bidding. For cheap to moderately expensive items, choose an opening bid that is nontrivial, but still a potential bargain. Auction houses routinely use 60% of their estimates, but I regularly see much lower opening bids from trusted dealers on eBay. For expensive items, when you are unsure of sufficient competition, buy insurance with a secret reserve, and, perhaps, lower the opening bid even more. Finally, unless you are interested in building a shady career, encourage bidder entry by maintaining your credibility and describing items carefully and fully.

5.13 Questions

1. How might a seller pass the cost of collecting payments with PayPal to the buyer without explicitly asking for a surcharge?

2. Suppose an item is listed on eBay with an opening bid of $46.00, no bids yet, and a buy-it-now price of $100.00. Why might you decide to enter a first bid well before closing that is *above* the buy-it-now price? (It turns out that eBay allows you to do this, but first tells you what you are doing and recommends that you buy it immediately at the buy-it-now price.)

3. Collect data from auction catalogs and study the relationship between auctioneers' estimates and prices realized in a field other than the ones I cited (fine art, coffee- and teapots, and jewelry). Ancient coins would be my choice.

4. Compare the prices realized for items sold at prestigious auction houses with comparable items sold on eBay.

Prices!

We return to the bidder and her most important question: How much should I bid? Much of the empirical research shows overbidding with respect to equilibrium. We will see how researchers put these results in harmony with theory. The evidence from price bubbles in the laboratory underscores the importance of bidder interaction and psychology. New concepts: the winner's curse, risk aversion, spiteful bidding.

6.1 Appraising the Scaffolding

WE ARE at the following point. In chapters 1 to 3, we examined how eBay works, and observed how buyers and sellers commonly behave. In chapter 4, we saw that a successful online auction site, which runs auctions over several days, should be designed to encourage early bidder entry. This goes a long way towards explaining why eBay uses the second-price rule. In chapter 5 we saw that sellers should give their highest priority to attracting bidders. In a word, competition is profitable for the seller and the house. If it is good for the seller to stimulate competition, then it is reasonable to think that avoiding competition is good for the bidder, and this is an excellent argument in favor of sniping.

We now come back to the bidder and take a longer and harder look at the problem she faces in deciding just how much to bid. Before we do this, we ought to review closely the foundations of the theory we've been using, which, after all, gives us the only scientific way to think about auction behavior in the first place. I'll focus on the three abstractions that are most important in making the theory work: *value, equilibrium,* and the ideal rational creature who can be found only in the economic zoo: *Homo economicus.*

6.1.1 *Valuations*

We begin with the extraordinarily fertile but usually unquestioned idea of *value*, and this brings me to one of my favorite topics: the distinction between unique, or at least rare, items, and commodity items, which are widely available, and essentially interchangeable. An item in the first category is the quarry of the collector—it excites the passions. But an item in the second category can be had another day, another place. The potential bidder usually has the option of walking away without much cost. It is hard to imagine working up passion in an auction for a toaster oven that can also be purchased at the mall, perhaps for a few dollars more. But it is all too easy to imagine working up a passion for a rare meteorite, an elusive action figure of Mr. Spock, or an ancient Greek bronze from a city you haven't seen in a lifetime of collecting. It is not simply a matter of the price level; the toaster oven might very well be more expensive than any of these items.

This distinction invites us to examine more carefully the idea of the bidder's *value*, really a pillar of auction theory, as well as the empirical work that tests the theory's predictions. Every single one of the theoretical predictions about auctions depends on the idea that an item has a value to a bidder, whether the bidder knows that value with certainty or not. It is useful in real situations to think of these values as intermediate between the two extreme mathematical models we've mentioned: the private-value and the common-value model.

A good example of an item well modeled by a pure private value is one that will be consumed by the buyer. All that matters is the utility she will get from it. At the other extreme, a good example of an item that fits the common-value category well is one that is bought only for resale. The price it will fetch may be uncertain, but, often, it will be about the same for anyone who buys it and resells it. So, if you are bidding for a bottle of wine that you intend to drink, the wine has a pure private value. If you are speculating in wine and intend to resell it, it has, to a first approximation, a common value. Of course, buyers may differ in their ability to resell wine, depending on their knowledge, skill, reputation, and so on, but the pure common-value model, like the pure private-value model, is a very useful simplification.

It is easy to see how values can be, and often are, some combination of private and common value. For example, most collectors who intend to hold on to their prizes when they buy them, eventually sell and trade some of them as their budgets and tastes change. It is logical that the resale value enter into the value equation. If I buy a coin for $100, enjoy owning it for several years, and then sell it for $100 plus inflation, I am actually way ahead. And in the back of every collector's mind is the knowledge that, eventually, someone else will come to own her prized possessions. The institution of the estate auction is based on this cruel fact. Furthermore, the contemplation of the potential resale value, the "market" value, of a possession can be, in itself, an important determinant of the pleasure of ownership, so the private- and common-value aspects of an object are often intertwined.

The models used in auction theory, at least the theory we make use of here, always assume that the value of an item to a bidder (or seller, for that matter) is fixed forever. It may be that the bidder is uncertain of her true value, and updates her estimate of it over the course of an auction, based on observations of bids, or research. But the mathematical models assume the value is fixed. However, I think that one could dream up auction models that do not rest on the idea that items have fixed values to bidders, especially when the bidders are collectors, who, I claim, are more apt than others to be influenced by reflection and emotion. For example, as we mentioned in chapter 3 in connection with the endowment effect, a collector may revise her *private* value after contemplating an item over the several-day duration of an eBay auction. This revision would be based on her own psychology, a reappraisal of anticipated pleasures of ownership or consumption. This process would be internal, quite different from, say, the possible re-estimation of a fixed value based on the arrival of information from the eBay listing, as would be modeled in the common-value auction framework. The same sort of revision of values can happen if the bidder researches the item during the duration of the sale. I am unaware of theoretical work on the evolution of values themselves during dynamic auctions like eBay, and perhaps this would make an interesting research project, especially if we take into account the personal cost of re-evaluation. But the fixed-value concept captures a great deal, and has been indispensable in spawning the rich auction theory we have today.

6.1.2 Equilibrium

Another pillar of auction theory is the idea of equilibrium behavior, which we introduced and discussed in chapter 4. The basic picture is this: An equilibrium is formed by a set of bidding strategies for bidders with the property that no deviation by any one bidder is profitable to that bidder.[1] Finding equilibria is the favorite occupation of auction theorists, and for good reasons: equilibria are an attractively logical way to predict behavior, they can often be found explicitly by solving mathematically tractable equations, and, to be honest, they are often the only definite way we have to predict behavior. But there are two serious problems with the idea of equilibria. First, it is not so clear how bidders can, in many real situations, find equilibria. And second, there is good evidence from the laboratory that bidders do not find and follow equilibria in situations where they clearly can, such as in private-value second-price auctions.[2]

The question of how people do, or don't, find equilibria in auctions, and in games in general, is presently the subject of intense research. It touches on important problems in understanding learning, and it is also closely related to problems in evolutionary biology, where Darwinian competition is modeled by games with equilibria. See Gintis (2000) for discussion of this topic as well as a lively introduction to the general field of game theory.

Depending on bidders to find and follow equilibria means depending on their acting rationally in their own interest. Which brings us to an imaginary human species.

6.1.3 Homo economicus

The third pillar of auction theory, and much of all economic theory as well, is the assumption that a bidder behaves *rationally* to maximize her *utility*, which is based on her value, or expected value. Such an agent is referred to as *Homo economicus*—the ideally rational economic

---

[1] We often restrict ourselves to symmetric bidders and correspondingly symmetric equilibria.

[2] See appendix D for a summary of this laboratory work.

human.[3] Much has been written on the question of whether this idealization is a good one for doing economics, and it would be foolish of me to try to summarize what is still a lively area of discourse. I do recommend a short article by Richard Thaler called "From Homo economicus to Homo sapiens" (2000), in which he predicts that economics will be more and and more concerned with modeling behavior that is not always rational. As he puts it, the *Homo economicus* used in economic models will evolve to *Homo sapiens*—that is, us. This is certainly an ambitious goal, but reflects the current trend towards what is called "behavioral economics." Thaler cites some well-known examples of behavior that is clearly not rational, at least from the point of view of traditional economic models, and we will mention some of them later in this chapter.

6.2 Overbidding: Some Classroom Experiments

As discussed in chapter 5, laboratory experiments give us a way to test theoretical predictions, and can even suggest new avenues for theoretical research. They allow us to control variables, such as bidder values, the number of bidders, and their level of experience, that are inaccessible in the field. What I will do next is present the outcomes of some homegrown laboratory experiments I conducted in my class.[4] A warning: These experiments were not particularly well controlled, and the results should definitely be regarded as anecdotal only. I include them to illustrate how these kinds of experiments are set up on a small scale, and how they go for small samples, in the classroom. They show the outcomes of individual auctions, while published results almost invariably present only aggregated statistics.

---

[3] Later in this chapter (in section 6.7.2) we will examine a model where the bidder's utility is based in part on the utility of other bidders as well as her own. You might think at this point about the rationale behind such a model, which might at first seem quite strange.

[4] The participants were upper-class computer science and economics students at Princeton University, a frisky crowd.

6.2.1 Experiment 1: First-Price with Uniformly Distributed Valuations

I'll illustrate first with a single experiment I ran in class on February 3, 2004, the first meeting. I wanted to observe my class's bidding behavior in the absolutely standard first-price auction, with independent private values that are distributed identically and uniformly between $0 and $100. There were 26 participants in the auction, so we know that the symmetric Nash equilibrium is to bid $(25/26) \cdot v$. To assign valuations, I printed out 3×5 cards with random numbers on them, generated with a pseudorandom number generator, distributed, as specified, uniformly between $0 and $100. I then had my assistant shuffle the cards and pass them out to the class. The rules were simple. First, I announced how I generated the valuations, and how many bidders were participating in the experiment, since this is assumed to be common knowledge in the model. Second, I asked the subjects to write their bids on the cards, in secret, next to their valuations. My assistant then collected the cards and produced a graph from the data, in this case the one in figure 6.1. It shows one data point in the bid vs. value plane for each bid. Also shown are the straight lines representing equilibrium and truthful bidding. In this context, it is reasonable to refer to bidding above equilibrium as *overbidding*.

With 26 bidders in this first-price auction with uniformly distributed values, there is not much room between the equilibrium and the truthful bidding line. In fact, the equilibrium is 25/26 times the true value, or within about 4%. The actual bids are scattered below and above the equilibrium line. It is a well-established experimental result that people tend on the average to overbid in private-value first-price auctions,[5] but such experiments are not usually conducted with as many as 26 participants. As a matter of fact, though, the bidders with the two highest valuations did overbid.

The highest bidder had a value of $92.73 and bid $89.98, fairly close to the equilibrium bid of $89.16; while the second-highest bidder, also the one with the second-highest value, had a value of $91.47 and bid $89.97. The equilibrium bid for the second-highest bidder was actually $87.95, but he bid $2.00 more, thus shading much less than called for,

---

[5] See appendix D.

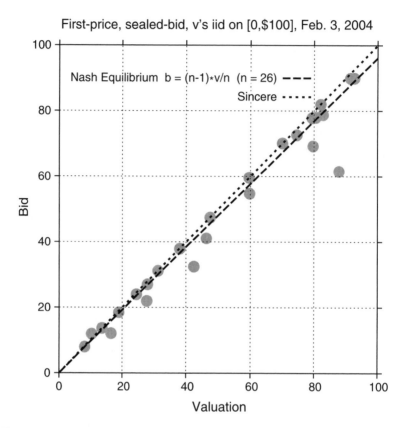

First-price, sealed-bid, v's iid on [0,$100], Feb. 3, 2004

Nash Equilibrium b = (n-1)*v/n (n = 26) – – –

Sincere · · · · ·

Figure 6.1 The result of a classroom experiment: a first-price auction with independent private values, distributed identically and uniformly between $0 and $100. There were 26 bidders, but if you count the data points, there are only 25. A bidder with value $29.32 bid $200.00, just to be perverse, I suppose. She bid anonymously, and we couldn't pin down her identity with certainty, so she escaped winning the auction and getting a bill from me for $170.68.

and almost stealing the item from the bidder with the highest value, missing it by one cent. If he had won, of course, he would have earned less surplus than the highest-value bidder.

6.2.2 Experiment 2: First-Price with Less Competition

Let's look next at a second classroom experiment, which I ran two weeks later, on February 17, 2004. The conditions were the same as for the

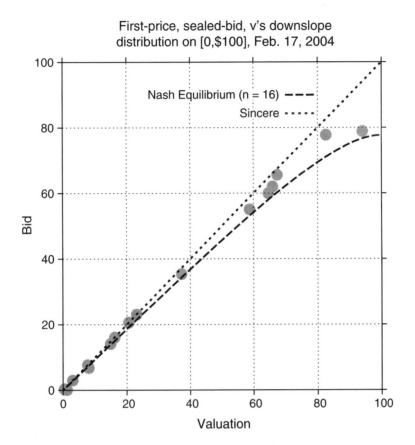

First-price, sealed-bid, v's downslope
distribution on [0,$100], Feb. 17, 2004

Nash Equilibrium (n = 16) ――――
Sincere ・・・・・

Figure 6.2 The result of a classroom experiment: a first-price auction with independent private values distributed identically between $0 and $100, but with a downsloping probability distribution. That is, low values are more likely than high. There were 16 bidders.

first experiment, except that the distribution of values was not uniform. It tended to be make low values more likely than high values. To be a little more precise, the probability density was linearly decreasing in the range from $0 to $100, so that, for example, getting the value $80 was only half as likely as getting the value $40. We can think of this as meaning that, on the average, there will be less competition if your value happens to be high. The results are shown in figure 6.2, together with the truthful, 45° bidding line, and the equilibrium for $n = 16$ bidders, calculated using equation A.42.

Notice that now the equilibrium bidding curve bends over quite a bit for high valuations, telling you to shade more relative to the uniform case if your valuation happens to be high. The intuitive content of the mathematics is that if you do happen to value the item highly, there is less chance than in the uniform-value case that others will also. Therefore, you can afford to shade more. The balance between the risk of losing the item and earning more surplus when you do win is shifted towards a lower bid. Roughly put, the less the expected competition, the lower you need to bid to maximize surplus in the long run.

The results are actually quite consistent with the solidly established experimental literature mentioned above:[6] Bidders in these first-price auctions shaded their bids, but tended to overbid. And once again, the highest bidder narrowly escaped losing the item because the second-highest bidder shaded much less than she did. I should point out that this was only the fifth meeting of the class, and the students, who had already demonstrated that they understood shading bids in a first-price setting on day 1, had nevertheless not seen the calculation of the equilibrium in this example, which is not trivial. But one should not read too much into the consistent overbidding in this one experiment. Two unfair forces were at work: The students had seen the narrow equilibrium shades in experiment 1, and the equilibrium strategy in experiment 2 calls for much more shading, perhaps counterintuitively more.

6.3 Feedback and Learning

These experiments return us to a question that came up earlier in this chapter: How are bidders supposed to learn the equilibrium in this auction? One way to understand the learning process is to think about the *feedback*[7] that a bidder receives as she bids in a succession of auctions. Remember that these happened to be first-price auctions.

---

[6] See appendix D.

[7] I use the term "feedback" in this section in its general, popular sense to mean information collected as the result of an action. Don't confuse it with the reputation feedback posted by buyers and sellers on eBay.

6.3.1 Feedback in First-Price Auctions

Let's go through two typical situations that arise in the kind of experiment described above. First, there is the situation when a bidder is the second-highest bidder, and sees, after the results are in, that he has bid less than the winner. The temptation is to bid higher, relatively, the next time, so as to increase his chances of winning the item—albeit at a higher price and earning, on the average, less surplus. But there is also the situation when a bidder wins an item, and might be tempted to bid lower, relatively, the next time, so as to pay less, but with a slightly decreased chance of winning. We are asking each bidder to accumulate enough experience to learn what fraction of her value to bid, so that, in the long run, she earns the most surplus. In the first experiment above, she would have to learn to shade her bid by the fraction 25/26 of her value. For this to be a believable story, the bidders must have good memories, since the opportunity for really informative feedback is not frequent, especially if there are many bidders. Furthermore, they must be good at adjusting their bids so as to seek the most revenue, not an easy task, especially when the equilibrium bidding function is some arcane curve, as in the second experiment. Finally, *all* the bidders must find the equilibrium simultaneously, because it is a best bidding strategy for any one bidder only if everyone else adopts it. If other participants are bidding off-equilibrium, a given bidder might very well benefit by also deviating from equilibrium.[8] All considered, it's a picture that demands a great deal from bidders, although it's easy to believe that bidders do learn to shade, perhaps more or less than they would in equilibrium, in well-defined situations.

6.3.2 Feedback in Second-Price and English Auctions

Compare this to the task of learning that bidding truthfully in a second-price auction is dominant—unbeatable no matter what anyone else does. If a bidder bids more than her value, she will eventually get stung, when the second-highest bidder bids an amount between her value and

[8] We are assuming in the examples in this chapter, where the bidders are symmetric, that bidders are looking for a *symmetric* equilibrium. That is, everyone is looking for the same equilibrium strategy.

her bid. Similarly, if she bids less than her value, she will occasionally lose an item that she could have won with a positive surplus, had she bid higher but still not above her value.

The ascending-price English auction makes it even easier to learn the dominant strategy; all a bidder has to do is stop when the bidding level reaches her value. The feedback is as clear as it could possibly be. In fact, Kagel, Harstad, and Levin (1987) report that subjects do learn the dominant strategy in English auctions, but tend to bid above their value, to overbid, in second-price sealed-bid auctions.[9] Furthermore, learning to bid exactly your value from feedback in either the English or second-price auction seems much easier than learning, for example, the shading ratio 25/26 in the first-price experiment above. Based on this reasoning, we can conclude that it is easiest to learn the equilibrium in English auctions, more difficult in second-price auctions, and still more difficult in first-price auctions.

The observation that what is certainly an error in bidding strategy will not be punished with certainty applies also, to some extent, to eBay. I say to some extent because if the bidding is incremental, it might very well be that an eBay auction will evolve in much the same way as an English auction. On the other hand, if you snipe, the punishment for overbidding will be, as argued, weaker because it will be less certain. This line of reasoning suggests that sniping can lead to some amount of overbidding on eBay. (See question 3.)

Next, another classic example of missing the equilibrium.

6.4 Overbidding: Jars of Nickels

It is well known that professors are apt to auction off jars of nickels (or, in the old days, pennies) in their classes on auction theory. I've done it myself, and with great success. I'm way ahead. The process illustrates what is called the "winner's curse," a phenomenon first described and analyzed mathematically in a wonderfully succinct three-page paper by Robert Wilson (1969). The classroom experiment is a simple (and profitable) way to show that, in general, finding equilibrium behavior

---

[9] And our argument about the role of feedback is taken from their paper.

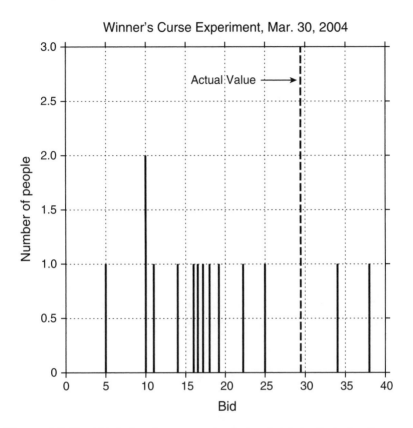

Figure 6.3 The bids in the classroom sale of a jar of nickels, illustrating the winner's curse. The winning bid was $38.00, but the jar actually contained only $29.45.

in an auction setting is not at all easy. This is especially true in one-shot situations, when there is no opportunity to learn from experience.

Here's how the experiment works. I show the class a sealed, clear jar of nickels, and offer it for sale in, say, a first-price auction. The highest bidder buys the jar at the winning bid. What usually happens after the bidding is that I announce how much money is in the jar, the winner believes me without opening the jar, and we settle accounts.[10]

Figure 6.3 shows the results of a classroom experiment I ran on March 30, 2004. The jar actually contained $29.45, and there were two bids

---

[10] The wise experimenter will not use the same sealed jar from semester to semester.

above that: one for $34.00, and one for a whopping $38.00. My profit was therefore $38.00 − $29.45 = $8.55.[11]

Why does this usually net a profit for the experimenter? It is a matter of a bidder not realizing that her winning is an *informative* event, even though this event happens after the bid is placed. The only time her bid counts is when it is the highest estimate. Being the highest estimate means that, statistically, it is very likely to be *too* high, unless she takes into account the fact that the bid wins. Put very simply, unless she discounts the event, by appropriately shading her bid, winning is bad news.

This experiment and analysis aligns well with our general picture of auctions. The model for bidder valuations is the common-value (mineral-rights) model, which fits into the more general affiliated-values model. There is an equilibrium that takes into account the fact that a winning bid is likely to represent an upwardly biased estimate, and this is, in fact, exactly the point of Wilson's analysis (1969). But it is asking a lot of a bidder to do this kind of calculation in a real-time auction, especially when there is no opportunity for learning in repeated trials.

6.5 Results from the Field: Tests of Revenue Equivalence

If I want to run a laboratory auction experiment, I can pass out index cards with values on them, and in this way control the bidder values as I please. But this is impossible in a field experiment, where bidders come and go as they please, with their own ideas in their heads about how they want to bid and what utility they will derive from winning. It is therefore not possible to say directly whether bidders in a field experiment are following equilibrium behavior. It is possible, however, to compare two situations that are, according to some theory, supposed

---

[11] I should mention that when doing experiments like this in earnest, it is important to collect ruthlessly. Otherwise, the experimenter will lose credibility with the subjects, and subjects may very well adjust their behavior to take advantage of the experimenter's softness, bidding more aggressively than otherwise. This is an example of a *limited-liability effect*. Holt and Sherman (2000) make this point, and reference some published argument over the matter.

to yield identical revenue. Here are two recent and pretty examples of field experiments that do exactly that, testing revenue equivalence in two different contexts.

6.5.1 *Magic on the Internet: A Surprise*

We return to Lucking-Reiley's magic window in time, and his field study of revenue equivalence, again selling *Magic* cards on the pre-eBay internet (Lucking-Reiley, 1999). He compared two pairs of auction forms head-to-head: English vs. second-price, and Dutch vs. first-price. His results showed that the English and second-price auction forms were, as predicted by private-value theory, (roughly) revenue equivalent.

There are, however, a couple of reasons to be at least slightly puzzled at this confirmation of the simplest theoretical model. First, Milgrom and Weber (1982) predict that in the affiliated-values case, the English auction should outperform the second-price form, because of the linkage principle.[12] But Lucking-Reiley argues, convincingly I think, that bidders have essentially private values for the cards, since they usually use them in play or to complete a deck. Furthermore, Milgrom and Weber's results depend on bidder symmetry. And if that were not enough, it turns out that the "English" auction form used in Milgrom and Weber's theory is actually the Japanese button auction, described in section 1.8, where bidders know at any point who has dropped out and who remains in. This makes it significantly different from the English auction used by Lucking-Reiley in two respects. First, bidders knew whether or not there was still more than one active bidder, but not who the bidders were, or how many there were. Second, he used a "Going, Going, Gone!" warning system, so that reentry was always possible until the auction closed (Lucking-Reiley, 1999, p. 1070).

A second reason to be a bit puzzled is the fact that in laboratory experiments, second-price auctions outperform English auctions, a conflict in the opposite direction.[13] No explanation is offered by Lucking-Reiley. The experimental ranking of second-price revenue above English

---

[12] See section C.2 for details.
[13] See appendix D.

revenue is due to Kagel et al. (1987), and they report that bidders find the equilibrium of truthful bidding in the English form, but seem to have more trouble learning the truthful equilibrium and tend to overbid in the second-price format.[14] As we described in section 6.3, they suggest that this may be due to the kind of feedback bidders get, which is more direct in the case of English auctions. One possible explanation of the rough equivalence found by Lucking-Reiley is that his bidders were more experienced than typical laboratory subjects, and hence found the equilibrium in both the English and second-price formats, or at least were better able to take account of the difference. It may also be that as collectors they were more strongly motivated.

Next, a real surprise. The Dutch auction significantly outperformed the first-price auction, raising an average of about 30% more revenue per card. Quite a shock, since the Dutch and first-price auctions are strongly strategically equivalent.[15] Their expected revenue is predicted by theory to be the same under very general conditions, such as interrelated values and bidder asymmetry. Lucking-Reiley does offer some suggestions for explaining the effect. For one thing, the Dutch format attracted more bidders, which would go a long way towards explaining the difference in revenue, even though the measure of participation used by Lucking-Reiley is slightly different in the two forms. But I tend to favor another argument presented by Lucking-Reiley: that bidders bidding for things they really care about are more likely to grow impatient in a Dutch auction. These auctions stretched over days. This would also tend to explain the reverse results in the laboratory, where subjects are not bidding on particular items they really care about, and where the time scale is not as long.

The explanation that bidders tend to bid early because they lose patience is supported by the laboratory experiments reported by Katok and Kwasnica (2002). They conducted Dutch auctions with different clock speeds, and found that a slow clock yielded higher revenue than a fast clock. In fact, a slow clock resulted in revenue that was higher than

---

[14] It is interesting to note that the kind of English auction used in Kagel et al. (1987, p. 1280) is actually the Japanese button auction, used in Milgrom and Weber's theory (1982) but not in Lucking-Reiley's field experiment.

[15] As we discussed in section 1.9.

that in the corresponding sealed-bid first-price auction, and the reverse was true with a fast clock.

The pity is that I can't see how Lucking-Reiley's experiment can ever be replicated again in the field. It would require a venue where many different forms of auctions are commonly used by sellers in the field, and where buyers are real buyers, not experimental subjects. This describes the pre-eBay internet, roughly 1994 (when Lucking-Reiley began buying and selling *Magic* cards) to late 1995 (when eBay began)— as I've said before, a magic window in time.

6.5.2 *Music CDs and Xboxes on eBay*

While it is impossible to compare two different sets of auction formats on eBay, which, of course, sets its own rules, Hossain and Morgan (2003) did devise an elegant test of revenue equivalence that can be run on eBay, based on the following principle: For any auction in what we called the "benchmark" model in chapter 5, the IPV model of Riley and Samuelson, the expected revenue depends only on the *entry value*, which is defined as the lowest valuation which makes it worthwhile for a bidder to enter an auction.[16] This is a remarkable form of the revenue equivalence principle, and says, essentially, that the expected revenue of a sale depends only on what set of bidders is excluded.

For example, if the opening bid in a second-price auction is $20, and there are no other costs associated with buying the item (shipping is free), then the entry value is simply $20. Any bidder who attaches a value of $20 or more to the item can expect to earn an average surplus that is certainly never negative, and usually positive.

Now suppose that the same item is being auctioned off, but the seller announces beforehand that he will charge a fixed shipping charge of $10, keeping the same opening bid of $20. Then the entry value is now $30; no bidder with a valuation less than $30 can expect to earn positive surplus, simply because she will have to part with at least $30 to get the item.

What Hossain and Morgan did was sell pairs of identical items, varying the opening bid and shipping charges for the two items, but

---

[16] For a proof of this remarkable result, see section B.2.

holding the entry value for both items of the pair fixed. For example, they sold pairs of identical music CDs in two ways: the first CD had an opening bid of $4 and zero shipping cost; the second CD had an opening bid of $0.01 (the lowest allowed) and a shipping cost of $3.99. Thus, the entry value in both sales was exactly $4. In all, they auctioned a total of 40 popular music CDs and 40 Xbox games. These seem to fit the private-value model well, because it seems unlikely that anyone would buy these readily available items, with ephemeral popularity, for resale.

They summarize their main results as follows: When the entry value was a relatively small fraction of the retail price ($4 for a CD), "auctions with a low opening bid and high shipping charges attracted more bidders, earlier bidding, and yielded higher revenue than those with a high opening bid and low shipping charges." On the other hand, when the entry value was double this, and therefore a larger fraction of the retail price, no such effect was observed. Why?

Hossain and Morgan offer the following instructive explanation for this behavior. It uses a mathematical model based on work by Kahneman and Tversky (1979; Tversky and Kahneman, 1991) and Thaler (1985). I'll summarize their intuition here. Let's suppose that a prospective bidder (1) thinks of her gains and losses with respect to a *reference point*, (2) cares more about losses than gains (is *loss averse*), and (3) keeps separate mental accounts for shipping and the price of the item itself. Then, when her separate accounting puts more weight on the item price than the shipping fee, (in effect discounting the shipping fee), she will bid higher when the shipping costs are higher and lower when the shipping costs are lower. But, if we assume further that she is loss averse with respect to some reference point of the shipping fee, she will balk at bidding higher if the shipping fee gets *too* high. Therefore, in the test sales when the entry fee is high, consideration of the high shipping fees will dominate consideration of the relatively lower item price, and she will bid higher when the shipping costs are lower and lower when they are higher.

To put it even more loosely, bidders tend to forget about the shipping costs unless they are high enough to raise a red flag. This is a nice example of what Hossain and Morgan call "rationalizing observed results." More and more, economists (and psychologists) are adjusting economic theories to take observed behavior into account, and the result is often referred to generally as "behavioral economics."[17]

6.6 Reconciliations

As we've just seen, the makers of economic theory respond constructively when observations diverge from predictions or experience. They adjust the theory so that it can better explain observed behavior, a feature of all good science. These adjustments sometimes introduce new features of the information structure (like bidders having interdependent values), or new aspects of agent behavior (like failure to account properly for postage, or to learn from mistakes when truthful bidding is dominant). When someone is able to present a mathematical formulation of an explanation that generalizes the old theory, a new and more comprehensive quantitative theory emerges (as in Milgrom and Weber's 1982 paper). Sometimes the explanation takes the form of a relatively simple quantitative model, like that of Hossain and Morgan (2003) to explain the failure of revenue equivalence in their field experiment. Sometimes, the only recourse is a qualitative story, like the explanation for overbidding in second-price auctions by Kagel et al. (1987).

We will next discuss two reactions to observed overbidding in first- and second-price laboratory experiments.

6.7 Equilibrium Regained

As we mentioned earlier, and discuss in appendix D, it is widely accepted that experimental subjects tend to bid above equilibrium in both first- and second-price auctions. The widely accepted explanation for this overbidding in first-price auctions is risk aversion. In fact, the

---

[17] Two leading contributors to this approach shared the 2002 Nobel Prize in Economics, and you can see the direct relevance to auction theory from the citations: Daniel Kahneman ("for having integrated insights from psychological research into economic science, especially concerning human judgment and decision-making under uncertainty"), and Vernon Smith ("for having established laboratory experiments as a tool in empirical economic analysis, especially in the study of alternative market mechanisms").

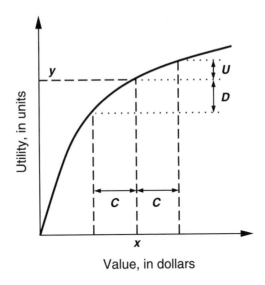

Figure 6.4 A concave utility curve. Increasing the value changes the utility less than decreasing the value by an equal amount, reflecting the fact that money has a decreasing marginal utility.

susceptibility to risk-averse behavior is considered to be a basic characteristic of economic agents in general, and permeates most of economics. Most descriptions of auction theory begin with a description of agents as either "risk neutral" or "risk averse," and we next describe this important and useful concept in more detail.

6.7.1 Risk Aversion

Up to now, we've assumed, tacitly, that *Homo economicus* seeks to maximize her surplus *measured in dollars*, the difference between the value attached to, and the price paid for, an item. However, it is a widely accepted principle that money has *diminishing marginal utility*; that is, the more money you have, the less a given amount is worth to you. For example, if your net worth is a million dollars, an additional $500 means a lot less to you than it would if your net worth were only a thousand dollars. The idea is embodied in the *utility function*, which represents how much importance a person attaches to a given value measured in dollars. A typical utility function is sketched in figure 6.4.

The horizontal axis is the value, measured in dollars, and the vertical axis is the utility, measured in some hypothetical unit of satisfaction, sometimes called the *util.*

The decreasing marginal utility of money (dollars) then means that this curve flattens out as value increases, or, in more technical terms, is *concave* (down). This is shown in figure 6.4. Suppose a bidder attaches a value of x dollars to a given item, with the corresponding utility of y utils. Then, if her value is increased by C dollars, her utility is increased by U utils; and if her value decreases by the same C dollars, her utility is decreased by D utils. Since the utility curve is concave, U is smaller than D. She derives less utility from a given increase in value than she loses from a decrease in value of the same size. A bidder or seller having a concave utility function in an auction model behaves as if she is loss averse, in the sense described above.[18]

When an agent's utility curve is *linear*, we say that she is *risk neutral.* In the case opposite to risk aversion, when it bends up, we say she is *risk loving.* All the equilibria mentioned up to now were derived for risk-neutral bidders. This means that we assumed that bidders seek to maximize their surplus. But what happens to the equilibria when bidders are risk averse, and seek to maximize, not their surplus, but the utility of their surplus? It turns out that in first-price auctions, the new, risk-averse equilibria call for bidding above the risk-neutral equilibria.

Here's the intuition.[19] You can think of the choice of equilibrium in a first-price auction, which we discussed in section 4.4, as a trade-off between bidding too much and not enough. If you shade less than the equilibrium dictates, bidding higher, you increase your chances of winning, but when you do win, your surplus will be less. On the other hand, if you shade more than equilibrium you decrease your chances of winning, but your surplus will be higher when you do win. The balance for risk-neutral bidders determines the equilibrium bidding strategies we've pictured in figures 6.1 and 6.2, for example.

Now, we ask how this balance is changed when the bidder is risk averse. In this case the prospect of higher surplus when shading

[18] Loss aversion is defined in terms of behavior and preferences, risk aversion in terms of the shape of a utility curve. For a discussion of the distinction, which can be important, see Schmidt and Zank (2002).

[19] For a proof, see section B.6.

127

more is not as important (because the utility curve flattens) as the prospect of winning more often when shading less. Therefore, shading less becomes relatively more attractive, and the balance shifts to the strategy of bidding higher—overbidding with respect to risk-neutral bidders.

At first blush, this would seem to resolve the problem of observed overbidding in laboratory first-price auctions. But there is a danger here that is easy to ignore, but is fundamental. What we are doing when we try to explain data from experiments, and this is true in any setting, amounts to curve fitting. That is, we jiggle the pieces and parameters of the ideal model so that the predictions are as close as possible to the data. The risk-averse explanation adds an entire utility curve to the things we are free to play with, and a curve gives us lots of freedom to fit data. An arbitrary concave utility curve adds a frightening number of degrees of freedom to our model—an uncountably infinite number of them, in fact. We should certainly expect a certain amount of improvement in the fit, even if there is no genuine extra explanatory power in the new idea. It is also difficult to think about how to make such a rich choice. For these reasons scientists find great pleasure in parsimony.

To avoid this embarrassing increase in explanatory power, economists like to characterize utility curves by a single parameter, and the most popular of these one-parameter families are the *constant-relative-risk-aversion* and *constant-absolute-risk-aversion* utility curves.[20] Overbidding in private-value first-price auctions is commonly accounted for by a single coefficient of constant-relative-risk-aversion.

The next natural question is whether there is some other one-parameter modification of the theory that can explain more—perhaps overbidding in second-price auctions.

A MEASUREMENT OF RISK AVERSION

Before we try to answer this question, I want to show a result from a laboratory experiment by Holt and Sherman (2000) that was specifically

---

[20] We won't go into the details here, but the reader can find them in Krishna (2002), for example.

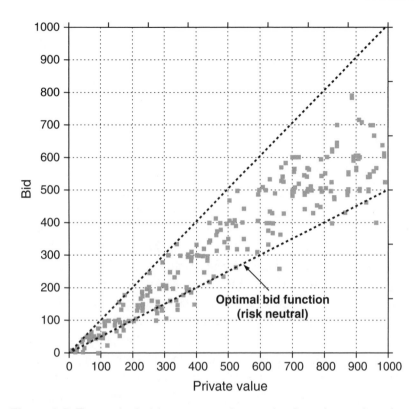

Figure 6.5 The result of a laboratory experiment using first-price auction rules, as reported in Holt and Sherman (2000).

designed to *measure* risk aversion through overbidding in first-price auctions. It was also done in the classroom.[21]

Figure 6.5 shows their data, which was gathered as follows: Each of twenty-four subjects participated in ten first-price auctions, each of which had two bidders. But each bidder did not face another human, but was instead paired with a *simulated* player. The bids of the simulated player were determined by the rolls of ten-sided dice. The dice were rolled three times, to get an amount between $0.00 and $9.99. Furthermore, the subjects were told that their rivals were, in fact,

[21] At the University of Virginia and the University of Houston. This particular experiment was actually a small part of their research paper, which was aimed at testing whether risk aversion can explain the winner's curse. They conclude that it cannot, at least by itself.

simulated players who played by rolling dice. Thus, the experimental setup does not conform exactly to a real auction. But it is not difficult to calculate the equilibrium bidding strategy in this setup for subjects who are risk averse, and the result depends on an assumed risk-averse utility curve that follows an rth power rule.[22] The parameter value one corresponds to risk-neutral bidders, and any given value less than one corresponds to utility curves that are concave down; the smaller r, the more risk averse the bidder.

The result of this calculation is that the equilibrium corresponding to risk-neutral bidders is bidding half one's value, exactly the same as in the corresponding first-price auction with human rivals. If you look at figure 6.5, you can see that people did realize that they should shade their bids, since almost all the bids are below the truthful bidding line (shown as a dashed line with unity slope). But they did not shade nearly as much as dictated by the risk-neutral equilibrium (shown as a dashed line with slope one-half). In fact, the data allowed Holt and Sherman to estimate what coefficient of constant-relative-risk-aversion best accounts for the data, and they arrived at the value of about one-half, which implies that the subjects' utility curve was roughly square-root shaped; that is, the subjects' utility corresponding to x dollars was $\sqrt{x}$ utils. The bidding results are quite similar to those seen earlier in my own classroom experiments, but they are more regular and consistent, as we should expect with more subjects and artificial bidding rivals with known behavior.

Remember Holt and Sherman's measurement of risk aversion and their result of a square-root utility curve. We'll return to it shortly.

6.7.2 Spite: An Alternative Theory

I'll now describe an alternative one-parameter adjustment to the theory, one that has nothing at all to do with risk-averse behavior. In fact, it attempts to capture a darker side of the psyche: spite. The incorporation of spite into auction theory is a step in the direction forecast by Thaler in his paper on the evolution of *Homo economicus* to *Homo sapiens*

---

[22] The parameter r is actually the coefficient of constant-relative-risk-aversion, mentioned above.

(2000). The last prediction in that paper is, in fact, "*Homo economicus* will become more emotional."

The term "spite" is used rather loosely in ordinary conversation, but what do we really mean by it? Thaler discusses spite in connection with the Ultimatum Game, which provides an excellent laboratory specimen of the behavior, and suggests a useful working definition as well. The Ultimatum Game is played by two people: the Proposer and the Responder. The Proposer is given a fixed amount of money, say $100. She is then required to offer the Responder a deal, in which the Proposer gets to keep x dollars, and the Responder gets the remainder, $100 - x$. If the Responder accepts the offer, the deal goes through. But if the Responder rejects the offer, no one gets anything.

Here we have a pointed challenge to the rationality of the Responder. Suppose the Proposer offers a split of $99 for herself, and only $1 for the Responder. Logically, the Responder has a choice between accepting the $1 or getting nothing. Cold logic demands that he take the $1. But, as you might guess, subject Responders in laboratory experiments balk if they are offered too little; Thaler mentions $20 as as example of a sum frequently rejected. Clearly, the Responder cares about what the Proposer gets, and if the discrepancy is too great, he considers it "unfair." It isn't rational from the point of view of an agent maximizing only his surplus, but it can thought of as a Responder maximizing his surplus *discounted*, somehow, by the surplus of the Proposer. A simple way to think about this is to imagine that the Responder weighs the difference between what he gets and what the Proposer gets.

This can be put a bit more precisely by saying that the Responder is willing to accept a loss of surplus, provided that the Proposer loses surplus also. Biologists go a step further and characterize spite among living things by requiring that the Proposer lose *more* than the Responder. Actually, evolutionary biologists are very interested in the concept of spiteful behavior, and, in particular, whether it can come about through the process of evolution.[23] Although some evolutionary biologists may question the existence of spiteful behavior

---

[23] Hamilton (1970) originally raised the question when he asked, "would we ever expect an animal to be ready to harm itself in order to harm another more?" The controversy is still very much alive. See, for example, Gadagkar (1993), Foster, Wenseleers, and Ratnieks (2001), and the dynamic model proposed by Morgan and the author (2003).

in nonhumans, I think we are on safe ground when we look for it in our own species.[24]

This idea of spite is incorporated into the private-value auction model in Morgan, Steiglitz, and Reis (2003) in the following natural way. Ordinarily, we require the rational bidder to maximize only her own expected surplus. But now we require her to take into account, not only her own surplus when she wins, but the surplus of the rival bidder who does win when she does not. The rival's surplus is weighted by a parameter α that characterizes the strength of the spite motive. A value $\alpha = 0$ corresponds to the standard case, with no spite; and the value $\alpha = 1$ corresponds to the case when the bidder gives equal weight to her own and her winning rival's surplus.

The symmetric equilibria for this model can be worked out using the same techniques as for the usual model. The first interesting consequence is that the equilibrium in the first-price auction goes up: Spite calls for higher bidding, just as risk aversion does. But one can go further. It turns out that the spiteful model and the risk-averse model are perfectly equivalent in the IPV case for first-price auctions. For every constant-relative-risk-aversion parameter r, there is a spite parameter α that leads to the very same equilibrium bidding strategy, and vice versa. The explanatory power of the two models—for first-price auctions—is exactly equal.

But the really interesting consequence of the spite motive is its effect on equilibrium behavior in second-price auctions. In this case, it is equilibrium behavior to bid *above* one's value, violating everything we learned from Vickrey about second-price auctions. Figure 6.6 shows the equilibrium bidding function for two bidders when their values are private, and distributed independently and identically between 0 and 1. The curve is in this case a straight line, starting at the bid of 1/3 when the value is 0, to the bid of 1 when the value is 1. This is equivalent to saying that the equilibrium bid is 1/3 plus 2/3 times the value.

The intuition behind the overbidding is not hard to see. Suppose that your rival is following the standard strategy of bidding truthfully. I'll argue, then, that if you deviate from truthful bidding by bidding

---

[24] Gadagkar (1993) comments that "Conventional wisdom has it that to be spiteful is the prerogative of humans alone."

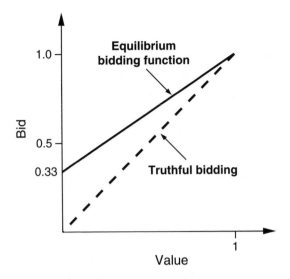

Figure 6.6 The equilibrium bidding function in a second-price auction with spiteful bidders. Private values are independently and uniformly distributed between 0 and 1, and the bidders are symmetric. In equilibrium they bid more than their values.

higher, it is plausible that you can improve the excess of your surplus over that of your rival—which is now the criterion for spiteful bidders. This will show that truthful bidding is no longer an equilibrium, and that overbidding could lead to one.[25]

Suppose, for example, that your value is, for the sake of round numbers, 1/2, and that instead of 1/2 you bid higher, say X. You don't know, of course, what your rival's bid is; it could be anywhere between 0 and 1. But when your rival's value is between 1/2 and X, you now win the auction, whereas before, when you bid truthfully, your rival won. Your winning results in a loss of surplus to yourself (because you've overbid), but you've also deprived your rival of surplus. On the other hand, when your rival's value is between X and 1, he now wins and is forced to pay more than he would have if you had bid truthfully. This also deprives your rival of surplus, while it leaves yours unchanged. The fact is that if you choose X appropriately, your overbidding will force

[25] For derivations of equilibria in the general IPV model with spiteful, symmetric bidders, see Morgan et al. (2003).

him to lose more, on the average, than you will. As we discussed, this is exactly what we mean by spite.

We see from this result that introducing the spite motive into the theoretical model explains overbidding in second-price auctions, but risk aversion does not. We've also seen that spite and risk aversion are equally powerful in explaining overbidding in first-price auctions. It would seem, therefore, that spite is the preferable behavioral adjustment to the theory. This is what my coauthors and I propose in Morgan et al. (2003).

But the last word has certainly not been written on the subject. For one thing, the model we've been using, with independent and identically distributed private values, and symmetric bidders, is very restrictive. But more important than this is the fact that risk aversion is a solidly established attribute of agents in many fields of economics, and has been verified in many experiments, such as, for example, the one by Holt and Sherman (2000) described above. We do suggest some experiments in Morgan et al. (2003) that might be able to distinguish between the two psychological effects, and it will be interesting to see what further research can teach us.

We will return to the subject of spite below, when we discuss its implications when bidding on eBay.

6.8 The Theoretically Informed (and Human) eBay Bidder

If I had to formulate a strategy for bidding on eBay, based on the chapters before this one, it would be this: Behave as if it's a Vickrey auction, and snipe with your true value. On balance, bidding early encourages competition and reveals information. And when it comes down to the situation when everyone snipes, eBay is a second-price auction in which bidding truthfully is dominant. But in this chapter we've seen some complications in following this advice: you might be unsure of your value for various reasons, and therefore vulnerable to the winner's curse. Or you might be susceptible to some of the same difficulties and pressures that cause subjects to overbid in laboratory experiments, or that somehow lead to failure of revenue equivalence in field tests. We'll wrap up this chapter by going over these mistakes and problems one by one, and see how we might try to avoid them. We'll also return for another look at bidding wars, a classic danger associated with auctions. We haven't discussed the subject since chapter 1, when Elaine got carried away in her competition for John F. Kennedy's golf clubs.

I've tried to order the problems faced by bidders according to how much emotions play a part, starting with errors that can be corrected by cold calculation, and ending with bidding wars. Many of the lessons apply, of course, to other kinds of auctions as well.

6.8.1 *Simply a Mistake: Bidding Untruthfully in Vickrey's Setting*

Even though finding the dominant strategy of truthful bidding in second-price auctions is much easier than finding the equilibrium shade in first-price auctions, the private-value experiments we've described show that people consistently miss the idea. There are two ways this mistake shows up on eBay, bidding too low or too high.

The first case can come about this way. Let us say that you have an idea of the most you want to pay for an item, $200, which we'll take as your private value. If you consult the listing for the last time and see that the posted price is only $25, you may snipe with a bid of $100, mistakenly assuming that there is no need to bid your limit of $200. If another sniper bids $150, you will see your mistake, and regret not bidding higher.

In the same way, you may bid more than your private value, say $300 in our example, mistakenly thinking that there is no real risk in bidding so high because you will very likely get the item for less. Again, this misses Vickrey's point. By bidding $300 instead of $200, you admit only situations where you can lose surplus.

This kind of overbidding is the simplest to explain and correct; it is nothing more than a logical mistake, assuming, of course, that you really are sure of your private value.

6.8.2 *The Winner's Curse*

Avoiding the winner's curse is another matter entirely. Here the problem stems from uncertainty about one's value, and shading correctly in the

135

face of this uncertainty can be quite tricky—or perhaps impossible. The notion that you, as a bidder, have a good idea of value distributions and number of bidders in a common-value model, and can do a good job of calculating the mathematically correct shade, is simply not realistic.

Still, we should carry with us the very important lesson of the winner's curse. Let's say that an ancient bronze is being offered that is clearly a Roman Alexandrian obol of Hadrian, and the seller, in the Middle East, does not offer any attribution beyond "Greek bronze." The piece is heavily patinated and the photograph is only fair, so that the details on the reverse are unclear. The piece might be a coin commemorating a nome, which would make it rare and desirable, or it might be a much more mundane variety. You expect that you would probably be able to attribute the coin with certainty if you had the piece in hand. You know the seller is a reliable businessman, with good feedback, but not an expert on coins. He guarantees it to be genuine, which you know it is, but otherwise he offers it "as is," so there will be no justification for a refund if it turns out to be common fare. You've observed the bidding up until snipe time, and the price level has been very low relative to the usual market value of a nome obol. You are faced with the problem of choosing a bid for your snipe. There may well be other collectors out there who specialize in this sort of item (you've bumped up against them before), and perhaps even expert dealers, each clutching his mouse in anticipation of sniping as well. Before you snipe, remember the idea behind the winner's curse: If you win, it means that your appraisal was the highest among all the bidders watching the item, and winning may very well be bad news if you bid too high.

To make the example even more concrete, suppose the market value of the coin is $200 if it's actually a nome coin, but only $40 if it's common. Suppose there have been altogether 11 bids before snipe time, from 9 different bidders, and the coin is sitting at a posted price of $33. If you estimate the chances of its being rare at about 50/50, your expected value—*before the informative event of winning the auction*—is 50% of $200 (if it is rare), and 50% of $40 (if it is common), which gives $120. You might then be tempted to snipe truthfully with this value. But it would likely be a mistake. Winning would mean that your estimate was the highest from a group of at least 10 bidders, and would therefore very likely be too high.

Of course, this scenario depends on your sizing up your competition accurately. If you think that you are likely to know more about this item than the other bidders, then the threat of the winner's curse diminishes. On the other hand, if you think your are relatively uninformed, you should guard against the curse even more vigilantly.

6.8.3 Lessons from the Failures of Revenue Equivalence

What lessons can we draw from the tests of revenue equivalence? As usual, we may not be able to derive detailed bidding strategies from the results, but we can certainly learn something.

Lucking-Reiley's field comparison of Dutch and first-price auctions (1999), as well as Katok and Kwasnica's laboratory study of clock speed in Dutch auctions (2002), confirm what we already know: people are not very patient. Put another way, bidders generally put a premium on ending an auction earlier rather than later. This explains a lot of what we can observe informally on eBay. It takes a certain amount of patience to wait until the last 10 seconds of a seven-day sale. It can also take iron nerves to resist a buy-it-now offer that is just a bit more than we might ordinarily be happy to pay, buying an early and happy ending to the auction, and removing the prolonged threat of being preempted by another taker, or the prospect of a long and possibly competitive real auction.

Whether jumping the gun in a slow Dutch auction is a mistake or not comes down to the same kinds of questions we asked about spiteful bidding. A model with utility for ending the auction sooner rather than later can rationalize the behavior in one sense, but you may forget the fleeting pleasure and in the morning remember only the price.

Hossain and Morgan's field test is more directly instructive. If we accept the explanation that bidders fail to take the shipping costs into account properly, then this failure is a mistake, clear and simple. The shipping costs are measured in the same dollars at the same time. The same potential for error exists when accounting for other costs in time or money that may be forgotten or ignored. For example, items from Lebanon can easily take a month to get to New Jersey, while some sellers live in New Jersey. But the dealer in New Jersey may charge a resident like me state tax, while the dealer in Pennsylvania will not. Some dealers do not accept PayPal, and may not even accept a personal check. Some do not offer insurance, or charge a lot for it, in some cases legitimately, because it may entail an extra trip to the post office. And of course, a dealer with poor feedback presents a risk that should be factored into the cost. Empirical evidence to support this last factor is given in the field study of U.S. cents on eBay by Lucking-Reiley et al. (2000). They show not only that a seller's feedback has a real effect on the prices she realizes, but also that negative feedback has a much greater effect than does positive.

6.8.4 *Spiteful Behavior*

It is not hard to argue that bidders have a tendency to bid spitefully. People, being people, have the base but natural impulse to be envious, and might very well be willing to spend some surplus to deny someone else the pleasure of owning a coveted object. This seems to be the driving force behind some bidding wars, where we can interpret escalating prices as "overbidding" to prevent sale to a rival. Such motives are sometimes referred to in anecdotal accounts of auctions, especially for highly prized and rare collectibles. The nineteenth-century art expert Edmond Bonnaffé is reported to have observed that "after Michelangelo's pictures and the Medici porcelain the rarest thing he had ever seen among collectors was goodwill, and he drew the conclusion that collectors' mania embraced the desire to own things for oneself, the desire to own them for others, and the desire to stop other people owning anything."[26]

While this motivating factor for spiteful bidding—denying someone else the pleasure of ownership—may seem worse than base, perhaps even sinful, there are other reasons for what may appear to be spiteful bidding that can be explained in different terms. It may be that taking future transactions into account, one's value is really higher than might, at first, appear.

For example, a bidder can derive utility from a rival's increased payment because that rival will be poorer because of the one sale, and will therefore be less competitive in a later sale. This applies to

---

[26] Rheims (1961, p. 7).

commodities like real estate, as well as rare or unique *objets d'art*. At the level of takeovers of giant corporations, where billions of dollars are involved, this consideration may be quite important. In his classic survey of real auctions, Cassady (1967, p. 145) recommends that "a buyer should concentrate his attention on items of interest to him, and not become embroiled in the emotional atmosphere of an auction. He may, however, bid on a lot in order to force a competitor to pay a higher price."

Another way consideration of future transactions can raise the value of an item to a bidder has to do with resale. It may be that the bidder already has one example of a desirable item, and bids on the offering of a second, with the intention of forcing a rival to pay a higher price than otherwise. This has the effect of maintaining a high record of the item's market value for future resale. In fact, prices realized in previous auctions for particular or similar items are an important guide to sellers and bidders, and are often quoted in sales catalogs. We might term this "supporting the market value of inventory."

If it happens that, in the attempt to force a higher price, the owner of one item winds up buying another similar one, she is, perhaps without intending, beginning a move to corner a very specialized market. I should mention that it is not so strange that several examples of a genuinely rare item surface on the market in rapid succession. This happens regularly in the ancient coin market, where a dealer may be dispersing a new find. A recently unearthed pot may contain a few examples of a rarity, among thousands of other coins. You may see three or four specimens of the type in one month, and then none for years. Anticipating an event like this and trying to capitalize on it is, of course, risky, and not recommended for the eBayer with a small budget and weak nerves.

These latter two reasons for bidding "spitefully" can be defended as rational attempts to increase revenue over a long time horizon, and are not really examples of spite, which requires that the bidder hurt herself, albeit hurting rivals more. Whether *genuinely* spiteful bidding is actually a mistake is hard to say—it depends on how seriously you take the notion of utility. I would argue that the utility a spiteful bidder derives from the loss of others is ephemeral, but that the utility of ownership is durable. But who am I to rank your pleasures?

6.8.5 Wars, Frenzies, and Bubbles

We all know what a "bidding war" is, and it is not hard to find examples of them on eBay, such as the one we discussed in section 3.1.2. The dynamics of such two-person wars are clear enough: Each bidder reacts to the other's bid, creating self-reenforcing feedback. The question of exactly why bidders behave this way takes us well beyond single-item, single-seller auctions and eBay, to the controversial and puzzling phenomenon of price bubbles in two-sided asset markets. We can, though, think of a bidding war on eBay as a tiny example of a stock-market boom, a minor frenzy, a micro-bubble.

We should draw a distinction between a bidding war in one particular auction, and a sustained boom in prices realized at auction, perhaps followed by a bust, over many auctions for a particular kind of item. The latter is a closer parallel to the usual conception of a price bubble as it might arise, for example, in the market for fine art, or baseball memorabilia. I don't know of any studies (yet) that examine long-term price trends of specialized categories of items on eBay.

To summarize the state of knowledge, I think it's fair to say that economists have not satisfactorily resolved the problem of even *defining* price bubbles precisely, much less explaining the phenomenon itself. This is reflected in the diversity of viewpoints in the 1990 *Symposium on Bubbles*, an informative and often fascinating collection of papers edited by Stiglitz (1990). We would like to say that a price bubble is an excursion from the "fundamental value" at some point, usually a fast excursion with frenzied trading, and usually followed by a sudden return to fundamentals—a crash. But what is the "fundamental value" of a rare tulip bulb? We would like to say that it is fueled by emotion, but perhaps there are some who, buying on the way up and selling before the crash, can claim to be coldly rational traders. We would like to say that it is the uncertainty in fundamental value that fuels price bubbles, but as we'll see from the laboratory experiments of Vernon Smith and his coworkers, they can be demonstrated when there is no uncertainty about the fundamental value at all. A basic problem is that we have ventured from the safe harbor of quiescent equilibrium behavior, and the sea of dynamic market behavior is stormy indeed.

I will close this chapter by reviewing the wide variety of methods being used today to study price bubbles. These include the ones we've seen for single-item auctions—empirical observation, laboratory experiments, and mathematical modeling—plus an approach we have not yet mentioned: agent-based computer simulation.

A REAL BUBBLE

The idea of a price bubble is often associated in the popular mind with "tulipmania," the speculation in tulip bulbs in the Netherlands of the 1630s, described in 1841 by Mackay. His description of the frenzy is classic (p. 94):

> Nobles, citizens, farmers, mechanics, seamen, footmen, maid-servants, even chimney-sweeps and old clotheswomen, dabbled in tulips. People of all grades converted their property into cash, and invested it in flowers. Houses and lands were offered for sale at ruinously low prices, or assigned in payment of bargains made at the tulip-mart. Foreigners became smitten with the same frenzy, and money poured into Holland from all directions.

And then the crash (p. 95):

> At last, however, the more prudent began to see that this folly could not last for ever. Rich people no longer bought the flowers to keep them in their gardens, but to sell them again at cent per cent profit. It was seen that somebody must lose fearfully in the end. As this conviction spread, prices fell, and never rose again. Confidence was destroyed, and a universal panic seized upon the dealers.

Mackay also describes other famous price bubbles, such as the South Sea Bubble in early-1700s England. But one needn't go back very far to see a good example; figure 6.7 shows the NASDAQ Composite Index for its entire history, and what is now known as the dot-com bubble is painfully evident. There is always the question, of course, of what the fundamental value of the NASDAQ is at any given moment. But, as I've mentioned above, uncertainty about value is evidently not necessary for the generation of a price bubble.

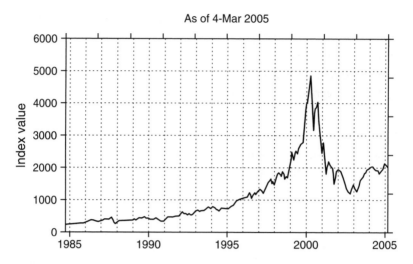

As of 4-Mar 2005

Figure 6.7 The NASDAQ Composite Index. Source: Yahoo! Finance.

BUBBLES IN THE LABORATORY

We come now to the remarkable experiments with price bubbles in the laboratory, reported in a series of papers by Vernon Smith, David Porter, and others over the past twenty years or so, and reviewed in Porter and Smith (2003). Their baseline experiment, originally reported in Smith, Suchanek, and Williams (1988), is summarized in Porter and Smith (2003, p. 7) as follows:

> [E]ach trader receives an initial portfolio of cash and shares of a security, with a dividend horizon of 15 trading periods. Before the nth trading period, the expected dividend value of a share, e.g. $0.24(15 − t + 1)$, is computed and reported to all subjects to guard against any possibility of misunderstanding. ... Each trader is free to trade shares of the security using double auction trading rules similar to those used on the major stock exchanges. At the end of the experiment, a sum equal to all dividends received on shares, plus initial cash plus capital gains minus capital losses[,] is paid in U.S. currency to the trader.

Thus, the expected dividends are linearly decreasing as a function of time, measured by the trading period t, an approximation to the

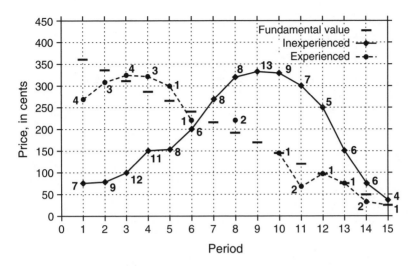

Figure 6.8 Mean contract price vs. trading period in a typical experimental asset market. The numbers next to the data points are the total number of contracts for that trading period. Source: Porter and Smith (2003).

situation in a closed-end fund.[27] In these baseline experiments, the one-period dividends are randomized, being chosen to be $0.00, $0.08, $0.28, and $0.60 with equal probability. The dividends are therefore uncertain, although the total future expected dividend is known to the traders.

The results show that, while experienced traders learn to trade at fundamental value, inexperienced traders produce high-amplitude and long-lived price bubbles, and much higher trading volumes. Figure 6.8 shows this contrast in behavior between experienced and inexperienced bidders in a typical laboratory experiment.

The most amazing result, however, appears when the dividends are made *certain*, instead of being randomized as in the baseline experiment described above. One might expect the removal of uncertainty about the true value of a share to eliminate trading above that value. But the results in Porter and Smith (1994) show that bubbles are not eliminated. The amplitude of the bubbles produced by inexperienced traders are

[27] In fact, price bubbles have been observed in real closed-end funds like the Spain fund, and their behavior is still puzzling and controversial. A good example is shown in Smith et al. (1988).

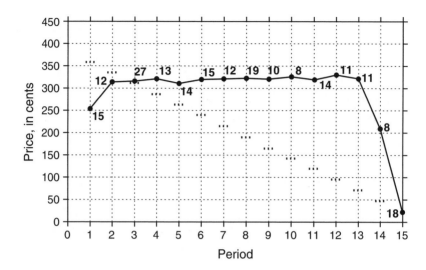

Figure 6.9 Mean contract price vs. trading period in an experimental asset market where the dividends are certain. The bubble is sustained and the crash is precipitous. Source: Porter and Smith (2003).

only slightly reduced, and, in fact, their duration is increased. Figure 6.9 shows a typical example from that study.

In their review of two decades of work, Porter and Smith (2003) describe many elaborations of this basic experiment, designed to test the effects of short selling, margin buying, brokerage fees, and the use of subjects experienced in business. The upshot is that strong price bubbles are a real phenomenon, repeatable in the laboratory, and largely insensitive to these factors—except experience of traders in these experiments. Perhaps their most important conclusion is that "bubbles seem to be due to *uncertainty about the behavior of others*, not to uncertainty about dividends, since making dividends certain does not significantly affect bubble characteristics." The italics are mine; the point confirms the importance we've placed throughout this book on bidder interaction, the precarious nature of equilibrium behavior, and psychological factors.

BUBBLES IN THE COMPUTER

Finally, I want to describe agent-based computer simulation, a favorite topic of mine. I think the technique holds promise for complementing the other mathematical and empirical approaches to studying auctions, and markets in general.

The idea is to model agent behavior at the microscopic level, and to simulate the dynamics of a market, trading period by trading period. For brevity, we'll call a trading period a *day*. We create a fictitious world which has just two commodities, the minimum number required for trade. Call the commodities *food* and *gold*. All the agents produce food or gold, consume food, and trade. The traders are differentiated by a permanent endowment of *skills*, which determine how much food they can produce in one day, and how much gold they can mine in one day. We can think of the agents with high farming skills relative to mining skills as *farmers*, and the ones with high mining skills relative to farming skills as *miners*. Every agent consumes one unit of food per day. The agents try to maintain an inventory of food, try to maximize their inventory of gold, and decide each day whether to farm or mine, and what offers to make to buy or sell food.

Each day a central auctioneer collects the buy and sell orders and clears the market, arriving at the public *market price* for the day. The agents use this market price to make their production decisions, and their buy or sell offers. For example, if the price of food gets sufficiently high, a miner may switch from mining to farming.

When this approach was first tried with Michael Honig (Steiglitz, Honig, and Cohen, 1996) at Bellcore, we fully expected this minimal kind of model economy to function smoothly. But the first result was chaos, literally. The agents have no foresight, and the delays in the system lead to wild oscillations of over- and undersupply. It didn't take long for food inventories to vanish. Agents were dropping like flies.

What was missing was some regulation, and, having some faith in the operation of markets, we added the most natural profit seekers we could imagine: traders who would attempt to buy low and sell high. The traders based their decisions on estimates of fundamental value, and they estimated the equilibrium food price, which in this system is well defined, with a simple adaptive estimation scheme. We called these new agents *value traders*. They stabilized the market price remarkably well, and produced a smoothly functioning economy, a lesson in the power of trade that I think would win the warm approval of most capitalists.

Later on, the work turned naturally to the question of price bubbles in such a simulated market.[28] At least two other groups were looking at dynamic[29] mathematical models that would reproduce price bubbles, described in papers by Caginalp and Balenovich (1993) at the University of Pittsburgh, and Youssefmir, Huberman, and Hogg (1994) at Xerox Palo Alto Research Center. Both groups used differential equations, and the first attempted to calibrate their numerical results with the laboratory results reported by Vernon Smith and his colleagues.

The general idea that has emerged is to model some agents to react, not only to the absolute price level, but to the *trend* in price. Such agents are called *trend traders*, or sometimes, *momentum traders*. This reaction may be a carefully planned investment move, or an emotional or subconscious tendency. What is important is that the trend traders' buy and sell decisions are influenced by perceived price trends or slopes. The hypothesis that price bubbles are produced by the interaction of value traders, who react to fundamentals, and trend traders, seems to be the most well-motivated and successful explanation for price bubbles we have today.

We proceeded to incorporate trend traders in our simulated world of farmers and miners. In the simulations we run, the market value is quite stable, and the trend traders find little to excite them. We therefore varied the theoretical equilibrium price exogenously, by randomly varying agents' farming and mining skills. This did produce nice price bubbles. A typical simulated bubble is shown in figure 6.10, and the details of the work are reported in Steiglitz and Shapiro (1998).

Although the technique is fairly new and certainly not well developed, agent-based simulation is potentially useful for studying auction and asset markets, where individual behavior is crucial in determining dynamic behavior. It would join an already wide spectrum of tools: equilibrium theory, laboratory experiments, field experiments, empirical observation, and dynamic modeling with differential equations.

---

[28] I worked on this with a colleague, Hideyuki Mizuta, IBM Japan, and several students, including Leonard Cohen, Jocelyn Lenormand, Erez Lirov, Sheehan Maduraperuma, Liadan O'Callighan, and Daniel Shapiro.

[29] The term "dynamic" is used here to distinguish the models from the static equilibria in the usual single-auction models.

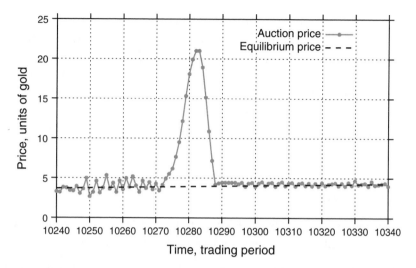

Figure 6.10 A price bubble in an imaginary world of robot traders. The agents are programmed to produce food and gold, consume food, save gold, and trade in a double auction. Agents who try to trade on fundamental value stabilize the market price; agents who try to trade on trend tend to cause bubbles. Source: Steiglitz and Shapiro (1998).

6.9 Questions

1. Is the field experiment of Katkar and Lucking-Reiley (2000) discussed in chapter 5, comparing the effect of equal secret and open reserves, a test of revenue equivalence? Explain.

2. Suggest explanations, other than the one discussed here, for the results of the field experiment of Hossain and Morgan (2003). Discuss the plausibility of each. (They examine five others.)

3. I argued in section 6.3 that because feedback for learning is less certain when sniping on eBay, snipers will tend to overbid, and prices will therefore tend to be higher than they would be with incremental bidding. John Morgan pointed out to me that this suggests that auctions with a soft-closing rule, which tends to diminish sniping, should yield less revenue. But in chapter 2, I quoted an anonymous party at Amazon, who argued that the soft-close auction was more attractive to the seller than the hard-close form. Discuss.

4. (For Latin scholars) Gintis (2000) proposed some species of the genus *Homo* distinct from *H. economicus*. *H. reciprocans* behaves reciprocally, *H. egualis* seeks equality in payoffs, and *H. parochius* divides the world into insiders and outsiders, and favors insiders. Name the species that bids spitefully. You might enjoy naming other species we've met, such as the sniper, the incremental bidder, the overbidder, the bidder who searches up to find the secret reserve, the risk-averse bidder, and the risk-loving bidder.

5. Discuss the effect of players' utility curves on the probable success of bluffing in poker.

6. Propose ways to measure risk aversion in the laboratory, besides the first-price auction experiments of Holt and Sherman (2000).

7. Intuition might tell us that bidding higher in a first-price auction is risk-loving, not risk-averse behavior. After all, it seems that bidding higher is more likely to result in your getting burned. And yet, in equilibrium, risk-averse bidders do bid higher in first-price auctions. Explain.

8. John Maynard Keynes introduced a metaphor in his 1936 book, *The General Theory of Employment, Interest, and Money*, which has become known in modern game theory as the "Beauty Contest." He says (p. 156):

> [P]rofessional investment may be likened to those newspaper competitions in which the competitors have to pick out the six prettiest faces from a hundred photographs, the prize being awarded to the competitor whose choice most nearly corresponds to the average preferences of the competitors as a whole . . . .
>
> . . . It is not a case of choosing those which, to the best of one's judgement, are really the prettiest, nor even those which average opinion genuinely thinks the prettiest. We have reached the third degree where we devote our intelligences to anticipating what average opinion expects the average opinion to be. And there are some, I believe, who practise the fourth, fifth and higher degrees.

Keynes anticipates here the modern idea of *bounded rationality*— roughly speaking, that people in a game-playing situation tend to think to a certain depth, and no deeper.

In a famous paper, "Unraveling in guessing games: An experimental study" (1995), Nagel reports the results of laboratory experiments with a variation of this game. Here's how her version of Keynes's Beauty Contest might translate into a classroom experiment. Each member of the class chooses, simultaneously and in secret, a number between 0 and 100, inclusive. These are collected, and the winner is the student who has guessed closest to *two-thirds* of the class average.

(a) What is the equilibrium guess in this game?
(b) Predict the results if the game were played in your class, or among a group of your friends.
(c) Predict the results if the game were played repeatedly.
(d) Run the game and compare your results with your predictions.
(e) Deduce from your experimental results what "degree" is practiced by your cohorts.
(f) When I ran this in class, I learned afterwards that two students had colluded in a second round, unsuccessfully as it turned out. Suppose you and one friend decide to collude. How would you do it?
(g) Why does the experiment become more interesting with a factor less than one, like two-thirds, than with one?

Transgressions

We have seen that stimulating competition is critically important for the seller. Sellers can therefore cheat by creating phantom bidders, or shills, to increase competition. And bidders can cheat by forming a bidding ring and colluding to reduce competition. We also discuss other forms of nefarious activity, ethical boundaries, and fakes.

7.1 Shills

A GOOD working definition of a *shill*, also called a *puffer* or *by-bidder*, is given by Cassady as a

> person who, without having any intention to purchase, is employed by the seller at an auction to raise the price by fictitious bids, ... while he himself is secured from risk by a secret understanding with the seller that he shall not be bound by his bids.[1]

A new twist is provided by the internet auction, in which the seller and the shill can be one and the same person, using two different identities. Shilling is expressly forbidden by the rules of eBay in their online rules:

> Shill bidding is the deliberate placing of bids to artificially raise the price of an item and is not allowed.[2]

Both definitions suffer from the problem that they involve *intent*. This makes it very difficult to prove that any particular bid is a shill

---

[1] Cassady (1967, p. 212), quoting *Corpus Juris Secundum*, "Auctions and auctioneers," American Law Book Co., Brooklyn, NY, 1937.

[2] eBay home page, November 2003. Besides being against eBay's rules, eBay mentions that shill bidding is "illegal in many areas with severe legal penalties." See Cassady (1967, pp. 212–213) for a discussion of the legal aspects of shilling, including some references to case law that go back to the eighteenth century.

bid, without evidence outside the auction. Consider, for example, the following "questionable pattern" suggested by eBay itself:

> A member bids several times just under the highest bidder towards the end of a listing, incrementing the final sale price by a dollar and retracting if he/she inadvertently bids more than the high bidder.[3]

The word "inadvertently" requires mind reading to apply with confidence. Certainly, the pattern described is very suggestive of shill bidding, especially if it is repeated. On the other hand, we have already seen reasonable bidding patterns in chapter 3 in which bidders inch up on other bidders. It is not inconceivable that such a bidder might get cold feet and retract a bid after becoming the highest bidder. In fact, as we've seen in chapter 3, there's an extraordinarily wide range of bidding behavior on eBay. We can guess at bidders' motivations, but being certain is another matter. Some people may not understand the rules, some may be behaving frivolously, some may be typing carelessly, and others may simply be daydreaming.

The scenario described above by eBay is rather blatant. The following story, based on the experience of a friend, is a bit more subtle. The friend, let's call her bidder 1, sees an item she wants, and the bidding is standing at a very low value, with hardly any bidding. She snipes with a bid of $10, and finds that bidder 2 has won, at the price $10.50, an increment above bidder 1's bid, which was the second highest. It turns out that bidder 2 has a new ID (flagged as such by eBay) and no feedback at all. So far, this is only slightly suspicious. But a week later, the very same item (which is one-of-a-kind) is listed again by the same seller. More suspicious. A couple of weeks later the seller's Member Profile includes the notation "No longer a registered user." More suspicious. My friend, bidder 1, then becomes interested in a similar item a few weeks later, being offered by a seller with a different ID. She exchanges email with this seller, asking a question, and the new seller turns out to be a reincarnation of the original seller—actually, the same person. She bids, and again she is outbid by a low-feedback newcomer. More suspicious. This time, she receives a "second-chance"

---

[3] Ibid.

offer through eBay.[4] At this point the evidence that the seller is using shill bids becomes overwhelming. But he used his shill bids simply, to establish what amounts to a reserve, rather than to egg on bidders during a sale. We will return to this point shortly.

Evidence for shilling beyond a single auction can thus be collected by examining the bidding histories of the seller's previous sales, provided that the seller has not chosen to make his feedback private.[5] It may be possible to spot a likely shill as a bidder who has relatively low feedback (perhaps inflated with purchases of cheap items), and who has bid mostly in the current seller's sales, often unsuccessfully. But again, there is always the possibility that such a bidder is innocent, just happens to favor this seller's items, and happens to bid low.

Figure 7.1 illustrates the details of what are very likely the operations of a seller using shills. As usual, the example is drawn from a real eBay sale, the identities of the bidders are anonymized, and the details of the item are a bit disguised. Bidder 1 appears to be a legitimate, if somewhat inexperienced, bidder. She has 21 feedback points from 25 purchases, from a variety of sellers, and no negative feedback. Bidders 2 and 3 have 0 feedback points and 1 feedback point, respectively, and there is good evidence from other sales by this same seller that these two are alter egos of his. The seller's big problem is simply that there is no competition, so he manufactures some. Bidder 1 bids early, with a bid of $30, the first day. Bidder 2 (a shill) enters the picture about 3.5 days later, and tries $25, $30, and $35, at which point he knows bidder 1's bid. He then bids once more, with a bid of $55. Bidder 1 responds about 5 days later with a bid of $50, which doesn't meet the current high price, and then $70, which does, at which point the second-highest bid sits at $55. The seller wants more, and with his shill bidder 3, enters bids of $60, $70, and two more that we will never know, about 10 hours before the closing time. (This was a 7-day sale, 168 hours.) Evidently the seller was hoping to stimulate further bids by bidder 1, but failed. Of course he didn't

---

[4] This is a relatively new mechanism that enables eBay to capture some of the revenue from sales that had previously been conducted around it, illicitly, as we discussed in chapter 3. If the second-chance offer is accepted, eBay collects its share of the sale price.

[5] Keeping one's feedback private on eBay is an option, and so is keeping the IDs of bidders private in a particular sale, as mentioned in chapter 3. Both choices are sure to raise flags for prospective bidders.

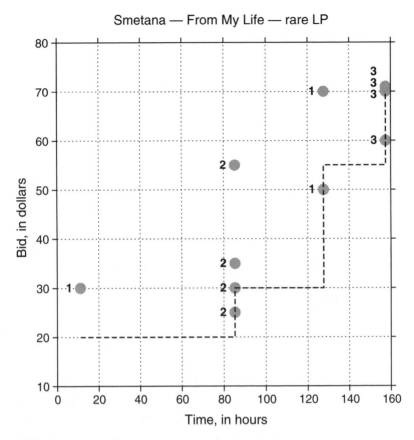

Figure 7.1 A bid history, illustrating the use of shills by a seller. Bidder 1 is the victim, and bidders 2 (feedback 0) and 3 (feedback 1) are the shills.

snipe, but left bidder 1 plenty of time to respond to the email from eBay informing her that she had been outbid. In this case the item was, in the parlance of traditional English auctions, "bought in."

Shilling can be done by the seller himself using an alternate ID, or, of course, by a confederate. In the former case, eBay is in a better position to investigate a report of shilling than are buyers, having records of account ownership. But when someone on the other side of the world is shilling by private arrangement, someone with many feedback points from many different sellers, it is all but impossible to prove it. As a student once commented to me, "my friend in Arizona shills for me all the time." The offense is all but undetectable by ordinary means, and one can only guess at how common it is among frequent sellers.

Sometimes, however, the level of fraud rises to the spectacular level, and attracts the attention of the FBI. The following excerpts from the Department of Justice web site describe one of the first indictments for shill bidding on eBay:

> United States Attorney John K. Vincent announced today that a federal grand jury returned an indictment charging two California men and one Colorado man for their participation in a ring of fraudulent bidding in hundreds of art auctions on eBay, including one last May in which an eBay user was induced to bid over $135,805 for a fake Richard Diebenkorn painting. . . .
>
> According to Assistant U.S. Attorneys Christopher P. Sonderby and Michael J. Malecek, who are prosecuting the case, the Indictment alleges that the defendants created more than 40 User IDs on eBay using false registration information, and then used those aliases to place fraudulent bids to artificially inflate the prices of literally hundreds of paintings they auctioned on eBay from November 1998 to June 2000. . . .
>
> According to the Indictment, the defendants shielded their true identities from eBay by providing bogus names, postal addresses, and telephone information, and by providing email addresses obtained from free email providers known to collect little or no verifiable information on their account holders. By creating multiple User IDs, the defendants intended to trick other eBay users into believing that the "shill" bids they placed on each other's items were legitimate. . . .
>
> Using these on-line aliases and others, the Indictment alleges that the defendants hosted more than 1,100 auctions on eBay from late 1998 until May 2000, and that they placed fraudulent bids on more than half of those auctions. The total value of the winning bids in all auctions hosted by [the defendants] in which they placed shill bids exceeded approximately $450,000. The total value of the high shill bids in these auctions exceeded approximately $300,000. The high shill bid averaged approximately 66% of the final high bid.[6]

---

[6] http://www.usdoj.gov/criminal/cybercrime/ebayplea.htm.

At the time of this writing, two defendants have pleaded guilty and one is still at large.

Here we have an indictment that charges that the shill bids were placed "to artificially inflate" prices, and that "an eBay user was induced to bid over $135,805 for a fake Richard Diebenkorn painting." The Department of Justice evidently agrees with our conclusions that bidders are influenced by rival bids, a position which supports our arguments against early bidding. Another interesting tidbit is the report that the "high shill bid averaged approximately 66% of the final high bid," a rare statistic, one that would be near impossible to gather in a field experiment that was legal.

7.1.1 Shill Bidding and Theory

Shill bidding on eBay is strictly against the rules, and, as we've just reported, can rise to a serious criminal activity. We will, nevertheless, discuss the question of how best to shill, if briefly. Our purpose is not to provide good advice to criminals. Studying shilling is morally defensible; it is only by knowing how vulnerable a particular auction form is to cheating, and how effective that cheating can be, that one can avoid bad auction mechanisms and design good ones.[7] Besides, it is always possible, in principle, to change the rules to allow shill bidding, which would be fair, provided everyone knows it. Graham, Marshall, and Richard (1990), and, more recently, Izmalkov (2004), discuss optimal bidding by a seller who is allowed to participate actively in an English auction. This simply legitimizes by fiat the taking of bids off the wall, which corresponds to shill bidding on eBay. But this theory of optimal shilling, maximizing revenue for the seller, assumes that the seller, in this case the auctioneer, knows a lot more about value distributions than he possibly could on eBay, and, further, that the auction is a Japanese button auction.

A shill bid, as we mentioned in section 3.7.2, has an effect that is very similar to a reserve. We can see this clearly in the sealed-bid second-price auction where the bidders have private values—that

---

[7] As observed by Izmalkov (2004). The same argument shows why cryptographers are justified in spending so much effort breaking encryption schemes.

is, they are absolutely certain of their values. Then we know (Vickrey's argument, of course) that truthful bidding is dominant, under very general circumstances, including those where bidders may be asymmetric or have interdependent values. In such cases a shill bid plays *exactly* the same role as a reserve. The seller chooses his (illicit) bid at the reserve prescribed by theory, as described in chapter 5 and, in more technical detail, appendices B and C. The tradeoff faced by the seller is the same one he faces when choosing the reserve: he excludes certain buyers, at the cost of losing a sale, but on the average he more than makes up for it by forcing winners to pay more. This amounts to a take-it-or-leave-it offer to the highest bidder. When viewed in this light, the shill bid seems rather innocent, at least *in theory*, because the seller can extract the same revenue simply by appropriately choosing an open reserve (opening bid), or a secret reserve, in the amount of his shill bid.

With private values, this equivalence between shill bidding and using a reserve also holds on eBay *if everyone snipes*, in which case eBay reduces to a sealed-bid sale. But on the real eBay, bidders may well be uncertain of their values, and may also be able to gather useful information about their values, and the values of others, by observing early bids. Besides, bidders are specimens of *Homo sapiens* and not *Homo economicus*. The reasons for sniping hinge on all these observations— early bidding can stimulate further early bidding, bidding wars, and, in general, price-raising activity that the sniper is trying to avoid. The seller who shill bids instead of using a reserve cheats the buyer precisely because of these effects on behavior.

Finally, we should mention a point raised by Kauffman and Wood (2003). Sellers on eBay may shill bid, not particularly to run up the final price to the buyer, but to avoid paying the higher listing fee associated with a higher opening bid—a strategy they call "reserve price shilling." They give an example where the seller can list an item at a starting bid of $0.01 and then (illicitly) enter a shill bid of $199.99, thus saving the $3.00 difference in listing fees that eBay charges for the higher opening bid. This gives the seller the protection of a $200.00 reserve while paying eBay only for the $0.01 reserve. Of course, the seller who shill bids always faces the negative consequences of actually winning his own item.

7.1.2 Mock Auctions: The More Important Diamond

Closely related to shill bidding, and in a sense an extreme form of it, is the practice of holding what Cassady (1967) calls "mock auctions."

I witnessed the following auction room drama in Atlantic City in the mid-1960s. At that time, there were no gambling casinos in the town, but there were walk-in storefronts on the boardwalk that conducted English auctions for jewelry. I never miss an opportunity to watch auctions, and these were particularly instructive. I walked into one of these operations, and observed heated bidding for a diamond ring that ended in an (apparent) sale for, let us say, $1000.[8] A second ring was then produced, and it sold for a similar amount, also after what appeared to be heated bidding. The auctioneer then paused dramatically, and announced that his assistant would now produce "the more important" diamond. He touted it effusively and skillfully as being, simply, in a different league from the earlier diamonds. He then asked for a "ridiculously low" starting bid of $2000. No bids. He appeared to grow frustrated, repeated the performance, and finally, after much theatrics, asked for $1000. Again, no bids, and appeared to be on the verge of retiring the item, when, with a wave of disgust, he asked for a mere $500 start, "just to get the ball rolling." Nothing.

While the auctioneer was working so hard with no effect, his assistant was walking around the auction room, showing the sparkling treasure. When no bid for $500 was forthcoming, he stopped at a gentleman on the center aisle, and asked, "Look at the quality of this stone. Surely, sir, you would pay $200 for this, right?" The gentleman nodded, and the assistant quickly turned to the auctioneer and announced, "we have a $200 bid!" The gentleman on the aisle seemed a bit surprised at first, and then quite pleased when he "stole" the item with no competition, despite further impassioned pleading by the auctioneer.

I later learned that I had observed a standard scam. The buyers of the first two rings, together with their competing bidders, were shills, and the ring that sold for $200 was worth something like $50. The success

---

[8] I don't remember the actual numbers, so I've invented modern prices that are roughly equivalent.

of this swindle depends, first, on the larceny that is ever in the heart of the bidder, the desire to take advantage of the seller. (As the saying goes, "You can't cheat an honest man.") Second, the performing auctioneer is illustrating once again the ease with which bidders can be influenced by other bids, and how they are liable to build up false expectations about value, in this case over a period of three auctions.

Cassady (1967) actually describes a scam that goes one step further than the one described here, in which a legitimate, brand-name item is sold to the sucker, and then surreptitiously replaced by "flash"— worthless merchandise. In any event, this sort of operation is best run in exactly the kind of seedy venue I observed, attracting transient customers with spare cash, vacationing tourists, for example. I don't know whether this multi-auction scheme could work on eBay, although it wouldn't surprise me. The lessons about bidder behavior are, however, eternal.

7.2 Bidder Rings: 84 Charing Cross Road

Buyers can cheat by colluding to decrease competition within a ring of insiders. A firsthand account of how this worked in the London antiquarian book business of the 1930s is provided by Leo Marks, son of the co-owner of 84 Charing Cross Road, in his autobiographical book, *Between Silk and Cyanide* (1998, p. 153).[9]

> Marks & Co. were kings of the book ring. They were one of the five leading firms of antiquarian booksellers who never bid against each other in the auction rooms. One member of the ring would be allowed to buy the book for a nominal sum, say £100. As soon as the auction was over the five conspirators would hurry to their nearest safe-house—usually a Lyons tea shop—and conduct a private auction. If one of them bought the book in question for £500, the £400 profit would be divided in cash amongst the other four. This process was called a 'knock-out', ...

[9] A thrilling and poignant book for reasons which have nothing to do with auctions.

In effect, the members of the ring stole the £400 from the house.[10] There are certain dangers for the colluders that come with the operation of a ring. Marks continues,

> ...and Frank Doel once blew an entire operation.
>
> A famous heart specialist named Evan Bedford instructed him to bid up to £300 for an edition of Harvey's *De Motu Cordis*, the earliest printed book on the circulation of the blood, which was coming up for auction at Hodgson's. Too busy with his own Harley Street salesroom to attend the auction himself, he telephoned Frank at home late at night demanding to know why the book had been sold to another dealer for £200 when he'd authorized Frank to bid three. Frank confided that it had been sold in the knock-out for £650. The irate physician immediately undertook to have the whole question of the book ring raised in the House of Commons, which caused cardiac arrest amongst its five participants.[11]

The ability of buyers to collude this way depends very much on their ability to communicate and observe each other. For one thing, they need to coordinate their plans. For another, they need to watch each other to prevent a member from defecting—that is, opportunistically bidding against the ring *center*, as the appointed bidder is called. This sort of close cooperation and monitoring can, and does, occur naturally in a small circle of book, coin, or rug dealers, say, in one city.

Buyer collusion is actually not difficult at all on eBay, although it appears to have received much less attention than shill bidding, either on eBay's web site, or in the press. It is, of course, impossible to gauge its actual extent. In the early days of eBay it was common to use one's email address as one's ID, but this practice was sensibly prohibited a few years ago. However, it is still possible to send email to any registered member using eBay as an intermediary, and it is therefore easy for buyers to exchange email addresses—if perhaps under eBay's watchful eye. After a while, it seems likely that you will come to know the identities and email addresses of your frequent competitors, especially if you make

---

[10] Cassady (1967) reports that the Antiquarian Booksellers Association of England did some housecleaning themselves in 1956, and agreed to disqualify dealers who participate in rings.

[11] The story gets even better; read the book.

an effort to find them out. I have myself been approached in email by buyers asking me, as a favor, to refrain from bidding on certain very specialized items. Presumably, the favor would be returned, and a two-person variety of bidder collusion could easily evolve.

The version of the ring described by Marks depends for its success on the colluding members having relatively little competition outside their own circle. The ring center must estimate how high to go, perhaps after consulting her co-conspirators. The knockout auction described by Marks is more precisely termed a *post-auction* knockout, and is evidently the way rings work in practice. McMillan (1992, pp. 146–47) describes a similar but much more elaborate ring in a New York auction for a silk Tabriz rug. It also uses a post-auction knockout, but has a more arcane scheme to share the illicit profit. Further examples of buyer rings and their operations can be found in Cassady (1967), where an entire chapter is devoted to the subject.

Theoretical work on buyer collusion is exemplified by Graham and Marshall (1987), who describe a theoretical scheme assuming the standard IPV model, a second-price sealed-bid main auction, and a second-price sealed-bid *pre-auction* knockout. Briefly, the plan is the following: The conspirators gather before the main auction and determine, in the sealed-bid knockout, who places the highest value on the item. The appointed ring leader, who acts as the banker, then pays a certain amount, P, to each ring member. The winner of the knockout, say ring member W, is then instructed to bid her value at the main auction; others can, perhaps, place meaningless bids to mask the ring operation. If W wins the main auction, she pays the required second-highest bid in the main auction, and gives the ring leader any excess of the second-highest price in the ring over the amount she paid in the main auction. The average value of this amount is actually the average profit of the ring, the average amount stolen from the main auctioneer. The amount P is calculated to balance the books for the ring leader; it is the average ring profit per ring member.

Graham and Marshall's ring operation has some nice theoretical properties. It boils down to one big Vickrey auction, and truthful bidding is therefore dominant. If a ring member places a value on the item that is the highest of anyone participating in either the ring or the main auction, she wins the object. Further, all ring members share equally in any profit, and therefore they all have an incentive to participate in the ring. One reason that real rings use post-auction instead of pre-auction knockouts is the difficulty in determining the value of the payoff P. This requires knowledge of the value distribution of the bidders, and we know that in the real world, this is simply not determinable with any accuracy. Even if the ring leader could calculate P, he would be assured of breaking even only on the average, and over many identical auctions. It is not likely that anyone would accept the role in practice.

There are some important things to learn from Graham and Marshall's paper, however. Just the existence of such a smoothly running ring in theory suggests that rings are likely to be persistent in real auctions. Their theory also predicts that auctioneers combat rings in practice by raising their reserves, a commonsense strategic response to the presence of a ring. Further, the larger the ring, the higher the auctioneer should raise his reserve. From this it follows that rings should try to hide their existence, or at least their size, from the auctioneer. All very reasonable conclusions.

Along these lines, Ashenfelter (1989) suggests that auction houses such as Sotheby's and Christie's keep reserves secret for just the purpose of thwarting the operation of rings. He suggests also that auctioneers typically keep the identity of buyers secret for the same reason—to combat rings. The idea here is that being able to buy anonymously gives ring members an incentive to bid for themselves and thereby double-cross their fellow ring members. Evidently there is no honor among thieves.

Once again, I have risked giving the appearance of using auction theory to advise criminals, but again the moral defense is clear. Knowing how rings work helps the house as well. In fact, rings are evidently a persistent and important problem, quite common in floor auctions. Graham and Marshall (1987) comment, "So prevalent are rings, in fact, that a retired auctioneer once noted that in 40 years of auctioneering, he had yet to attend an auction at which a ring was not present." As I mentioned above, the practical success of rings relies on buyers being able to communicate and to watch each other. The internet and the policies of eBay make this easy, and the reported prevalence of collusion in English floor auctions suggests that bidder collusion on eBay may be a significant, if practically invisible, problem, particularly in narrow collecting specialties with repeat buyers.

7.3 Ethics

We've just discussed two criminal activities that directly violate the auction rules, and do so to increase competition for the seller or decrease competition for the buyer. We now take up other possible shadowy activities, some of which may not actually violate the auction rules, and some of which may be considered, by some, to be perfectly acceptable behavior.

There is quite a broad spectrum of ethical problems for any auction participant, ranging from those that might induce a slightly soiled feeling, to those that manage to skate just on the boundary of crime. We'll take them up in no particular order. We'll then finish with the serious problems of frauds and fakes on eBay, which, however, are not directly related to the operating rules of the auction.

7.3.1 The Twinge of Guilt: The Buyer Withholds Information

Suppose a seller posts an eBay item as "unidentified," or a "mystery item." This is a fairly common occurrence in the ancient coin section, where odd and beat-up pieces of metal are popping up all the time. If you win such an item, you may be asked by the seller if you know what it is. If you do know, you are faced with a small moral crisis, because you may not want to reveal the extent to which you are informed about the sort of material this seller comes up with. On the other hand, lying, even only by omission, has an emotional cost (for most people).

In the extreme case, you as a buyer may be so much better informed about an item that you might feel you are taking advantage of the seller's ignorance. Here we can find a spectrum of moral codes that comes up again and again. You can be softhearted, or you can play hardball. By informing the seller before the sale of the value of the item, you essentially give him money. Or, by keeping your information to yourself, you can extract the maximum surplus from the deal.[12] eBay makes it a point to warn buyers that they are generally

---

[12] I'm now ignoring positive rewards for feelings of virtue, as well as the possible penalties of a tortured conscience.

unprotected, *caveat emptor*.[13] It would seem that *caveat venditor*[14] is also in order.

One way to deal with this question psychologically is to make a distinction between buying from a private party and buying from a dealer, assuming you can tell the difference from the seller's item page and feedback record. A dealer is implicitly representing himself as more or less knowledgeable about his wares, at least ideally, and you might take the position that he is more fair game than granny, say, who found an ancient Roman coin at the back of a drawer.

7.3.2 Conversely: The Seller Withholds Information

In selling a "mystery item," the seller implies that he really does not know what the item is and what it might be worth. When he posts a high-quality photograph, it may be that the seller is sincerely trusting the market, and such items can present good opportunities for experienced collectors to cash in on their expertise. But sometimes the posted photograph is blurry, or the items encrusted, and the seller may be feigning ignorance to attract bidders with mild larceny in their hearts.

Related ethical transgressions come up in selling ancient coins that are (presumably) freshly dug from the ground. They are usually advertised as "unsearched," or even with the added enticement "gold found." Just how unsearched they are, and just what the chances are of finding a gold aureus in a one-dollar lot, is the buyer's guess. The technique is not new to internet auctions, and I have often seen "surprise boxes" auctioned off in venues not unlike the Atlantic City boardwalk auctions of the 1960s. The lure of the bargain is always available as a tool for the seller.

Beyond this, I have often seen a seller post a fake, with the warning that he is unsure of its authenticity. Again, this may be an honest representation, or it may be an attempt to fetch a good price for a fake by attracting speculators.

---

[13] "Buyer beware." PayPal, owned by eBay, now offers a kind of insurance of satisfaction to the buyer after each sale.

[14] Seller beware.

Of course, all these selling maneuvers ultimately become blatant misrepresentation when carried to the extreme, and we will return to the problem of intentionally peddling fakes in section 7.5. It is hardly necessary to point out again that we can't count on Milgrom and Weber's principle of full disclosure (1982) on eBay, where the credibility of sellers is far from certain (in fact, it's often in question), and buyers are likely asymmetric.

7.3.3 Sniping

There is a tendency for newcomers to eBay to consider sniping a dastardly act. It reminds me of the common reaction of young children learning to play chess when they are first the victim of a knight fork. "No fair!" they cry out. But they learn that it *is* fair, and that in the narrow world of chess, the rewards of kindheartedness are slight. Many bidders on eBay come around to the same ruthless position in regard to sniping, or at least come to accept sniping as acceptable social behavior.

7.3.4 Shadowing Bidders

Shadowing a bidder, as mentioned in chapter 3, is the practice of tracking what another person is bidding on, to take advantage of the other's expertise, or maybe just to save your searching time if you know that the bidder you track has similar tastes. It provides a good reason not to bid early. Shadowing is made possible by eBay's extraordinarily liberal policy in revealing information, a policy that engenders trust, and in this sense follows the spirit of Milgrom and Weber's theoretical result recommending full disclosure on the part of sellers. But the policy also invites this practice of shadowing other bidders, which many might consider quite nasty. It is, after all, a way of taking advantage of someone without their knowing it.

One can argue, however, that all bidders are given equal access to the rules, and shadowing is no more an evil act than sniping, which is generally considered fair play. The truth is, however, that not all eBayers, especially newcomers, know that the list of items on which they are currently bidding is actually public.

One can also question eBay's motive in making current bidders' activities so public. It does seem that, on the average, it encourages competition and therefore raises eBay's revenue.

7.3.5 The Ethics of Feedback

After every transaction, the participants can, if they wish, leave a "feedback" report—+1, −1, or neutral, plus a text comment—which then becomes a *public* and permanent part of the buyer's and seller's record.[15] The purpose of feedback is to provide the community with a means for estimating the reliability of a seller or buyer, and thus to provide an incentive for honest behavior.[16]

Exactly because it's public and permanent, a negative feedback point is a serious mark against someone, and, generally speaking, the threshold for getting negative feedback is high.[17] There is good empirical evidence from field experiments (Lucking-Reiley et al., 2000) that it's the negative feedback that really counts, much more so than the positive.

However, a negative point is very often answered with a reciprocal negative point, contradicting the statements made by the first party. Since negative feedback is so often reciprocated, why would anyone leave a negative point in the first place? I suppose it's possible that many do it out of a sense of community service. But the usual tone of negative feedback suggests to me that the principal motivation is anger. It is often the only way that an injured party can hurt an offender, and it's worth the hit to vent the fury.[18]

The phenomenon of trading both positive and negative feedback is an example of the *tit-for-tat* strategy, common in life as well as in game theory (see question 1 and Axelrod's book, *The Evolution of Cooperation* (1984)). The idea is to punish your adversary over repeated encounters, and thereby encourage good future behavior. But on eBay,

---

[15] Except that, as mentioned before, someone can choose to keep her feedback private.

[16] For an introductory article on the general field of online reputation systems, with further references, see Resnick, Zeckhauser, Friedman, and Kuwabara (2000).

[17] Except for the occasional, inevitable maniac.

[18] This qualifies as *spiteful* behavior, as we discussed in chapter 6.

buyers choose their sellers, and it is not very likely that you would choose to buy a second time from someone with whom you have traded negative feedback. The potential damage is likely far greater than any expected future benefit in dealing with one particular seller. There is thus a strong, rational incentive *not* to leave negative feedback under any circumstances, which is in direct conflict with the altruistic motive to warn others about a dishonest character, and also with the base motive to hurt the offender, even while hurting oneself. In this case, strict self-interest is aligned against both altruism and spite.

7.3.6 *Exporting and Importing Ancient Artifacts*

The ethical and legal questions raised by trading in ancient artifacts are yet more complex. The resulting heightened demand may contribute to activities in the source county that are either illegal or, if legal, morally reprehensible. For example, operations in a new market like eBay might stimulate looting in the country of origin, the forgery of export permits and receipts, or the forgery of the artifacts themselves. It might also encourage the destruction of important archaeological data associated with the artifacts, or deny museums the opportunity to buy and display items of national and cultural pride.

As usual, I'll use ancient coins as a case in point. When a pot of coins is dug up, it is important to document exactly which coins are in the find, so that the fact that they were hoarded at one time can be used to deduce things about the time and culture of the site. For example, if the coins are Roman, the date of the latest emperor can usually provide a good estimate of when the pot was buried. Furthermore, details about the striking mint and condition of accompanying coins can tell numismatists a great deal about trade routes in the ancient world, the sequencing of non-Roman rulers when that information is obscure, and how long coins were likely to circulate. Dispersing a hoard of coins without proper documentation irretrievably destroys valuable historical information, and is a crime against human culture. Similar problems of course arise with many kinds of artifacts that might come to sellers from their original burial sites.

According to the Illicit Antiquities Research Centre (IARC) at Cambridge University, the problem of illicit international trade in antiquities has "increased enormously over the past twenty years and is thought to have caused the large-scale plundering of archaeological sites and museums around the world."[19] Their newsletter, *Culture without Context*, is a good source for current news and comment on the topic.[20] Especially interesting is the article by Chippindale and Gill, "On-line auctions: A new venue for the antiquities market" (2001), which surveys present traffic in antiquities on eBay, and also on Sotheby's web site.

The United States has laws about importing archaeologically and culturally significant artifacts. Here's an extract from the United States Customs web site:[21]

```
U.S. law may also restrict the importation of
specific categories of art/artifacts/antiquities. For
example, U.S. laws restrict the importation of: 1) Any
pre-Columbian monumental and architectural sculpture
and murals from Central and South American countries;
2) Native American artifacts from Canada; Mayan
pre-Columbian archaeological objects from Guatemala;
pre-Columbian archaeological objects from El Salvador
and Peru; archaeological objects (like terracotta
statues) from Mali; Colonial period objects such as
paintings and ritual objects from Peru; 3) Byzantine
period ritual and ecclesiastic objects such as icons
from Cyprus; and 4) Khmer stone archaeological sculpture
from Cambodia.
```

The view from the other side of U.S. border, from the same source:

```
Most countries have laws that protect their cultural
property: art/artifacts/antiquities; archaeological
```

---

[19] I am indebted to archaeologist Peter Bogucki for pointing out just how important this problem is, and for leading me to the IARC web site, http://www.mcdonald.cam. ac.uk/IARC/home.htm.

[20] Available online at the IARC web site.

[21] http://www.customs.gov/xp/cgov/travel/vacation/kbyg/prohibited_restricted.xml, March 2005. See also the State Department cultural property web site, http://exchanges. state.gov/culprop/, which has articles, recent reports of looting, theft, prosecution, and recovery on the web, and an image database.

and ethnological material are also terms that are used. Such laws include export controls and/or national ownership of cultural property. Even if purchased from a business in the country of origin or in another country, legal ownership of such artifacts may be in question if brought into the United States. Therefore, although they do not necessarily confer ownership, you must have documents such as export permits and receipts when importing such items into the United States.

Right now, the United States government appears to exercise a laissez-faire policy in this arena on eBay, at least as far as relatively inexpensive items are concerned. But, of course, eBay buyers and sellers have an obligation to learn the law in their specialty and follow it conscientiously. As for the ethical problems that arise, they are complex and controversial. Personal feelings differ about whether artifacts belong to individuals, nations, cultures, or the world at large, and these feelings often run high.

Ancient coins are distributed across the spectrum between unique artifacts and very commonly traded material. The great majority of coin types that are found on the market are readily attributed to mint cities and time periods, and have already been documented in books and catalogs. So, for example, if a coin is found at a human burial site, it is most likely the coin that will tell us about the skeleton, and not the other way around. Usually, the only information about coin hoards that is vital to the preservation of the archaeological record is their content and location. In some very special cases, however, such as newly discovered coins from rare city mints, the find location *can* help attribute a coin, and the exact conditions of its recovery should certainly be preserved.

7.4 A Note on Downright Fraud

The main function of feedback on eBay is to provide a means for establishing reputation against the worst offenses, outright fraud. Selling fake collectibles is a particularly interesting and complex kind of fraud, and we will devote the next section to the problem. But, besides that, there is no end to the ingenuity brought to bear on the problem of extracting value from others in illegitimate ways. On eBay, besides the common and sometimes borderline offenses we've mentioned, some sellers simply collect payment and abandon their accounts, or send items different from the ones they posted, or doctor the photos they post, and so on. With PayPal offering insurance, there are sure to be false insurance claims as well.

On the other end of transactions, buyers pay with stolen credit cards or bad checks, or falsely claim that items are not delivered. As in all business, participants need to be circumspect, and the best policy is to know the person you are dealing with. That is one good reason why good feedback records are coveted, and why so many buyers on eBay deal repeatedly with the same sellers.

7.5 Fakes

Where fakes[22] are involved, the question of what constitutes ethical behavior is usually clear. If a seller has any question about the authenticity of his wares, he should go out of his way to inform prospective buyers. If the seller is simply not knowledgeable, he should say so. Unfortunately, people cannot always be expected to behave in such a straightforward way. The worst offense, of course, is knowingly representing a fake as genuine. Not far behind, I suppose, is disingenuously expressing doubt when there is no doubt at all, thus enticing the inevitable bargain hunters with some larceny in their hearts. While the ethical questions may seem clear, the area of forgeries has a romance all its own, and I can't resist dipping into some details here.

I'll discuss fakes with reference to ancient coins, but the points raised apply, to a greater or lesser extent, to most areas of collectibles. Consider stamps, for example. It appears that the main problem in the eBay market for collectible stamps is the alteration of stamps to

---

[22] I won't try to distinguish between fakes, forgeries, counterfeits, replicas, copies, and reproductions. The terms are used almost interchangeably in a variety of contexts. I will usually use the word "fake" because it carries with it a certain opprobrium.

increase their value dramatically. This can be done in a myriad of ways that are difficult to detect: replacing torn corners, removing or adding cancellations, removing or adding perforations, or changing some other subtle but crucial characteristic, such as a tiny design element.

In contrast with stamps, ancient coins, especially those made of bronze, are almost never in pristine condition. Most have been buried in the ground at one time and are usually found covered with dirt, a patina, or varying degrees of encrustation. Furthermore, they were manufactured by hand rather than machine, and subtle alterations cannot usually increase their value dramatically. In fact, ancient coins are almost always cleaned, and many are "touched up" in ways that may not be considered fraudulent, or even objectionable, by most collectors.

On the other hand, fake ancient coins are often manufactured from scratch, and there is a thriving business making modern reproductions on a wholesale scale, especially in Bulgaria, where a prolific engraver apparently named Slavey Petrov produces a wide range of struck forgeries, usually called "Slaveys."[23] These are not especially convincing in style, but they are likely to fool beginners. There are also large-scale operations selling cast copies of genuine coins on eBay, especially the sellers known as "Online Liquidators" or the "Toronto Group."[24] These fakes look like casts, and will also fool only relative beginners, having characteristically dull, granular, and porous surfaces, but their hawkers will sometimes post a photo of a real coin and send the buyer the fake. These operations are easy to spot: the sellers typically keep their own feedback private, keep the bidders' identities anonymous (another eBay option),[25] and so on. In the case of the Toronto group, many items are posted at once, with a short auction duration (usually one or three days), so as not to allow time for complaints to eBay to be effective. Not only are many items posted together, but they often have exactly the same dreary appearance, even though the coins are supposed to originate from places thousands of miles apart, at times separated by centuries.

[23] http://www.calgarycoin.com/reference/fakes/fakeswebsites.htm.

[24] http://www.chijanofuji.com/online_liquidators.html, 2003.

[25] The point of keeping bidders' IDs private is to prevent other bidders from warning them early through email.

I should point out that fake ancient coins are very interesting themselves, and are often sought after by collectors.[26] They fall into several categories, which I summarize below, just to give you an idea of the rich variety of nonauthentic items that are out there.

- Ancient silver-plated bronze versions of silver coins, called fourrés. These were struck from official dies, and were evidently unofficial productions of the official mints. They are really on the borderline between genuine and fake.
- Ancient forgeries intended to be passed as currency. These were often produced by just plain forgers, or by Celtic tribes, Vandals, and the like. These are sometimes struck from crude, forged dies, and sometimes cast from molds. In fact, the molds themselves are sometimes found and also show up for sale.
- Renaissance copies, which were often quite beautifully made, and which often did not copy any particular coin, but were in some sense "fantasies." For example, there are well-known sixteenth-century forgeries from Padua, often made by Giovanni da Cavino, that are collected for their own sake, and are usually easily recognized as imitations (Klawans, 1977).
- More or less well-made forgeries of more modern times, either cast or struck from hand-made dies in the manner of the ancients. The outstanding examples of such productions are the really remarkable coins made by "Becker the Counterfeiter" (see Hill (1924) for a fascinating account of Becker's career, and plates of his known productions). Becker was a master at imitating the spirit and fabric of his ancient prototypes, and his forgeries found their way into many important collections.
- Electrotypes, often made by museums for scholarly purposes. These are often very convincing head-on, but the edges where copies of the two sides are joined are usually a giveaway. Attempts at disguising the telltale seam are invariably unsuccessful.
- Poor imitations, recognizable as fakes from across the room, often sold to the tourist trade in the Middle East. Imitations like these sometimes show up in costume jewelry.

[26] I suppose fakes should be guaranteed to be such, with a money-back guarantee if they turn out to be genuine.

- Fantasies and inventions, pieces made more or less in imitation of ancient antecedents, sometimes with no intent to deceive. My favorite in this category is an advertising token imitating the famous Syracusan dekadrachm,[27] produced by the Stearns Bicycle Company of Syracuse, New York in 1898. It is inscribed ΣΤΕΑΡΝΣ, MDCCCXCVIII.

It should be clear, even from this quick summary, that the world of forged ancient coins is complicated, and the products range from frivolous to those about which experts disagree. All the major collections in museums and universities have their tray of forgeries, or "rogue's gallery," and visiting scholars are often treated to a review of the questionable holdings, perhaps together with some war stories.

Fakes are sold and bought on eBay in a variety of ways. At one extreme, fakes are advertised as such in bold letters by honest dealers, many of whom crusade for the proper identification of coins that are not genuine, or even those that are just questionable, and the weeding out of dealers who pass them on as authentic. At the other extreme are downright crooks, who sell fakes knowingly, and often on a large scale. These bandits change their IDs often, and, as mentioned above, often keep their own feedback and the bidders' IDs private. When their feedback is public, they usually have a small number of feedback points, harvested from transactions for very inexpensive items. So far, eBay has kept its distance and does not actively police such goings-on, in keeping with its *caveat emptor* policy, but there are vigilante newsgroups and dealers that monitor the more blatantly dishonest dealers on eBay.

Needless to say, the collector is well advised to stick with the reputable dealers with proven track records and a good return policy, and to take advantage of certification services[28] for expensive items. On the other hand, bottom fishing for cheap items can be a lot of fun when only pocket change is at stake. I've accumulated a fair collection of interesting fakes, plus a few bargains, by buying items on speculation. It has even happened that I've bought an item represented as a fake that turned out to be genuine, at least in my opinion.

---

[27] Struck c. 400 B.C., perhaps the most beautiful and famous of all ancient coins.
[28] The best known is David Sear, http://www.davidrsear.com/certification.html.

7.6 Questions

1. In game theory, a game between two people, each of whom has exactly two possible strategies, is often modeled by a 2×2 matrix. The rows and columns represent strategies by player 1 and 2, respectively. Each entry in the matrix is a pair of numbers, representing the expected payoffs to the two players. Formulate the "Feedback Game" on eBay in this form, assuming that players must leave either positive $(+)$ or negative $(-)$ feedback. Is the pair of strategies $(+,+)$ a Nash equilibrium? How about $(-,-)$?

2. How might behavior in leaving feedback be affected by the nature of the items being sold?

3. Here are the bids after Mar-12-05 09:41:30 PST in an actual eBay auction. The closing time was Mar-13-05 01:35:58 PST. As you can see, the bidders' identities are private, which greatly limits our ability to reconstruct the sequence of events. But can you spot at least one bid that is suggestive of shilling? (I suspect from the photo that the item is a fake denarius of Antony and Cleopatra, but of course I can't be sure.)

```
private listing - bidders' identities protected US $1,025.00 Mar-13-05 01:35:52 PST
private listing - bidders' identities protected US $1,000.00 Mar-13-05 01:35:52 PST
private listing - bidders' identities protected US   $900.00 Mar-12-05 14:35:07 PST
private listing - bidders' identities protected US   $799.99 Mar-12-05 15:53:02 PST
private listing - bidders' identities protected US   $700.05 Mar-12-05 14:34:50 PST
private listing - bidders' identities protected US   $700.00 Mar-12-05 13:46:38 PST
private listing - bidders' identities protected US   $680.05 Mar-12-05 14:34:40 PST
private listing - bidders' identities protected US   $660.05 Mar-12-05 14:34:29 PST
private listing - bidders' identities protected US   $650.00 Mar-12-05 09:41:30 PST
private listing - bidders' identities protected US   $640.05 Mar-12-05 14:34:18 PST
private listing - bidders' identities protected US   $620.05 Mar-12-05 14:34:05 PST
...
```

4. Can you think of ways to detect bidder collusion on eBay from bidding histories? What patterns might you look for?

5. Write a program, as in question 7 of chapter 3, to find the frequency of a buyer returning to the same seller after trading negative feedback with him. Be careful to exclude cases where the negative feedback is first exchanged for several items at about the same time, which is fairly common.

Epilogue

8.1 Looking Back

To RETRACE the path we've taken, the first three chapters provided background:

Chapter 1   The history of auctions, and the two standard pairs;
Chapter 2   The development of eBay as a natural evolution from mail-bid sales;
Chapter 3   Observations of behavior on eBay.

These chapters are mostly a description of what is, not what should be, or could be.

In the next three chapters we did the bulk of the hard thinking, applying the theory and the results of laboratory and fieldwork:

Chapter 4   From the point of view of the house: Why does eBay use the second-price rule?
Chapter 5   From the point of view of the seller: How should he choose his opening bid and reserve?
Chapter 6   From the point of view of the buyer: How much should she bid?

In the last chapter of the main text, chapter 7, we explored the activities that are questionable, unethical, clearly illegal, or on the fuzzy borderlines.

When warranted, I've tried to extract morals, explanations, and advice from the supporting research, the elements of which are laid out in appendices A–D. The lessons are usually simple. In the end, human behavior is what really matters in auctions, especially *competitive* behavior. Bidders should try to discourage competition as much as possible, which is why sniping on eBay is a good idea. Sellers should try to encourage competition, which is why opening bids on eBay should be set attractively low, why secret reserves should be used sparingly and only for high-priced items, and why sellers should maintain their credibility by revealing their information fully. The main forms of cheating in auctions arise when the seller illicitly increases competition by shill bidding, or the buyers illicitly suppress competition by colluding. Of course, this summary oversimplifies, but it gives us a compass by which to navigate.

The theory, a brilliant body of work, does much more, or much less, than provide us with specific advice or predictions. What I mean is that the main role of theory, when all is said and done, is to give us a grammar for thinking about auctions. The ideas are few, precious, and hard-won. I've mentioned the main ones in the little forewords at the starts of chapters: strategic dominance, strategic equivalence, the flavors of value distributions, equilibrium bidding, bid shading, revenue equivalence, the linkage principle, risk aversion, spite, the winner's curse. These are reminders of what ideal patterns of behavior we might want to follow or avoid. While eBay has been our main focus and source of examples, these basic ideas apply to auctions in general. Those of you who are interested in theoretical ideas and work through appendices A–C should be in a good position to read much of the current literature on experimental auctions, and to take on Krishna's more advanced book (2002).

For some examples of how the theoretical ideas can help us: If you think you know your valuation for an object in a second-price auction of any kind, you should at least consider seriously the strategy of bidding truthfully. If you overbid, you should be aware that in doing so you may also be paying for the pleasure of depriving someone else the pleasure of ownership. If you are bidding in a situation where you are uncertain of your valuation, you should be aware of the danger of the winner's curse, imagine the news that you are the highest bidder, and consult your intuition for a reading of whether that would be good or bad news. If you are selling, you should be aware that hiding information about items may, in the long run, work against you by suppressing competitive bidding by buyers wary of the winner's curse.

8.2 Looking Ahead

It appears that the present course of auction research supports Thaler's view (1985) that *Homo economicus* is slowly evolving towards *Homo sapiens*. More and more theoretical papers are appearing which are aimed at modeling behavior that is not based entirely on strictly rational behavior. And an entirely new genre of experimental work has been born, based on conducting field experiments on eBay—where one will encounter only our own species. The general trend is towards what we might call "psychologically informed" auction theory.

So the base of auction theory, as well as economics in general, is expanding from a model of perfect rationality to one that includes emotion. What better way to assess the influence of emotions on decision making than to peek inside the brain? This is exactly what is happening in the emerging field of *neuroeconomics*, using functional magnetic resonance imaging (fMRI). A good example of this work is reported by Sanfey, Rilling, Aronson, Nystrom, and Cohen (2003), who image brain activity when subjects play the Ultimatum Game (which we discussed in section 6.7.2). In this paper the authors show that when the Responder is offered an unfair deal, say $1 out of a total of $10, a region of the brain lights up that is associated with negative emotional states. Furthermore, the activation of this area—the anterior insula—is correlated with the subject's subsequent decision to reject the offer. Here we have very direct evidence that a subject will often choose to deny himself a clear $1 surplus on the basis of emotion, in opposition to the dictates of goal-directed, rational centers of the brain. That is, he will deny himself surplus in order to deny surplus to a rival, exactly what we mean by spite, and exactly what we argued plays a role in auction behavior.

Besides building irrationality into mathematical models, we can also use computers to simulate it. I described such simulations in section 6.8.5 when discussing price bubbles. I can also mention preliminary work of Mizuta and myself (2000) to model snipers vs. early bidders on eBay; and the simulations that Bajari and Hortaçsu (2002) used to study the winner's curse and the effect of reserve prices on eBay. Agent-based simulation is a particular interest of mine, and I'm hoping the technique will prove a useful supplement to the theory and empirical work.

Computers are also standing in for the human actor in practice: increasingly sophisticated robot programs (*bots*) execute programmed tasks on the internet. It is easy to search eBay, or the entire web, for items that match your specifications with a fair degree of precision. Automated sniping services are commonplace, and so are price-comparison services. The evolution of intelligent shopping and bidding bots is well on its way.

Bots promise to save labor by processing enormous amounts of information, but ultimately they are under human control (one hopes), and still subject to decisions that take place in your anterior insula and not your laptop. You might just trust a robot bidding program to purchase mass-produced music CDs or toaster ovens at low prices. But as I discussed in section 6.1.1, there is an immense gulf between commodity items and rare or unique collectibles. I am not going to trust a shopping bot to hunt for and buy a poorly preserved, barely recognizable ancient bronze from the Roman Middle East, and I am certainly not going to relinquish the pleasure.

This brings me full circle back to my starting point, the unique niche of eBay as a marketplace for objects with the special aura of rarity or mystery that only a collector can sense. And what better marketplace can there be in which to study human behavior?

Vickrey's Genesis

A.1 Introduction

THE PURPOSE of appendices A–C is to provide the theoretical under-
pinnings of auction theory for models with independent private values
(IPV), so that readers with some background in calculus and probability
theory can see the origin of the concepts used in our discussions, and
also learn something about the tools of the auction theory trade. No
attempt has been made to extend detailed description of theory beyond
the circumscribed IPV model to the more general and later work with
affiliated values, although this model itself and the main results of
Milgrom and Weber (1982) are described in appendix C. For further
theory the reader is referred to Krishna (2002), which has become the
standard text in auction theory at the senior-graduate level. He does an
admirable and precise job in providing a relatively complete exposition
of the really basic theory as it exists now. I will try to stick close to his
mathematical notation, which is usually standard, and in some cases
I follow his order of treatment.

Appendix A deals essentially with the state of knowledge after Vickrey's 1961 paper covering the simplest results in equilibrium bidding
and revenue equivalence for the most common auction forms. Appendix B covers the extension in 1981 by Riley and Samuelson to a wide
class of optimal auctions, and the use of the seller's reserve, all for
the case of symmetric bidders and the IPV model. Finally, appendix C
expands the theory to the results in Myerson's 1981 paper, which
finds optimal mechanisms when the bidders in the IPV model are not
symmetric. To be sure, these mechanisms maximize expected revenue,
but they do not always award items to the highest bidders. They would
hardly be acceptable to the usual eBay denizens. For reference, figure A.1
shows the landscape of appendices A–C.

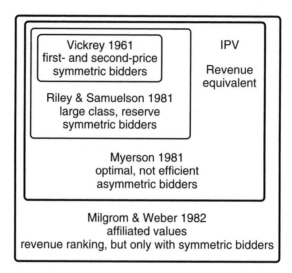

Figure A.1 The general territory comprising present-day auction theory. Appendices A–C cover the inner three categories. Milgrom and Weber's main results are discussed in section C.2.

A.2 A Preview of Revenue Equivalence

Perhaps the most remarkable theoretical result in auction theory is *revenue equivalence*, a principle which can be loosely expressed as follows: For a broad class of auctions, bidders, ideally, adjust their behavior to the rules in such a way that the expected revenue to the seller remains the same.[1] In this appendix, we'll look at the simplest case, the equivalence between first- and second-price auctions. In this section, we'll sketch the very simplest example of this simplest case, the situation with only two bidders, each having values uniformly and independently distributed between 0 and 1.

Consider the second-price auction first. We know that it is a dominant strategy for the bidders to bid truthfully.[2] The expected price paid

---

[1] The first real revenue equivalence theorem is due to Riley and Samuelson (1981) and Myerson (1981), who are usually credited with (roughly) simultaneous publication. Riley and Samuelson's paper is less technical and has illuminating examples, many of which we will see in the next appendix; Myerson's paper is more general.

[2] I assume that you have read chapter 1, where this terminology is introduced.

to the seller is therefore the expected value of the lower of the two bidders' values. This turns out to be $1/3$.[3]

Now consider a first-price auction with the same value distributions for the same two bidders. In these auctions the winner pays her bid, no less. For that reason, it would be pointless to bid truthfully; the surplus in the event of winning would always be exactly zero. The right strategy, then, is to bid somewhat less than your valuation—to "shade" your bid. We will study exactly how much to shade later in this appendix, but the basic idea is to use a shading strategy that is a best response against itself. That is, in the case of two bidders, if your rival bidder shades by a certain amount, then you can do no better than to use exactly the same shade. This is called a *symmetric Bayesian Nash equilibrium* (SBNE). The term "Bayesian" reflects the fact that it is the *expected* surplus that is used as a criterion, and the term "symmetric" the fact that all bidders use the same strategy. For short, when there is no chance for confusion, we often call this simply an "equilibrium."[4]

I now claim that an[5] equilibrium strategy in this simple situation is to bid half one's valuation. We will prove this later in this appendix, but at this point we can at least verify the claim that this is in fact an equilibrium.

Suppose then that you are bidder 1, with value v_1, and you need to choose your bid b, assuming that your rival, bidder 2, with value v_2, adopts the putative equilibrium strategy and bids $v_2/2$. Your expected surplus can be calculated as an average over those values of v_2 where you win; that is, over values of v_2 that satisfy $b \geq v_2/2$. This average can be written as an integral with uniform weight (because values are assumed to be uniformly distributed), over values of v_2 such that $v_2 \leq 2b$, of your surplus, $(v_1 - b)$:

$$\int_0^{2b} (v_1 - b)\,dv_2 = 2b(v_1 - b). \tag{A.1}$$

To choose b to maximize your surplus, you can just differentiate this with respect to b, and set the resulting derivative to zero. This derivative

---

[3] We will verify this in section A.4 using the more general results derived there.

[4] We will be dealing with symmetric equilibria in appendices A and B, but by no means are equilibria always symmetric.

[5] An equilibrium need not be unique, but usually is in the cases we consider.

is $2v_1 - 4b$, so the optimal choice of bid b against the strategy of bidding $v_2/2$ is $v_1/2$, verifying that bidding half one's value is a SBNE.

Notice that this reasoning asks the bidders in first-price auctions to work much harder than in second-price auctions. In second-price auctions, bidding truthfully is a dominant strategy, and no thought at all is necessary to bid with what is for all practical purposes an optimal strategy. In first-price auctions, on the other hand, we ask that bidders carry out the nontrivial calculation of an equilibrium, anticipate that others carry out the same calculations, and, moreover, tailor their behavior in accordance with the results.[6] Auction theorists would like to believe that humans find and use Nash equilibria and follow their prescriptions. But it is one of the main contributions of Vickrey's 1961 paper that so much less is required for intelligent bidding in second-price auctions than in first-price auctions.

This said, we can at least calculate the expected realized price, and hence the revenue to the seller in a first-price auction, assuming that both bidders do follow the equilibrium derived above. Given that bidders 1 and 2 have values v_1 and v_2 respectively, bidder 1 pays her bid, $v_1/2$, when she wins, which is when $v_1 > v_2$. Thus, the payment of bidder 1 for a given v_1 averaged over those values of v_2 which lose to v_1 is

$$\int_0^{v_1} (v_1/2)\,dv_2 = v_1^2/2. \tag{A.2}$$

Averaging this over all values of v_1 then yields the expected payment of bidder 1:

$$\int_0^1 (v_1^2/2)\,dv_1 = 1/6. \tag{A.3}$$

The expected revenue received by the seller is twice this, since, by symmetry, bidders 1 and 2 pay the same on the average. Thus, the expected revenue in the first-price auction is $1/3$, exactly the same as in the second-price case.

This is far from an accident. In fact, it is an extremely simple case of the central result in auction theory: For a very wide class of auctions,

---

[6] The situation is even more complicated when the equilibrium is not unique. In such cases we need some way to argue that one equilibrium is preferable to the others.

equilibrium behavior on the part of bidders leads to the same revenue to the seller. The rest of this appendix will be devoted to demonstrating this equivalence between first- and second-price auctions, and appendix B will extend the result to a much wider class of auctions.

A.3* Quick Review of Some Probability Theory

Our next immediate goal is to answer a very practical and fundamental question: Given the simplest formulation of a second-price auction (either English or Vickrey), how much can the seller expect to receive when bidder valuations are not necessarily uniformly distributed? To put it a bit more mathematically, what is the expected realized price for the item as a function of the number of bidders n, given that the bidders have some specified distribution of values? For this, we will, of course, need to use some probability theory, which we review in this and the next section.

For now we will restrict attention to random variables with smooth *probability density functions* (pdfs) $f(x)$.[7] By this we mean that the probability of finding that the random variable w lies between some given value x and $x + dx$, where dx is very small, is $f(x)dx$. It follows from this definition that the probability of finding that the random variable w lies between *any* two values, say a and b, is

$$\text{pr}\{a \leq w \leq b\} = \int_a^b f(x)dx. \qquad (A.4)$$

Clearly, we always have $f(x) \geq 0$ (because probabilities are never negative), and $\int_{-\infty}^{\infty} f(x)dx = 1$ (because the total probability of any value at all occurring is one).

---

* Sections providing mathematical background are indicated with an asterisk. Skim these sections if you don't need the review.

[7] We will not be concerned with mathematically subtleties here, and will assume that pdfs are continuous and differentiable to any order we need. Note, however, that when there is a nonzero probability that a particular value occurs (for example, a coin showing heads), the pdf has an impulse, and is not smooth at all. The usual terminology for our smoothness assumption is that the distribution is "atomless."

A very useful function related to the pdf is the *cumulative distribution function* (cdf), defined by the probability that a random variable w is below or at a given value x:[8]

$$F(x) = \text{pr}\{w \le x\} = \int_{-\infty}^{x} f(y)\,dy. \tag{A.5}$$

Clearly, $F(-\infty) = 0$, $F(\infty) = 1$, and $F'(x) = f(x)$, so $F(x)$ is monotonically nondecreasing.

By far the most common and important example is the *uniform* pdf, where a random variable is equally likely to take on any value in the unit interval $[0, 1]$.[9] In this case,

$$f(x) = \begin{cases} 1 \text{ if } 0 \le x \le 1 \\ 0 \text{ otherwise} \end{cases}, \tag{A.6}$$

and

$$F(x) = \begin{cases} x \text{ if } 0 \le x \le 1 \\ 0 \; x < 0 \\ 1 \; x > 1 \end{cases}. \tag{A.7}$$

The uniform distribution of values is an idealization that is conceptually simple, usually easier to analyze than general distributions, and serves as a kind of plausibility test. If a property of interest does not hold for uniform distributions, then we can't reasonably expect it to hold in a great many practical situations.

The expected value of any function φ of a random variable is

$$E[\varphi] = \int_{-\infty}^{\infty} \varphi(x)\,dF(x) = \int_{-\infty}^{\infty} \varphi(x) f(x)\,dx. \tag{A.8}$$

The first form of the integral covers pdfs with atoms (discrete events, single values of x with positive probability), in which case the atoms are represented by discontinuities in $F(x)$; these integrals are properly interpreted as Lebesgue-Stieltjes integrals with (probability) measure F. This kind of integral can cover cases in which a pdf has discrete

[8] In keeping with tradition, we will use lowercase letters for pdfs and the corresponding uppercase letters for cdfs.
[9] Of course, it doesn't matter what this interval is, as long as it is finite, because we can always rescale to make it the unit interval.

components, and any reasonably advanced book on probability and statistics will cover them. See, for example, Cramér's venerable classic, *Mathematical Methods of Statistics* (1946), or the more modern Whittle (1992).

Continuing with the example of the uniform distribution, let us find the expected square value of a random variable uniformly distributed on [0, 1]. In this case, $\varphi(x) = x^2$, $F(x) = x$, and therefore

$$E[x^2] = \int_0^1 x^2\, dx = 1/3. \tag{A.9}$$

The *variance* (the expected square of the deviation from the expected value of x, or mean, $\bar{x} = 1/2$) is

$$E[(x - \bar{x})^2] = E[(x^2)] - [\bar{x}]^2 = 1/12. \tag{A.10}$$

Finally, when events X_1, X_2, ..., X_n are independent, the probability that they all happen is the product of their individual probabilities:

$$\mathrm{pr}\{X_1 \wedge X_2 \wedge \cdots \wedge X_n\} = \prod_{i=1}^{n} \mathrm{pr}\{X_i\}, \tag{A.11}$$

where the symbol "$\wedge$" is used to denote the conjunction of events, logically the AND operation. When the events are mutually exclusive, the probability that one happens is the sum of their individual probabilities:

$$\mathrm{pr}\{X_1 \vee X_2 \vee \cdots \vee X_n\} = \sum_{i=1}^{n} \mathrm{pr}\{X_i\}, \tag{A.12}$$

where the symbol "$\vee$" denotes the disjunction of events, logically the OR operation.

A.4* Order Statistics

In practice, auctions are almost always won by the highest bidder, and the price paid is almost always determined by either the highest or the second-highest bid. The distributions of those values therefore play a crucial role in all of auction theory, and we can now derive them quite easily. We will use these results over and over.

In particular, we seek the pdfs and cdfs of the highest and second-highest of a set of n *independent and identically distributed* (iid) draws from a given pdf, say $f(x)$. While we're at it, we might as well derive the pdf of the kth highest, for any k; it isn't much more difficult. Fix x, and first consider the probability that a drawn value lies between x and $x + dx$. This is just $f(x)dx$. The probability that another, independently drawn value lies above x is $(1 - F(x))$, while the probability that another drawn value lies below x is $F(x)$. Thus, the probability that a particular value x is the kth highest, *with a particular set* of $k - 1$ drawn values above that, is $f(x)dx(1 - F(x))^{k-1}F(x)^{n-k}$. But we also need to consider the many different ways it can happen that a particular value x turns out to be the kth highest. This is not hard: there are n possible choices for which draw out of n draws turns out to be the kth highest; and then $\binom{n-1}{k-1}$ ways[10] in which $k - 1$ of the remaining $n - 1$ draws lie above x. Putting all the factors together shows that the probability that the kth highest lies between x and $x + dx$ is

$$n\binom{n-1}{k-1}f(x)dx(1 - F(x))^{k-1}F(x)^{n-k}. \qquad (A.13)$$

Denoting the pdf of the kth highest by $g_k(x)$, we have shown that

$$g_k(x) = n\binom{n-1}{k-1}f(x)(1 - F(x))^{k-1}F(x)^{n-k}$$

$$= \frac{n!}{(k-1)!(n-k)!}f(x)(1 - F(x))^{k-1}F(x)^{n-k}. \qquad (A.14)$$

When there is any question about the number of draws, n, we indicate it explicitly with another subscript, as in $g_{k,n}(x)$.[11]

Another piece of useful and standard notation: Indicate the highest of n draws by Y_1, the second highest by Y_2, and so on. Thus, the sorted version of the n draws $X_1, X_2, \ldots, X_n$ is denoted by $Y_1 \geq Y_2 \geq \cdots \geq Y_n$. Again, if there is any danger of confusion, we indicate the number of draws explicitly with a subscript, so, for example, the highest of n

---

[10] The binomial coefficient, sometimes written C_{n-1}^{k-1}.

[11] Krishna (2002) denotes this by a superscript in parentheses, as in $g_k^{(n)}(x)$. The notational problem here is to avoid confusion when writing a function raised to a power.

draws is denoted by $Y_{1,n}$.[12] The function $g_{k,n}(x)$ is therefore the pdf of $Y_{k,n}$, or, briefly, when n is understood, $g_k(x)$ is the pdf of Y_k.

Returning to the two most important cases, the pdf of the highest of n drawn values is obtained by setting $k = 1$ in equation A.14:

$$g_1(x) = nf(x)F(x)^{n-1}, \tag{A.15}$$

and that of the second highest by setting $k = 2$:

$$g_2(x) = n(n-1)f(x)(1 - F(x))F(x)^{n-2}. \tag{A.16}$$

Using equation A.5, we can integrate each of these to obtain the cdf of the highest value:

$$G_1(x) = F(x)^n, \tag{A.17}$$

and the second highest:

$$G_2(x) = nF(x)^{n-1} - (n-1)F(x)^n. \tag{A.18}$$

Once again, when there is danger of confusion, we write $G_{1,n}(x)$, and $G_{2,n}(x)$, and so on.

EXAMPLE We can now verify the claim in Section A.2 that the expected second-highest value of two independent draws from a distribution uniform on [0, 1] is 1/3. In this case, $n = 2$, $f(x) = 1$, and $F(x) = x$. Equation A.16 then tells us that the pdf of the second-highest of two independent draws is $2(1 - x)$. The expected value of this is

$$E[Y_2] = \int_0^1 x \cdot g_2(x)dx = \int_0^1 x \cdot 2(1-x)dx = 1/3, \tag{A.19}$$

as claimed. □

EXAMPLE Suppose you participate in an in-class experimental auction in which you are one of n bidders receiving iid values from the distribution F. The probability that your value, say x, is the highest in the class is the probability that the highest of the $n - 1$ values of your rivals are all less than x, which is, by definition, $G_{1,(n-1)}(x) = F(x)^{n-1}$. To get a feeling for some numbers, when F is the uniform distribution on $[0, 100]$ and $n = 20$, the probability that a draw of 96 will be the highest in the class is $(x/100)^{19} = (0.96)^{19} = 46\%$, almost an even bet. If you draw 48, the probability of having the highest value sinks to 0.88×10^{-6}, not even a million-to-one shot. □

From the last example we can put this fact away for safekeeping: In an auction where the bidder with the highest valuation always wins, and values are iid with distribution F, the probability of winning with value x is simply $G_{1,(n-1)}(x) = F(x)^{n-1}$.

A.5 Revenue of Second-Price Auctions

With this bit of mathematical equipment, we can now return to the goal of this appendix, to compare the expected revenue in first- and second-price auctions in fairly general circumstances. Beginning with second-price auctions, the expected price realized in such an auction, which is also the expected revenue to the seller, is just the expected value of the second-highest of n iid draws from the distribution $F(x)$. Denoting this revenue by R_{sp}, we can calculate it using the distribution of the second-highest in equation A.18:

$$R_{sp} = E[Y_2] = \int_0^1 x \, dG_2(x), \qquad (A.20)$$

where we assume that the support of the distribution of valuations is the unit interval, $[0, 1]$.[13] We can rewrite this using integration by parts[14] in a slightly simpler way as

$$R_{sp} = 1 - \int_0^1 G_2(x) \, dx, \qquad (A.21)$$

where we use the facts that $G_2(0) = 0$ and $G_2(1) = 1$, because G_2 is a cdf. In the special case of uniformly distributed valuations, $f(x) = 1$ and $F(x) = x$ on $[0, 1]$, and using equation A.18 in equation A.21

[13] We'll always make this assumption unless otherwise stated.
[14] Integration by parts is the duct tape of auction theory; when in doubt, integrate by parts. As a reminder, $\int_a^b u \, dv = uv|_a^b - \int_a^b v \, du$.

yields

$$R_{sp} = \frac{n-1}{n+1}. \tag{A.22}$$

This is a simple but celebrated result (Vickrey, 1961), as we will see when we come to consider the revenue of other auction forms.

The usual caveat: The expected revenue in equation A.22 is a valuable piece of information if it's reliable, but its reliability depends on all the assumptions that led up to it. Remember that we're assuming that valuations are distributed independently and uniformly, that bidders *know* their valuations with certainly, that they don't change them during bidding, and that they accept maximizing surplus as the criterion for bidding as well as the logic that leads to sincere bidding. As we've seen, any of these assumptions can be called into question in real situations, and we return to examine them many times in chapters 1–7.

A.6 First-Price Auctions and Nash Equilibria

We now return to one of the central questions in this appendix and in Vickrey (1961): Given that the usual English outcry auction is strategically equivalent to a second-price sealed-bid (Vickrey) auction, and that we know, in the usual IPV model, what revenue to expect, can a seller do better by conducting a *first-price* sealed-bid auction? The winning bidder now pays her bid, not the second-highest, so should we expect higher revenue? Maybe not, because bidders are, after all, free to adjust their bidding strategies to suit the new rules. The first question we need to consider, then, is how bidding strategies might be chosen in this new set of circumstances.

Recall that in a first-price sealed-bid auction, sincere bidding no longer makes sense. If we bid sincerely and win, we pay our valuation, and so receive no surplus at all. And of course if we don't win, we also receive no surplus. We conclude that with these rules, we ought to bid below our valuation, at least opening up the possibility that if we win the object we obtain some positive surplus. We call this *shading* our bid. With bid shading, the possibility of a dominant strategy goes out the window, because it is no longer the case that any given bid is best regardless of what rival bidders may do. For example, if it so happens that rivals all bid exceptionally low, and we can in some way anticipate this, then it is to our advantage to bid low also, but above the highest rival. This increases our surplus. Contrast this with the situation in a second-price auction, where the price we pay, in the cases when we win an auction, is not affected by our bid. In this sense first-price auctions are more *strategic* than second-price auctions, because the effects of decisions depend more strongly on rivals' decisions.

Formulating a criterion for bidding in a first-price auction is thus a more subtle problem than in second-price auctions. We are indebted to John Nash (1950) for giving us an elegant way to think about it, which we incorporate in the following definition:

DEFINITION A bidding strategy $b(v)$, prescribing the bid in an auction when one's private value is v, is called a *symmetric Bayesian Nash equilibrium* (SBNE) if there is no better response when all of one's rivals adopt that same strategy. □

As mentioned before, the "Bayesian" in the definition reflects the fact that it is *expected* surplus we are dealing with, and the "symmetric" reflects the fact that in equilibrium all bidders behave the same way. Take note that in general there is no assurance that there *is* a SBNE, or that, if one exists, it is unique. For simplicity, and following common usage, we often refer to a SBNE as a "Nash equilibrium."

A.7 Revenue Equivalence of First- and Second-price Auctions with Uniformly Distributed Values

Given Nash's framework, we can now look for a SBNE in a first-price auction with any number of bidders n, and, as usual, we begin with the special case that is particularly easy to work out: the case when the iid valuations are *uniformly* distributed over the interval $[0, 1]$. Assume that all n bidders know their valuations (private values), that ours[15] is v_1, and that the others are, respectively, $v_2, v_3, \ldots, v_n$. As in the case of two bidders that we worked out at the beginning of this

---

[15] We usually think of ourselves as bidder 1.

appendix, let our unknown bid be b, and let's guess that the other bidders, bidder i, $i = 2, \ldots, n$, bid (symmetrically) an amount θv_i. When we are finished, we will learn if there's a value of θ that yields a SBNE.

This being a first-price auction, if we win, we pay b for the item being auctioned, so our surplus will be $v_1 - b$, given that our value is v_1. We therefore want to choose b to maximize

$$E[\text{surplus}] = (v_1 - b) \cdot \text{pr}\{1 \text{ wins}\}. \tag{A.23}$$

It is critical to realize now that for this calculation the probability that bidder 1 wins depends, not only on our choice of bid, but also on the assumption that our rivals use the common bidding function, assumed for this argument to be θv. More concretely, the probability that we win is the probability that the bids of our $n-1$ rivals, $\theta v_2, \theta v_3, \ldots, \theta v_n$, are all less than our own bid, b, and this is, in the iid uniform distribution case, simply $(b/\theta)^{n-1}$. Putting this into equation A.23 gives us[16]

$$E[\text{surplus}] = (v_1 - b)(b/\theta)^{n-1}. \tag{A.24}$$

To find the b that maximizes this surplus, differentiate this with respect to b, and set the result equal to zero, yielding

$$b = \left(\frac{n-1}{n}\right) v_1. \tag{A.25}$$

Choosing $\theta = (n-1)/n$ then shows that this is a desired SBNE. The best shade in equilibrium is the fraction $1/n$ of our value.

What, then, is the revenue that a seller can expect if the bidders bid in equilibrium in a first-price auction? Well, our expected payment as bidder 1 is the probability that we win times our bid. The probability that we win in equilibrium is just v_1^{n-1}, the probability that all of the other bidders have values less than ours. Our bid is $((n-1)/n) \cdot v_1$, so

$$E[\text{payment of } 1] = \left(\frac{n-1}{n}\right) v_1^n. \tag{A.26}$$

Averaging this over all v_1 shows that our expected payment is $(1/n) \cdot (n-1)/(n+1)$, and multiplying this by n (because all n bidders are equally

---

[16] We will need to check when we are done that the probability $b/\theta < 1$. But if we do get a SBNE, our bid $b = \theta v_1$, so this will not be a problem.

likely to win) yields the expected revenue of $(n-1)/(n+1)$, the same as in the second-price case, equation A.22. We have thus verified revenue equivalence between first-price auctions and second-price auctions in the uniformly distributed value case.

A.8 A Nash Equilibrium for First-Price Sealed-Bid Auctions

We now move to the more general case when n bidders have iid valuations drawn from an arbitrary pdf $f(v)$ defined on $[0, 1]$. In cases such as this, when bidders all have the same distributions, we say that the bidders are *symmetric*. As above, assume that all n bidders know their valuations, that ours is v_1, and that the others are $v_2, v_3, \ldots, v_n$. Instead of guessing the form of the answer (linear in the uniformly distributed value case), denote our bidding function by $b(v_1)$, and the common bidding function of our rivals by $\beta(v)$. If we win, we pay $b(v_1)$ for the item being auctioned, so our surplus will be $v_1 - b(v_1)$. We therefore want to choose the function $b(v_1)$ to maximize

$$E[\text{surplus}] = (v_1 - b(v_1)) \cdot \text{pr}\{1 \text{ wins}\}. \tag{A.27}$$

Once again, the calculation of the probability that we win depends, not only on our choice of bid, but also on the assumption that our rivals use the common bidding function $\beta(v)$. In this more general case, this probability of winning is the probability that the bids of our $n-1$ rivals, $\beta(v_2), \beta(v_3), \ldots, \beta(v_n)$, are all less than our own bid, $b(v_1)$.

At this point we are forced to make an additional assumption, one that we will need to check when we get our answer. We know the common cdf of the v_i, $F(v)$, and we would like to express the condition $\beta(v_i) < b(v_1)$, $i = 2, \ldots, n$ using $F(v)$. To do this, we would like to be able to write

$$\text{pr}\{\beta(v_i) < b(v_1)\} = \text{pr}\{v_i < \beta^{-1}(b(v_1))\} = F(\beta^{-1}(b(v_1))),$$

$$i = 2, \ldots, n, \tag{A.28}$$

using the inverse of the assumed equilibrium bidding function $\beta(v)$. The problem is that if $\beta(v)$ is not monotonic, this inverse is not well defined. Suppose, for example, that $\beta(v) = v(1 - v)$, so that it rises from $v = 0$, peaks at $v = 1/2$, and then goes back down to 0 at $v = 1$. Its inverse is then not single-valued, and the probability $F(\beta^{-1}(b(v_1)))$ in equation A.28 does not make sense. We therefore assume that the equilibrium bidding function we're looking for is strictly monotonically increasing. We already assume that $\beta(v)$ is differentiable and smooth in any way we need, so its inverse is well defined and single-valued. The probability that our bid wins can be written as the product of $n - 1$ (identical) cdfs,

$$\prod_{i=2}^{n} F(\beta^{-1}(b(v_1))) = F(\beta^{-1}(b(v_1)))^{n-1}. \tag{A.29}$$

By the way, we should keep this monotonicity assumption in mind. If it ever turns out that a solution to our derived equation is not monotonic, then it is not valid.

Recall that this maneuver was not a problem when we went through our simple preview in the case of two bidders and iid uniform values in section A.2. In that example, the bidding function was $b = \beta(v) = v/2$, and the inverse of the monotonic function β turned up in the condition $v \leq 2b$ and in upper limit of integration in equation A.1.

The problem now becomes that of choosing bid $b(v_1)$ to maximize our surplus,

$$E[\text{surplus}] = (v_1 - b(v_1)) F(\beta^{-1}(b(v_1)))^{n-1}. \tag{A.30}$$

Setting to zero the derivative of this with respect to the value b, we get the general (necessary) condition

$$\frac{\partial E[\text{surplus}]}{\partial b}\bigg|_{\beta(v)=b(v)} = 0. \tag{A.31}$$

It is now routine to work this out for first-price auctions, using the surplus in equation A.30, the chain rule, and the fact that the derivative of $\beta^{-1}(b)$ is given by

$$(\beta^{-1}(b))' = \frac{1}{\beta'(\beta^{-1}(b))} \tag{A.32}$$

(see question 3). Because we are looking for a SBNE, we now insist that $\beta(v) = b(v)$; that is, that the bid of bidder 1, $b(v)$, be the same as the (common) bidding function $\beta(v)$ of bidder 1's rivals. Setting

$\beta(v) = b(v)$ introduces the derivative of $b(v)$ into the condition, through $\beta'(v)$, even though we began by seeking the scalar bid value b.

Condition equation A.31 yields, after some algebraic simplification, the following ordinary differential equation for $b(v)$:

$$b'(v) + \frac{(n-1)f(v)}{F(v)}b(v) = \frac{(n-1)f(v)}{F(v)}v. \tag{A.33}$$

Not only is this an ordinary differential equation, but it is first order and linear, which means it can be integrated exactly using an integrating factor.[17] The procedure, starting with any differential equation of the form

$$b'(v) + C(v)b(v) = D(v), \tag{A.34}$$

is to multiply by the integrating factor[18]

$$e^{\int C(v)dv}. \tag{A.35}$$

Equation A.34 then becomes

$$b'(v)e^{\int C(v)dv} + b(v)C(v)e^{\int C(v)dv} = D(v)e^{\int C(v)dv}, \tag{A.36}$$

or

$$\frac{d}{dv}\left(b(v)e^{\int C(v)dv}\right) = D(v)e^{\int C(v)dv}. \tag{A.37}$$

Integrating this directly then gives us the general solution

$$b(v) = e^{-\int C(v)dv}\int D(v)e^{\int C(v)dv}dv + \gamma e^{-\int C(v)dv}, \tag{A.38}$$

where γ is an arbitrary constant of integration.

In the particular case of interest, equation A.33, $C(v)=(n-1)f(v)/F(v)$, $D(v)=vC(v)$, the integrating factor is

$$e^{\int C(v)dv} = e^{\int \frac{(n-1)f(v)}{F(v)}dv} = F(v)^{n-1}, \tag{A.39}$$

[17] This differential equation is usually solved ad hoc; see question 4. I like the general method that I describe next because it's useful in other, similar situations.
[18] The integral is indefinite, and the result is also a function of v. This is a trick that goes back to the beginning of time. I learned it from Kells (1954), which was a standard text for many years.

and the solution in equation A.38 becomes

$$b(v) = \frac{1}{F(v)^{n-1}} \int v \, dF(v)^{n-1} + \frac{\gamma}{F(v)^{n-1}}, \qquad \text{(A.40)}$$

or, integrating by parts,

$$b(v) = v - \frac{\int F(v)^{n-1} \, dv - \gamma}{F(v)^{n-1}}. \qquad \text{(A.41)}$$

We now need an additional condition to make definite the limits of integration and pin down the constant γ. In this auction it's clear that $b(0) = 0$, since there is no point in a bidder bidding a positive amount if her valuation for the item is zero. This fact gives us the needed condition, which we can enforce easily by integrating from 0 to v, and choosing $\gamma = 0$. The equilibrium bidding function then becomes

$$b(v) = v - \frac{\int_0^v F(y)^{n-1} \, dy}{F(v)^{n-1}}. \qquad \text{(A.42)}$$

We should not forget to check our assumption that this bidding function is monotonically increasing (see question 5). We should also worry a bit about what happens to this solution when the value v is zero (See question 6).

The equilibrium bidding function in equation A.42 has the simple interpretation that, in equilibrium, we ought to shade our bid below our valuation by exactly

$$\frac{\int_0^v F(y)^{n-1} \, dy}{F(v)^{n-1}}. \qquad \text{(A.43)}$$

EXAMPLE In the case of valuations uniformly distributed on $[0, 1]$, $F(v) = v$, and the shade is v/n (compared with a sincere bid of v). That is, the equilibrium bid is $(1 - 1/n)v$. When you are up against only one other bidder, the equilibrium bid is only half your valuation.

How would you expect the equilibrium bidding strategy to change if lower values are more likely to occur than higher values? To be concrete, suppose the pdf of the values is linearly downsloping on the unit interval: $f(v) = 2(1 - v)$. Figure A.2 shows the equilibrium for

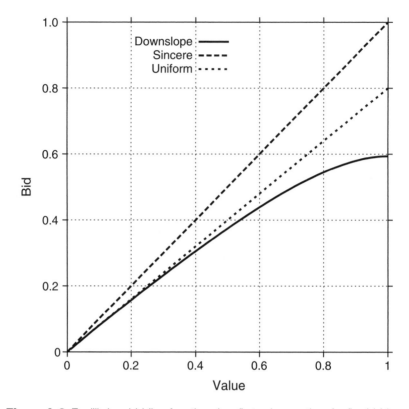

Figure A.2 Equilibrium bidding functions in a first-price auction, for five bidders, and two kinds of value pdfs on [0,1]: uniform and linearly downsloping.

this case, as well as the uniform case, when there are $n = 5$ bidders.[19] We see that there is significantly more shading in the downsloping case, especially at higher values. In fact, at $v = 1$ the shade is more than twice what it is in the uniform case. The intuition is as follows: If we know that our rivals are more likely to have lower than higher values, and if our own value is high, then for a given value we are more likely to win the auction than when the values are uniformly distributed. We can therefore shade our bid more, and the slightly lower probability of winning is more than compensated for by the prospect of a larger surplus. Loosely speaking, if we know we have an unusually high draw, we can bid less conservatively. □

[19] To calculate the equilibrium bidding function for the linearly downsloping case, I used the symbolic manipulation program Maple and eq. A.42.

A.9 Revenue of First-Price Auctions

At this point it is natural to wonder how a seller should choose between first- and second-price auctions to maximize his revenue. We therefore calculate the expected revenue when a seller auctions an item using first-price rules. Assuming bidders use the equilibrium bidding function we have just derived, equation A.42, this is n times the expected payment of any one bidder, say bidder 1, which is in turn the equilibrium bid times the probability that bidder 1 wins the object. Thus, denoting this expected revenue by R_{fp},

$$R_{fp} = n\mathrm{E}[\text{payment of } 1] = n\mathrm{E}[b(v_1)\mathrm{pr}\{1 \text{ wins}\}]$$

$$= n \int_0^1 b(v) F(v)^{n-1} dF(v), \qquad (A.44)$$

where the expectation is over all values of v_1. We leave it for question 7 to substitute the equilibrium bid from equation A.42 into this and simplify to get

$$R_{fp} = 1 - n \int_0^1 F(v)^{n-1} dv + (n-1) \int_0^1 F(v)^n dv. \qquad (A.45)$$

Recall (from equation A.18) that $G_2(x) = nF(x)^{n-1} - (n-1)F(x)^n$, so this can be rewritten as

$$R_{fp} = 1 - \int_0^1 G_2(x) dx. \qquad (A.46)$$

We have now arrived at a special case of one of the most remarkable and important results in theoretical economics. Comparing equation A.46 with equation A.21, we see that $R_{fp} = R_{sp}$. The expected revenues of the two auction forms, *assuming bidders follow the equilibrium strategy*, are exactly the same! This is usually referred to as the *revenue equivalence theorem*, or, simply, *revenue equivalence*. As we will see in the next appendix, the result applies to much more general situations than the first- and second-price auctions considered here. The simple intuition is that in equilibrium bidders adapt their behavior in just the right way to make the particular rules irrelevant. Put another way, bidders bid in first- and second-price auctions in such a way as to discount the difference in the auction rules. But the reader should be warned that revenue equivalence does not hold in many important situations, both in real-world practice and theory. In fact, much of auction theory is concerned with just when and how revenue equivalence might be expected to *fail*. To summarize:

RESULT 1 (Revenue equivalence, first version) Assume bidders have iid private valuations. Then, in equilibrium, the expected revenue in first- and second-price auctions is the same. □

A.10* Conditional Expectation

In auction theory, we are often interested in the average value of some quantity, *given that some event has taken place*, such as, for example, winning an auction, or having a value in a given range. The part of probability theory that captures this idea is *conditional expectation*.[20] We'll use it immediately to provide an intuitively satisfying interpretation of the equilibrium bidding function in first-price auctions (eq. A.42), and to show that the revenue equivalence result in the previous section can be strengthened. We'll also find it useful in many other situations.

Suppose we are interested in a random variable x with distribution F, conditioned on an event A. This event can be almost anything, but it usually takes the form of some statement that x is less than or larger than some quantity, or is the largest or smallest of some set. Very often the event is simply that the bidder with value x wins an auction by virtue of the fact that x is larger than the values of all her rivals. The *conditional expectation* of the random variable x, given the event A, is defined as

$$E[x|A] = \frac{1}{\text{prob}\{A\}} \int_A x\, dF(x). \qquad (A.47)$$

The idea here is to restrict the integral that determines the expectation of x to the domain where the event A is true (indicated by $\int_A$), and

---

[20] Our explanation of conditional expectation follows Whittle (1992), which is also a good source of further material on probability theory.

to normalize by the probability of A. In a sense, we are redefining the domain of x to be the space where A is true.[21]

EXAMPLE Here's a simple question; guess the answer before reading on. Suppose the random variable x is uniformly distributed on $[0, 1]$. What is the expected value of x given that $x \leq c$, where $c \leq 1$ is some constant?

Here the event A is $x \leq c$, prob$\{A\} = c$, and the required conditional expectation is

$$(1/c) \int_0^c x \, dx = c/2. \tag{A.48}$$

Intuitively, given that x is originally distributed uniformly on $[0, 1]$, when we restrict attention to the cases when $x \leq c$, it becomes uniformly distributed on the interval $[0, c]$. $\square$

EXAMPLE Suppose x_1 and x_2 are two independent draws from the uniform distribution on $[0, 1]$. What is the expected value of x_1, given that $x_1 \leq x_2$?

Before we compute the answer using conditions, we note that we already know the answer from order statistics. It is the expected value of the lower of two draws, which has the distribution $G_{2,n} = 2x - x^2$, and the pdf $g_{2,n} = 2(1 - x)$, using the fact that $n = 2$. Therefore the expected value of the second highest is

$$\int_0^1 x \, dG_{2,n} = 2 \int_0^1 x(1 - x) \, dx = 1/3. \tag{A.49}$$

Alternatively, we can compute the expectation of x_1 conditional on the event $A = x_1 \leq x_2$, which by symmetry has probability $1/2$. Thus,

$$E[x_1 | A] = 2 \int \int_{x_1 \leq x_2} x_1 \, dx_1 \, dx_2 = 2 \int_0^1 \int_0^{x_2} x_1 \, dx_1 \, dx_2 = 1/3. \tag{A.50}$$

In this calculation we consider as outcomes all pairs x_1 and x_2, and integrate over this space restricted to the set A, which means integrating over the subspace $x_1 \leq x_2$. $\square$

---

[21] When the probability of A is zero, we leave the expectation conditioned on A undefined.

A.11 An Interpretation of First-Price Equilibrium Bidding Strategy

We can now gain some intuition for the first-price equilibrium bidding function by interpreting it in terms of a conditional expectation. Consider the form of the bidding function in equation A.40,

$$b(v) = \frac{1}{F(v)^{n-1}} \int_0^v y \, dF(y)^{n-1}, \tag{A.51}$$

where we have integrated from 0 to v and taken $\gamma = 0$, as argued when equation A.41 was derived. A little thought shows that this is exactly in the form of a conditional expectation, equation A.47. To see this, take the event A to be $\{Y_{1,(n-1)} \le v\}$; that is, that the largest of the $n-1$ rivals' values is less than or equal to the bidder's value v. Since we are restricting attention to monotonically increasing bidding functions, the event A is also, simply, the event that the bidder wins the auction. Then the integral in equation A.51 is just the expectation of $Y_{1,(n-1)}$ over the space where $Y_{1,(n-1)} \le v$ (that is, over A), and the denominator is just prob$\{A\}$. Thus, we can rewrite the equilibrium bidding function in a first-price auction as

$$b(v) = E[Y_{1,(n-1)} \mid Y_{1,(n-1)} \le v] = E[Y_{1,(n-1)} \mid v \text{ wins}]. \tag{A.52}$$

The mathematics nicely supports the heuristic argument in section 4.4: the winner's equilibrium bid is her best estimate of the next-highest value—assuming that she wins.

A.12 Stronger Revenue Equivalence

We can now say something even stronger about the revenue equivalence between first- and second-price auctions. First, consider the expected payment, in equilibrium, of a bidder with valuation v in a second-price auction, which we will denote by $P_{sp}(v)$. This can be calculated as the probability that the bidder wins the auction with value v, times the expected highest value of her rivals (since in equilibrium bidders bid their values) given that v wins. Thus,

$$P_{sp}(v) = \text{prob}(v \text{ wins}) \times \text{E}[Y_{1,(n-1)} \mid v \text{ wins}]$$

$$= \int_0^v y \, dG_{1,(n-1)}(y), \tag{A.53}$$

using the definition of conditional expectation, equation A.47, and the fact that $G_{1,(n-1)}$ is the distribution of $Y_{1,(n-1)}$.

Next, consider the corresponding expected payment in a first-price auction, denoted by $P_{fp}(v)$. This is the probability that v wins, times the amount that the bidder pays if she wins, namely her equilibrium bid, which is, by equation A.52, $\text{E}[Y_{1,(n-1)} \mid v \text{ wins}]$. The resulting expected payment is exactly the same as equation A.53, so $P_{sp}(v) = P_{fp}(v)$ for every v. To underscore this remarkable fact: not only is the overall expected payment by bidders the same in first- and second-price auctions when equilibrium strategies are used, but the expected payments match *for each particular possible draw* of a bidder's valuation v. Notice that the former, weaker version of revenue equivalence follows directly from this latter result.

Equation A.53 leads to a very pretty graphical representation of the expected payment and surplus in first- and second-price auctions. Integrating equation A.53 by parts and using the fact that $G_{1,(n-1)}(y) = F(y)^{n-1}$ gives us the following expression for the expected payment by a bidder with value v:

$$P_{sp}(v) = v F(v)^{n-1} - \int_0^v F(y)^{n-1} dy. \tag{A.54}$$

The first term on the right-hand side is the area of the rectangle in figure A.3, and is also the expected value received by a bidder with value v. The second term is the area under the curve $F(v)^{n-1}$, and since it is the difference between the expected value received and the expected payment, it must be the expected surplus. This picture goes back at least to the paper of Bulow and Roberts (1989).

In light of this equivalence of expected payment for each draw of a bidder's value v, it may come as a surprise that the actual payment for any *particular* realization of values may be different in the two auction forms. To see this, consider a simple example. Suppose there are two bidders, and $v_1 = 0.8$ and $v_2 = 0.6$. In a Vickrey auction, the bidders

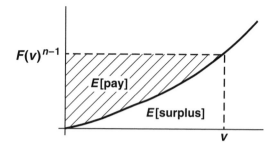

Figure A.3 Graphical representation of the expected payment and surplus in first- and second-price auctions.

bid truthfully in equilibrium, bidder 1 wins, and pays the second highest bid, 0.6. In the corresponding first-price auction, in equilibrium, each bidder bids $v/2$ (from section A.8), so bidder 1 wins and pays her bid of 0.4. It is only the *expected* payment given bidder 1's value of 0.8 that is the same in both auction forms.

A.13 Dutch Auctions and Strategic Equivalence

In a *Dutch* or *descending-clock* auction, the price starts high, higher than anyone is willing to pay, and is lowered until someone indicates that she is willing to buy the item at the current level. The first bidder to indicate a willingness to pay becomes the buyer. Figure 1.4 shows the most famous kind of implementation of this auction format, the descending-clock auction used most notably in Holland for the sale of cut flowers.

We've already pointed out in section 1.9 that the decision faced by a prospective buyer in a Dutch auction is exactly the same as that faced by a bidder in a first-price sealed-bid auction. She must choose exactly one number: the price to submit in the sealed-bid sale, or the price at which to indicate a willingness to buy in the Dutch sale. To argue this point in a little more detail, suppose you need to give complete instructions to someone who is going to act as your agent in a Dutch auction. What information must you supply? You need to tell her to sit on her hands until a certain price is reached on the clock, the price that you would submit in a first-price sealed-bid auction, and then to bid. The point is that there is no further information that can possibly affect her behavior, because any other instructions would have to be conditional on some observation of a bid, and at that point the auction would be over. In game theory terminology, we say that the Dutch auction and the first-price sealed-bid auction are *strategically equivalent*. There is a one-to-one correspondence between the set of all possible strategies in the two auction settings, and likewise between the corresponding payoffs.

It is worth repeating at this point that this equivalence is much stronger than the equivalence between the English outcry and the Vickrey auction forms that we discussed in section 1.8. As we pointed out in that section, bidders in an English auction can observe the bids of rivals during the course of a sale, and can, if they wish, adjust their behavior according to these observations. This is why we termed the equivalence "weak." More technically, there is no longer a one-to-one correspondence between the set of all possible strategies in the English and Vickrey auctions; the instructions you might give to someone bidding on your behalf in an English auction might be much more voluminous than the one number you need to supply for a Vickrey auction.

We have seen that the four traditional, standard auction forms are related in the following way:

$$\text{English} \approx \text{Vickrey} \quad \text{and} \quad \text{Dutch} \equiv \text{First-Price},$$

where we use the symbol "$\approx$" to mean weakly equivalent, and "$\equiv$" to mean strategically equivalent. Furthermore, when bidder valuations are iid distributed, they yield, in equilibrium, the same expected revenue to the seller. This is the first layer in the foundation of auction theory, and is the essence of Vickrey's 1961 paper. The next step in laying the (very basic) foundation of the theory is to generalize revenue equivalence to a much wider class of auctions, and to examine the question of setting the seller's reserve price. As we will see in the next appendix, the two issues are (perhaps surprisingly) closely related.

A.14 Another Kind of Auction—the All-Pay Auction

To see why one might want to consider alternative auction forms, here is an example of an auction that is quite different from the four standard ones, but nevertheless of some practical interest. Candidates running for political office must decide how much to spend on their campaigns. We can consider this an auction, the single item being the political office, and with one winner. However, the winner does not get a refund after the election; everyone who bids must pay. This kind of auction is called an *all-pay* auction.[22] The same kind of auction models lobbying activity (Krishna, 2002), and also bribery, for that matter.

The surplus in an all-pay auction can be written just as it was in a first-price auction, equation A.30, except that in this case the bid $b(v_1)$ is not multiplied by the probability of winning; the winner pays regardless of whether she is the highest bidder. That is,

$$E[\text{surplus}] = v_1 F(\beta^{-1}(b(v_1)))^{n-1} - b(v_1), \qquad (A.55)$$

where as usual we derive the equilibrium bid of bidder 1, given that all the others adopt bidding strategy $\beta(v)$, and valuations are iid with distribution F. The rest of the derivation is very similar; in fact, it's simpler. Set the derivative of the expected surplus equal to zero, and demand that the best choice for b occur when the bidding strategy β of the rivals of bidder 1 is the same as b. This yields

$$b'(v) = v(n-1)F(v)^{n-2}f(v) = v\frac{dF(v)^{(n-1)}}{dv}, \qquad (A.56)$$

which can be integrated directly to give

$$b(v) = \int_0^v y\, dF(y)^{n-1}, \qquad (A.57)$$

where we have set the constant of integration to zero because the bidding function should be zero when the value is zero; there is no reason to bid a positive amount in an all-pay auction when there is nothing to be won.

Taking our usual example of the uniform distribution, $F(v) = v$, equation A.57 shows that the equilibrium bid in an all-pay auction with n bidders is

$$b(v) = \frac{n-1}{n}v^n, \qquad (A.58)$$

instead of $((n-1)/n) \cdot v$ for the first-price auction. The intuition in an all-pay auction is that a bidder needs to have a very high value

---

[22] All-pay auctions should more properly be called *first-price all-pay* auctions, because the payments are equal to the bids. But the shorter terminology is standard.

(relative to what she might expect given the total number of bidders) to justify a reasonably high bid. This is seen easily in the uniform case from equation A.58. Suppose you are one of 20 bidders, and values are uniformly distributed from $0 to $100. If your valuation is $90, your equilibrium bid is only $11.55. This, of course, has to do with the fact that your probability of winning the auction, even with a valuation as high as $90, is still only about 13.5%, not all that high.

Intuition suggests that if your valuation is as low as $70 it would be foolish to bid at all, since you are almost certain to lose your bid. In fact, your equilibrium bid in this case is about $.08, so the mathematics largely confirms the intuition—except that it also puts a fine edge on the strategic calculation. It tells us that it is, after all, worth throwing exactly $.08 after the long shot.

It is now quite interesting that, despite the high threshold for bidding a substantial amount, the expected payment in an all-pay auction is exactly the same as that in the corresponding first-price auction (and, of course, by our earlier revenue equivalence result, the corresponding second-price auction). This follows from the fact that in an all-pay auction the expected payment of a bidder is identical to her bid, which is, by equation A.57, exactly the same as the expected payment in the corresponding first- or second-price auction, equation A.53. The all-pay bidding function might seem low, because it is multiplied by the probability of winning, but this is exactly compensated for by the fact that the bid is paid regardless of whether or not the bidder wins. Thus, the all-pay auction is revenue equivalent to the four standard forms, more than a subtle hint that revenue equivalence is a general phenomenon that applies to a wide class of auctions. This sets the stage for the wonderful paper of Riley and Samuelson (1981), which is our starting point for the next appendix.

A.15 Questions

1. You are one of n bidders who draw iid valuations from the distribution $F(x)$. We know from the example in the text that the probability that your draw x is the highest is $F(x)^{n-1}$. What is the probability that it is the second highest? The kth highest? Check this last result by showing that its sum over $k = 1, \ldots, n$ is 1. What values do these probabilities take on when $f(x)$ is uniform on $[0, 1]$?

2. Derive the cdfs for the highest and second highest of n iid draws, equations A.17 and A.18, from first principles (rather than by integrating the densities).

3. Show that the derivative of an inverse function is given by equation A.32. What assumptions do you need?

4. Write the differential equation for the equilibrium first-price bidding function, equation A.33, in terms of the cdf of the highest of $n - 1$ independent draws, $G_{1,(n-1)}$, and its corresponding density $g_{1,(n-1)}$. Is it now obvious what the integrating factor is?

5. Check that the equilibrium bidding function in equation A.42 is monotonically increasing.

6. Prove that the limit of the equilibrium bidding function in equation A.42 as v approaches zero is zero. Hint: Recall L'Hôpital's rule.

7. Derive R_{fp} in equation A.45 from equation A.44.

8. Starting with equation A.53, verify that n times the expected value over all v of the equilibrium payment of one bidder in a first- or second-price auction, $n P_{sp}(v) = n P_{fp}(v) = n \int_0^v y \, d G_{1,(n-1)}(y)$, is equal to the total expected revenue, $R_{sp} = E[Y_{2,n}]$ (from equation A.20). Hint: Remember, in auction theory, when in doubt, integrate by parts. This problem will give you some practice.

9. Supply the intuition for the equilibrium first-price bid in the uniform case, $((n - 1)/n) \cdot v$, using the conditional expectation form, equation A.52.

10. Show that the expected surplus in first- and second-price auctions with iid private valuations is, for each drawn value v, a monotonically decreasing function of the number of bidders n. What does this say about the effect of competition on the seller's expected revenue? Hint: See figure A.3.

Riley and Samuelson's Optimal Auctions

B.1 Definition of Riley and Samuelson's Class

IN THIS appendix we will build up a theory of auctions that are *optimal* in the sense that they maximize seller revenue. Along the way we will account for the fact that in any realistic auction, the seller will be allowed to set a minimum acceptable bid, the "starting bid" in an eBay sale. We will then answer the question of whether there might be alternatives to the four basic forms discussed so far (first-price $\equiv$ Dutch, English $\approx$ Vickrey) that yield greater expected seller revenue. It will turn out that within a certain reasonable class of auctions, and with the assumption that bidders all have identically distributed and independent valuations, these four basic forms all yield the highest revenue possible.

This appendix is devoted to the results in Riley and Samuelson (1981) and follows it closely.[1] This is a deceptively simple-looking paper and its flow seems, after the fact, almost inevitable. While it uses nothing beyond freshman calculus and repeated applications of integration by parts, the manipulations are very carefully chosen, and the ideas are subtle and reward close study.

We begin by defining Riley and Samuelson's class of auctions precisely.

DEFINITION The class of auctions $\mathcal{A}_{rs}$ is defined as follows:

1. There is one seller, selling one indivisible object.
2. The seller announces a minimum acceptable bid, b_0, which we call the *reserve*.

[1] As mentioned before, Myerson (1981), which appeared at about the same time as Riley and Samuelson (1981), is more general, more mathematical, but less concrete, and a bit more difficult. When I refer to Riley and Samuelson (1981) in this and the next appendix, I mean to distinguish their class of auctions, with iid value distributions. Credit is due all three of these researchers.

3. There are n bidders, with valuations v_i, $i = 1, \ldots, n$.

4. These valuations are independent and identically distributed according to the cdf $F(v)$, which is strictly increasing and differentiable (and thus with pdf $f(x) > 0$), and support $[0, 1]$.

5. There is a SBNE, corresponding to the strictly increasing bidding function $b(v)$.

6. The bidder with the highest acceptable bid wins the object.

7. The payment rules are *anonymous*; that is, they do not distinguish one bidder from another. □

In practice, the most restrictive assumptions here concern the bidders' valuations. There is usually some reason to believe that valuations are either not independent, or not identically distributed. Later on we will examine such auctions—outside the class $\mathcal{A}_{rs}$—and observe how revenue equivalence can break down, and what ideas allow us to generalize the result.

B.2 Revenue

The first step in studying the general properties of the class $\mathcal{A}_{rs}$ is to write the expected surplus of bidder 1. Observe that determining 1's bid is equivalent to finding z in the assumed bidding function $b(z)$, since by assumption, $b(z)$ is uniquely invertible. The expected surplus of bidder 1, if she bids $b(z)$, given that her valuation is v_1, can then be written

$$v_1 F(z)^{n-1} - P(z), \tag{B.1}$$

where we denote the expected payment of bidder 1, given that she bids $b(z)$, by $P(z)$. (Recall that $F(z)^{n-1}$ is the probability that the remaining $n - 1$ bidders have valuations below z, and hence the probability that bidder 1 wins.) For the bidding function $b(z)$ to be a SNBE, it must be that this expected surplus is maximized when $z = v_1$ (because that corresponds to bidding $b(v_1)$). We can therefore maximize the surplus if we differentiate this with respect to z, replace z by v_1, and set the result to zero.[2] This leads to the following differential equation:

$$x \frac{d}{dx} \left[F(x)^{n-1} \right] - P'(x) = 0, \tag{B.2}$$

where for simplicity we use x as the variable instead of v_1.

Next, we need a boundary condition. The idea may seem simple, but it's crucial. Observe that there is a valuation v_*, which we call the *entry value*, below which it is not profitable to enter a bid, and above which it is. To prove that such a value exists, we need to assume that the surplus function is a continuous and increasing function of valuation (see question 2).[3] At the value v_* the expected surplus in equation B.1 must be exactly zero, which gives us the desired boundary condition

$$P(v_*) = v_* F(v_*)^{n-1}. \tag{B.3}$$

We can now integrate equation B.2 directly, from v_* to v_1, yielding

$$\int_{v_*}^{v_1} P'(x)\,dx = \int_{v_*}^{v_1} x\,dF(x)^{n-1}, \tag{B.4}$$

or, integrating by parts (once again),

$$P(v_1) - P(v_*) = v_1 F(v_1)^{n-1} - v_* F(v_*)^{n-1} - \int_{v_*}^{v_1} F(x)^{n-1}\,dx. \tag{B.5}$$

The boundary condition equation B.3 then allows us to cancel the $P(v_*)$ and $v_* F(v_*)^{n-1}$ terms, yielding

$$P(v_1) = v_1 F(v_1)^{n-1} - \int_{v_*}^{v_1} F(x)^{n-1}\,dx. \tag{B.6}$$

Now here is something quite remarkable. Equation B.6 tells us the expected payment in any revenue-maximizing auction in the class $\mathcal{A}_{rs}$, given the valuation v_1, in terms of the critical entry value v_*—*regardless of the particular form of the auction!* We will next use the result for expected payment to calculate the expected revenue, *which will also be independent of the particular rules of the auction.* This is the central result of Riley and Samuelson's paper and the key to revenue equivalence.

---

[2] Strictly speaking, this gives us a necessary condition for the surplus to be maximized. I will usually leave proofs of sufficiency or uniqueness for more advanced work, or assign them as problems.

[3] As usual, we can always check this assumption when we are done.

By symmetry, all bidders have the same expected payment, and the expected revenue to the seller is just n times the expected payment of bidder 1. Thus, the expected revenue to the seller is n times equation B.6, averaged over valuation,

$$R_{rs} = n \int_{v_*}^{1} \left[v F(v)^{n-1} - \int_{v_*}^{v} F(x)^{n-1} dx \right] dF(v), \qquad (\text{B.7})$$

where we call this revenue R_{rs}, use the generic variable v for valuation v_1, and average over the range $v_* \leq v \leq 1$, since bidders will not bid when their valuations are below v_*.

We can rewrite the first part of the integral as

$$n \int_{v_*}^{1} v F(v)^{n-1} dF(v) = \int_{v_*}^{1} v \, dF(v)^{n}. \qquad (\text{B.8})$$

The second part of the integral in equation B.7 can be simplified using, yet again, integration by parts, yielding

$$\int_{v_*}^{1} \left[\int_{v_*}^{v} F(x)^{n-1} dx \right] dF(v)$$

$$= \left[\int_{v_*}^{v} F(x)^{n-1} dx \right] F(v) \bigg|_{v=v_*}^{v=1} - \int_{v_*}^{1} F(v) d \left(\int_{v_*}^{v} F(x)^{n-1} dx \right)$$

$$= \int_{v_*}^{1} \left[F(v)^{n-1} - F(v)^{n} \right] dv. \qquad (\text{B.9})$$

Finally, using these in equation B.7, and replacing $n F(v)^{n-1} dv$ by $(1/f(v)) dF(v)^{n}$, results in the following important form for the expected revenue of an optimal auction in the class $\mathcal{A}_{rs}$:

$$R_{rs} = \int_{v_*}^{1} \left[v - \frac{1 - F(v)}{f(v)} \right] dF(v)^{n}. \qquad (\text{B.10})$$

We think of this as

$$R_{rs} = \int_{v_*}^{1} MR(v) \, dF(v)^{n}, \qquad (\text{B.11})$$

where

$$MR(v) = v - \frac{1 - F(v)}{f(v)} \qquad (\text{B.12})$$

is called the *marginal revenue,* by analogy with monopoly theory (Bulow and Roberts, 1989), or, more appropriately in our context, *virtual valuation* (Krishna, 2002).[4] Since $F(v)^n$ is the cdf of the highest, and hence winning, valuation, we can interpret this as saying that *the expected revenue of an optimal auction is the expected marginal revenue of the winning bidder.*

We take this opportunity to state our new, more general, version of Result 1 (section A.9).

RESULT 2 (Revenue equivalence, second version) In equilibrium the expected revenue to the seller in any auction in Riley and Samuelson's class $\mathcal{A}_{rs}$ is the same. Furthermore, over different auctions this expected revenue is a function only of the entry value v_*. □

Notice also that equation B.6 tells us that the stronger form of Result 2, analogous to the one in section A.12, also holds: In equilibrium the expected payments by a bidder match *for each particular possible draw* of valuation v.

B.3 Optimal Reserve Price

We next turn to the question of how the seller can optimally determine the minimum acceptable bid, b_0. Recall that this is part of the seller's options according to the definition of Riley and Samuelson's class of auctions $\mathcal{A}_{rs}$. We are also going to introduce an additional variable, the value of the item to the seller, which we will denote by v_0. This introduces no real additional complication, but makes the results a little more general.[5]

We want to maximize the total expected revenue to the seller, so we need to add to the revenue in equation B.11 the contribution when there are no acceptable bids at all, in which case the seller retains the object. The probability of this event is the probability that all bids are

---

[4] I prefer *virtual valuation,* but *marginal revenue* seems the more common terminology. Besides, the symbol VV would never do, being too easily confused with values.

[5] Many theoretical treatments assume that $v_0 = 0$; that is, that the object being offered at auction is of no value to the seller. This is sometimes unrealistic, especially if we consider that the seller may be able to offer an unsold item for sale in a later auction.

below v_*, which is $F(v_*)^n$. The expected contribution in this case is therefore $v_0 F(v_*)^n$, and the total expected revenue becomes

$$R_{rs}^{total} = v_0 F(v_*)^n + \int_{v_*}^1 MR(v) \, dF(v)^n. \tag{B.13}$$

Now when we think of adjusting b_0, it is really the effect on the entry value v_* that counts, so we can think of adjusting v_* optimally instead. Thus, we set the derivative of equation B.13 with respect to v_* to zero,

$$v_0 n F(v_*)^{n-1} f(v_*) - MR(v_*) n F(v_*)^{n-1} f(v_*) = 0, \tag{B.14}$$

or

$$MR(v_*) = v_0, \tag{B.15}$$

or

$$v_* - \frac{1 - F(v_*)}{f(v_*)} = v_0. \tag{B.16}$$

This gives us a condition that determines v_* given only the distribution F and the seller's valuation v_0. It is quite remarkable that v_* therefore depends neither on the number of bidders, nor on the particular form of the auction. Once v_* is determined, it is then up to the seller to find the reserve b_0 that results in this required entry value.

For first- and second-price auctions, the optimal reserve b_0 is simply equal to v_*. In proving this we will use the fact that the winner in a second-price auction must pay at least the reserve, even if hers is the only acceptable bid. This is a simple but important point, because it provides an incentive to set the reserve above zero in a second-price auction.

PROPERTY 1 *In the cases of first- and second-price auctions, the entry value equals the optimal reserve: $v_* = b_0$.*

PROOF *In either first- or second-price auctions, there is no incentive to bid when our value is below the reserve b_0. If we did, we would be forced to bid at least b_0, and pay at least b_0 whenever we won, and this would result in a negative surplus. Therefore $v_* \geq b_0$. On the other hand, in either auction type, we can realize a positive expected surplus by bidding as soon as our value exceeds b_0. The point at which we are indifferent to bidding or not bidding is therefore $v_* = b_0$.* □

Notice that this implies immediately from equation B.16 that in first- and second-price auctions

$$b_0 = v_* = v_0 + \frac{1 - F(v_*)}{f(v_*)} > v_0, \qquad \text{(B.17)}$$

using the fact that $F(v_*) < 1$ and $f(v_*) > 0$. That is, in these auctions the seller sets the reserve strictly above his value.

B.3.1 Example: First-Price Auction with Reserve

Consider a first-price auction with our favorite illustrative case of valuations uniform on $[0, 1]$, so that $f(v) = 1$ and $F(v) = v$. For convenience, let the value of the object to the seller be $v_0 = 0$. (We will usually assume this from now on.) Equation B.12 then becomes

$$MR(v) = v - \frac{1 - F(v)}{f(v)} = 2v - 1, \qquad \text{(B.18)}$$

and equation B.15 gives us $v_* = 1/2$. As we know, this is independent of the number of bidders and the form of the auction. By property 1, for first- and second-price auctions the optimal reserve price is therefore $b_0 = v_* = 1/2$.

Continuing with the example, we ask what the equilibrium bidding function is in a first-price auction with optimal reserve, in order to compare it with the no-reserve case, as calculated in section A.8. Going back to that derivation, the general form of the equilibrium bidding function is, from equation A.41,

$$b(v) = v - \frac{\int F(v)^{n-1} dv - \gamma}{F(v)^{n-1}}. \qquad \text{(B.19)}$$

We now want to impose the condition that at the entry value v_*, the expected surplus is zero. Bidding truthfully in a first-price auction yields zero surplus, so this is equivalent to the condition $b(v_*) = v_*$. It is easy to see that we can accomplish this by taking the constant of integration γ to be zero (as in the case with no reserve), and the lower limit of integration to be v_* (instead of 0). Thus, the equilibrium bidding strategy is now

$$b(v) = \begin{cases} 0 & \text{if } v < v_* \\ v - \dfrac{\int_{v_*}^{v} F(x)^{n-1} dx}{F(v)^{n-1}} & \text{if } v \geq v_* \end{cases}. \qquad (B.20)$$

We can consider the no-reserve case as simply the special case when the entry value v_* is zero.

To keep the example simple, consider the case of two bidders. Then $v_* = b_0 = 1/2$, $F(v) = v$, $n = 2$, and equation B.20 becomes

$$b(v) = \frac{v}{2} + \frac{1}{8v}, \quad \text{for } v \geq 1/2, \qquad (B.21)$$

as compared to simply $b(v) = v/2$ when there is no reserve (see fig. B.1). Thus, the equilibrium bidding when $b_0 = 1/2$ (the optimal reserve) is more aggressive than when $b_0 = 0$ (when all bids are accepted by the seller).

Finally, we can compute the expected revenue of the two auctions, anticipating, of course, that the optimal choice of reserve has actually benefited the seller. The work for this has already been done, in deriving equation B.13. Using the marginal revenue in equation B.18, we get a revenue of 5/12 for the optimal choice $b_0 = 1/2$, and only 4/12 when $b_0 = 0$. So we see that the seller's expected revenue is actually increased by 25%, a significant gain. Question 3 asks you to generalize this to n bidders.

A glance at figure B.1 shows that when the optimal reserve is used in this example there is a marked increase in the bid levels—when values do exceed the reserve. To offer some intuition that explains this behavior, suppose you are bidder 1 and your valuation is $v_1 = 0.8$. If the seller's reserve is set at $b_0 = 0$, we know that your equilibrium bid is $v/2 = 0.4$. But if the reserve is set at the optimal $b_0 = 0.5$, bidding 0.4 is not allowed. Should you then not bid at all? Of course not. You can still earn a surplus if you bid between 0.5 and 0.8 and happen to win. Should you bid the minimum allowed amount, 0.5? It turns out that in equilibrium you should bid above 0.5. Just how much more than 0.5 requires the derivation leading up to equation B.21, but this general argument explains the shape of the bidding function in figure B.1.

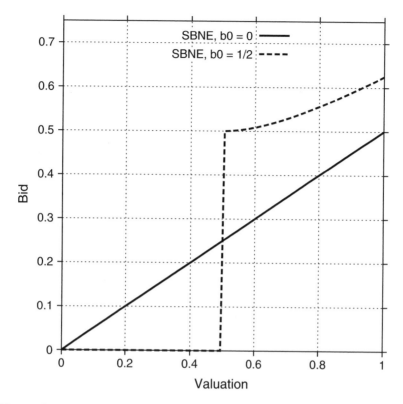

Figure B.1 Equilibrium bidding functions in a first-price auction with two bidders and independently and uniformly distributed values, for zero and optimal reserve.

B.3.2 Example: Second-price Auction with Reserve

It is also interesting to see what happens in a second-price auction with the same setup (two bidders, iid uniform valuations) when the seller adds a reserve. The same argument as in the no-reserve case, Vickrey's 1961 time-honored argument (chapter 1), shows that truthful bidding is still weakly dominant. Thus, bidder 1 bids v_1 whenever v_1 exceeds the entry value v_*. We can check the revenue directly. Bidder 1 wins whenever v_1 exceeds both v_* and v_2. When she does win, she pays v_* if $v_2 \leq v_*$, and v_2 if $v_* \leq v_2 \leq v_1$ (as usual, ignore ties). Averaging this payment over v_2 then gives us the expected payment of bidder 1 given that her value is v_1,

$$P_{sp} = \begin{cases} 0 & \text{if } v_1 < v_* \\ \int_0^{v_*} v_* \, dv_2 + \int_{v_*}^{v_1} v_2 \, dv_2 & \text{if } v_1 \geq v_* \end{cases} . \qquad \text{(B.22)}$$

The revenue to the seller is twice this, averaged over values of $v_1 \geq v_*$, which works out to be

$$v_*^2 - (4/3)v_*^3 + 1/3. \qquad \text{(B.23)}$$

Differentiating this with respect to v_* shows that the optimal choice of v_* is $1/2$, as we already know, and that the expected revenue is $5/12$, the same as in the first-price auction with optimal reserve.

Although setting an optimal reserve raises the revenue in this second-price auction from $4/12$ to $5/12$, exactly as it does in the first-price auction, and exactly as predicted by revenue equivalence, the mechanism seems quite different. In the second-price case, the bidding levels are not elevated, and it is the fact that the winner pays the reserve when the second price is below the reserve that increases the expected payments. This asks less in the way of strategic thinking than the equilibrium adjustment in the first-price case, and is the mechanism that one expects to operate on eBay, which has, after all, a second-price payment rule.

B.4 Sad Losers and Santa Claus

Riley and Samuelson (1981) give two examples of auctions in their class that may seem somewhat bizarre, but are nonetheless interesting for illustrating how the theory works. They are too entertaining and instructive to skip, and I'll describe them here. In both examples, we will assume that there are two bidders, with valuations independently and uniformly distributed on $[0, 1]$; and that the value of the item to the seller, v_0, is zero. We also assume that these two examples will be *optimal* auctions, in the sense that the seller will make the choices necessary to receive maximum expected revenue.

B.4.1 The Sad-Loser Auction

The sad-loser auction is distinguished by its payment rule: The winner pays nothing at all and walks away with the item for sale, while the loser pays what he bid and leaves the auction empty-handed.[6] The sad-loser auction, despite its strange payment rule, is in $\mathcal{A}_{rs}$, and we will now derive its equilibrium bidding function and check its revenue with an optimal reserve.[7]

When bidder 1 chooses to bid, which occurs by definition when her value is at least v_*, she wins, in equilibrium, when and only when her value exceeds that of her rival, which occurs with probability $F(v_1)$. Her expected surplus is therefore

$$v_1 F(v_1) - b(v_1)(1 - F(v_1)), \quad \text{for } v_1 \geq v_*, \quad \text{(B.24)}$$

being that she stands to earn v_1 if she wins the auction, and pay $b(v_1)$ if she loses. At the entry value v_*, the point of indifference between bidding and not bidding, bidder 1 wins if and only if there is no rival bid (ignoring ties, which occur with probability zero), so it is optimal at that point for her to bid as low as possible. That is, $b(v_*) = b_0$. Furthermore, at the entry value the expected surplus is zero. Using these two facts in equation B.24, and recalling that we are assuming uniformly distributed values, tells us that

$$b_0 = \frac{v_*^2}{1 - v_*}. \quad \text{(B.25)}$$

We know that for optimal revenue, $v_* = 1/2$, so the optimal reserve is $b_0 = 1/2$.

What about the equilibrium bidding function? It turns out that in this case, as in many such examples, the work on the expected payment $P(v)$ in section B.2 delivers the equilibrium bidding function as a valuable dividend, with hardly any further effort. To see how, notice that we have two expressions for $P(v)$: $b(v)(1 - F(v))$ from equation B.24, and

---

[6] This auction is sometimes called "loser-weeps," as in the street game of marbles, where "playing for keeps" means "winner keeps, loser weeps." See http://streetplay.com/thegames/marbles/marbleglossary.shtml.

[7] Riley and Samuelson do not use a reserve with the sad-loser auction, but instead charge an entry fee to those wishing to bid. This is another way to set the entry value optimally, and is nearly equivalent. See question 7.

equation B.6, which gives us $P(v)$ in terms of $F(v)$ and v_*. Equating these two expressions, and using $F(v) = v$ and $n = 2$, yields

$$b(v)(1 - v) = v^2 - \int_{v_*}^{v} x\,dx, \qquad (B.26)$$

and therefore, with our choice $v_* = 1/2$,

$$b(v) = \frac{v^2 + 1/4}{2(1 - v)}, \qquad \text{for } v \geq 1/2. \qquad (B.27)$$

Of course, we need to add the condition $v \geq 1/2$, the reserve.[8]

Figure B.2 shows a plot of the equilibrium bidding function. It instructs us to bid higher and higher, without bound, as our value approaches one, which makes intuitive sense for the following reason. When our value is very close to one, we can afford the gamble of bidding very high, because we are likely to win, and if we do win we pay nothing at all. The exact form of the equilibrium in equation B.27 tells us just how high we can go without risking so much that we will be ruined (on the average) by losses.

It is easy enough to check the fact that the sad-loser auction has the same expected revenue as all the optimal auctions in the class $\mathcal{A}_{rs}$ with the same entry value—for example, the first- and second-price auctions used as examples in section B.3. When a bidder bids, her expected payment is the probability of losing the auction times the amount of her bid. We average this over the values $v \geq v_*$, the range where she does bid, to give

$$\text{E[payment]} = \int_{v_*}^{1} b(v)(1 - F(v))\,dv, \qquad (B.28)$$

which works out to 5/24 in the case of interest, when values are uniformly distributed and $v_* = 1/2$. There are two bidders, so the expected revenue to the seller is twice this, or 5/12, as expected.

---

[8] The maneuver here has been to write the expected payment of a bidder in terms of the equilibrium function, to equate that to the expected payment in any optimal auction, equation B.6, and to solve for the bidding function. A trick worth remembering.

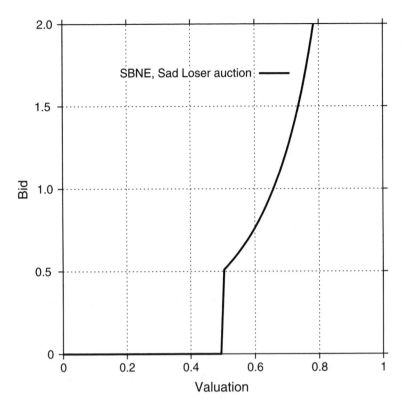

Figure B.2 Equilibrium bidding function in the sad-loser auction. There are two bidders, values are independently and uniformly distributed, and the reserve is chosen optimally at $1/2$.

B.4.2 The Santa Claus Auction

The second of Riley and Samuelson's examples is an auction that illustrates a central point of auction theory: the seller auctions off an item because she is unsure of its value. The expected surplus extracted by the bidders is a direct reflection of this uncertainty. Suppose, for example, that the seller happens to know the bidders' valuations for an item. In this case she can realize the most revenue by offering to sell the item to the buyer with the highest value on a take-it-or-leave-it basis, at a price some small ϵ below that highest value. The buyer has an incentive to accept this offer, albeit with the small surplus of ϵ, and the seller extracts practically full value for the item. We see from this that

219

there is real value in the information contained in the valuations of the bidders, and the second example makes this value explicit.

The rules of the Santa Claus auction are as follows: Each bidder who submits a bid is paid for participating by the seller. The highest bidder then wins the object and pays her bid (so this is a kind of first-price auction). The payment to each bidder depends on how much she bids, provided her bid meets the seller's reserve b_0. As we will see, if the amount paid to each bidder is chosen in just the right way, and the reserve b_0 is chosen so that the entry value is optimal, the auction becomes an optimal auction in Riley and Samuelson's class $\mathcal{A}_{rs}$. Furthermore, a very interesting thing happens: in equilibrium the bidders will bid truthfully.

We can see directly what the payment from the seller to the bidders must be. Since the winner pays her bid, bidding truthfully will yield no surplus at all, and so any surplus realized by a bidder will come from the seller's payment. For the auction to be an optimal one in $\mathcal{A}_{rs}$, a bidder's expected surplus must be the same as it is in all the others in the class with the same entry value. We can therefore calculate this expected surplus by using any optimal member of the class $\mathcal{A}_{rs}$ with the same entry value, say the ordinary first-class auction. Using the equilibrium bidding function in equation B.20 for $n=2$ bidders, the surplus in equilibrium of a bidder with value v in an ordinary first-price auction is

$$E[\text{surplus}] = \text{pr}\{\text{winning}\} \cdot [v - b(v)]$$

$$= F(v) \cdot [v - b(v)] \tag{B.29}$$

$$= \int_{v_*}^{v} F(y)\,dy. \tag{B.30}$$

The seller's payment to a bidder who bids b must therefore be simply $S(v) = \int_{v_*}^{b} F(y)\,dy$, since we will arrange things so that bidding is truthful in equilibrium. Furthermore, the seller's reserve price b_0 should be chosen to be equal to the desired entry value v_*, the point at which it first becomes profitable to bid.

To prove that truthful bidding is an equilibrium strategy, suppose that bidder 2 bids truthfully. Then the expected surplus of bidder 1 when she bids b_1 is

$$E[\text{surplus}] = S(b_1) + (v_1 - b_1) \cdot F(b_1), \qquad \text{for } v_1 \geq v_*. \qquad \text{(B.31)}$$

Bidder 1's best response can be obtained by differentiating this with respect to b_1 and setting the result to zero, yielding

$$(v_1 - b_1) \cdot f(b_1) = 0. \qquad \text{(B.32)}$$

The best response to truthful bidding is therefore truthful bidding (the pdf $f(v)$ is assumed positive everywhere on its support), which establishes this as an equilibrium bidding strategy. In effect, the seller is paying the bidders their expected surplus to reveal their true values.

Checking revenue equivalence is a straightforward calculation, as usual. The total expected payment to the seller from both bidders is the expected value of the higher of two bids, where the expectation is taken over the range $v \geq v_*$:

$$\int_{v_*}^{1} v \, dF(v)^2 = 2 \int_{v_*}^{1} v^2 \, dv = (2/3)(1 - v_*^3). \qquad \text{(B.33)}$$

The seller's payment to a bidder with value v is

$$S(v) = \int_{v_*}^{v} F(v) \, dv = v^2/2 - v_*^2/2. \qquad \text{(B.34)}$$

Averaging this over bidder values $v \geq v_*$, and multiplying by two (because there are two bidders), gives us the total expected payment from the seller to the bidders,

$$\int_{v_*}^{1} (v^2 - v_*^2) \, dv = 1/3 + (2/3)v_*^3 - v_*^2. \qquad \text{(B.35)}$$

The expected net revenue to the seller is the difference, which works out to 5/12 for $v_* = 1/2$. This is the same as in the previous examples with this entry value, checking revenue equivalence.

Despite the name, the Santa Claus auction is hardly a philanthropic institution. In equilibrium the bidders earn, on the average, exactly the same surplus as in the corresponding optimal first- or second-price auction. By the same token, the loser in the sad-loser auction has no good reason to be unhappy; in equilibrium she also earns the same surplus, on the average. What does vary across the different kinds of auctions is the variance of the bidders' surplus. For example, a bidder in the sad-loser auction experiences losses—but these losses are offset by the bonanzas of winning items gratis. The bidder in the Santa Claus auction, on the other hand, never takes a loss, and can rely on a much steadier surplus stream.

B.5 The All-Pay Auction Revisited

For yet another example of an optimal auction, we return briefly to the all-pay auction, discussed without a seller's reserve in section A.14. It is easy to check that this auction belongs to the class $\mathcal{A}_{rs}$. Once again, we stick to the simple case of two bidders and iid uniformly distributed values.

We first find the reserve b_0 that results in an entry value $v_* = 1/2$, to compare with the previous examples. The expected surplus of bidder 1 is

$$
\text{E[surplus]} = \begin{cases} 0 & \text{if } v_1 < v_* \\ v_1^2 - b(v_1) & \text{if } v_1 \geq v_*, \end{cases} \tag{B.36}
$$

because she wins value v_1 with probability v_1, and always pays her bid if she bids at all. As in the sad-loser auction, bidder 1 wins at the point of indifference between bidding and not bidding if and only if there is no rival bid. It is therefore optimal for her at that point to bid as low as possible, implying that $b(v_*) = b_0$. We also know that at the entry value v_*, the expected surplus is zero, and then equation B.36 at v_* tells us that $b_0 = v_*^2 = 1/4$. Notice that this is the first example in which the reserve is something other than the entry value.

The form of the equilibrium bidding function in an all-pay auction is, from equation A.58,

$$
b(v) = v^2/2 + \gamma, \tag{B.37}
$$

where γ is a constant of integration. Imposing the condition that $b(v_*) = v_*^2$ then shows that $\gamma = 1/8$, and the equilibrium bidding function is therefore

$$
b(v) = v^2/2 + 1/8, \quad \text{for } v \geq 1/2, \tag{B.38}
$$

which is plotted in figure B.3.

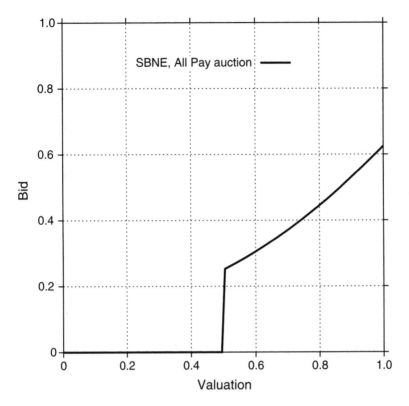

Figure B.3 Equilibrium bidding function in an all-pay auction with two bidders, and independently and uniformly distributed values. The entry value is optimal at 1/2, while the reserve is 1/4.

Checking the revenue is once again straightforward. The expected payment of bidder 1 is

$$\text{E[payment]} = \int_{v_*}^{1} b(v)\, dv = 5/24, \qquad (\text{B.39})$$

and twice this is the expected revenue of 5/12, checking the previous examples.

We see that equilibrium bidding in the all-pay auction is more conservative than in the other examples. There is bid-shading at all valuations. This makes intuitive sense—we don't want to bid too generously if we know that our bids are actually nonrefundable checks.

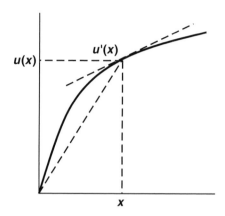

Figure B.4 A convex-down utility function, illustrating that the derivative u' at a point x is upper-bounded by the ratio u/x.

B.6 Risk Aversion

Before going on to more general bidder models, we need to discuss *risk aversion*, a very important characteristic of bidders, which is often mentioned in the literature and sometimes invoked to explain departures from standard theory of one kind or another. As we'll see shortly, risk aversion separates the first- and second-price auctions in terms of expected revenue even for the class $\mathcal{A}_{rs}$. The motivating idea is that real-world bidders might very well attach a nonlinear utility to surplus. In particular, they might attach a greater loss of utility when losing a dollar than the gain in utility when winning a dollar. In such cases we say a bidder is *risk averse*, and model her risk aversion with a convex-down utility function $u(y)$, such as the one illustrated in figure B.4. When a bidder's utility is linear, we say the bidder is *risk neutral*.

The main result shows that when bidders are risk averse, first-price auctions raise more revenue on the average than second-price auctions. The result is in Riley and Samuelson (1981), and we will follow the proof in Krishna (2002). We'll assume that the utility function is smooth, and that its convexity is strict, so that the inequalities we write are strict.

RESULT 3 (Revenue ranking for risk-averse bidders) Suppose all bidders in an auction in Riley and Samuelson's class $\mathcal{A}_{rs}$ are risk averse with the same convex-down utility function $u(x)$. Then the expected revenue in the first-price auction is greater than the expected revenue in the second-price auction:

$$R_{fp} > R_{sp}. \tag{B.40}$$

PROOF *Observe first that in second-price auctions, even when bidders are risk averse, the equilibrium strategy is still sincere bidding, and the expected surplus is the same as with risk-neutral bidders.*

In the first-price auction, the expected surplus is

$$W(z)u(x - \gamma(z)), \tag{B.41}$$

where the bidder's actual value is x, her bidding function is $\gamma(x)$, she bids as if her value is $x = z$, and $W(z)$ is the probability of winning when she bids as if her value is z, just $F(z)^{n-1}$. Notice that we use here, not the surplus $x - \gamma(z)$, but the utility function u evaluated at that point. As usual, to get a condition for the symmetric equilibrium bidding function, we insist that the maximum of the expected surplus occurs when $z = x$. Differentiating with respect to z and setting the result to zero gives us

$$\gamma'(x) = \frac{w(x)}{W(x)} \cdot \frac{u(x - \gamma(x))}{u'(x - \gamma(x))}, \tag{B.42}$$

where $w(x) = W'(x)$.

We next use a property of convex functions that should be obvious from figure B.4. The slope of the utility curve at any given point is less than the slope of the chord that goes from the origin to the point. This gives us the lower bound $u(x)/u'(x) > x$, which, when applied to equation B.42, yields

$$\gamma'(x) > \frac{w(x)}{W(x)} \cdot (x - \gamma(x)). \tag{B.43}$$

Now let $\beta(x)$ be the equilibrium bidding function in a first-price auction with risk-neutral bidders. By setting $u(x) = x$ in equation B.42, we can write its derivative as

$$\beta'(x) = \frac{w(x)}{W(x)} \cdot (x - \beta(x)), \tag{B.44}$$

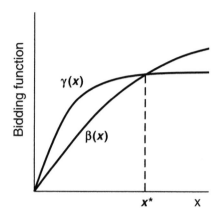

Figure B.5 Sketch completing the proof that the risk-averse bidding function $\gamma(x)$ is uniformly greater than the risk-neutral bidding function $\beta(x)$. The curves are assumed to cross at the point x^* for a contradiction.

which is the same as the right-hand side of equation B.43, except that $\beta(x)$ replaces $\gamma(x)$.

Next, it is easy to see that $\gamma'(0) > \beta'(0)$. If this were not true, then there would be some small interval $[0, \epsilon]$ on which $\gamma(x) \leq \beta(x)$. Equation B.43 would then show that on this interval

$$\gamma'(x) > \frac{w(x)}{W(x)} \cdot (x - \beta(x)) = \beta'(x), \qquad \text{(B.45)}$$

using equation B.44, which would contradict the hypothesis that $\gamma'(0) < \beta'(0)$. It is also true that $\gamma(0) = \beta(0) = 0$; bidders with value zero bid zero.

Finally, we will show that $\gamma(x) > \beta(x)$ for all x. Thus, in first-price auctions, the bidding by risk-averse bidders is uniformly higher than the bidding by risk-neutral bidders. The bidding by risk-neutral bidders in first-price auctions yields the same revenue as in second-price auctions, by revenue equivalence, and therefore the revenue in first-price auctions with risk-averse bidders is higher than in second-price auctions, which is what we want to show.

Figure B.5 shows a sketch of the bidding functions $\gamma(x)$ and $\beta(x)$. We already know that they both start at the origin, and that for some interval starting at the origin, $\gamma(x)$ is above $\beta(x)$. We want to show that $\gamma(x)$ stays above $\beta(x)$. Suppose not. Then let x^* be the first point *at which they cross, and use equation B.43 at the point $x = x^*$:*

$$\gamma'(x) > \frac{w(x^*)}{W(x^*)} \cdot (x - \gamma(x^*)) = \frac{w(x^*)}{W(x^*)} \cdot (x - \beta(x^*)) = \beta'(x).$$

(B.46)

But the slope of the γ curve cannot be greater than the slope of the β curve at a point where γ crosses from above, and this contradiction completes the proof. □

B.7 Point of Departure

In this appendix, we have seen quite a variety of auctions that fall into Riley and Samuelson's class, including the standard four. The equilibrium bidding strategies are correspondingly varied, but they all take the auction rules into account in just the right way to result in the same revenue to the seller.

The story of auction theory since 1981 is largely concerned with escaping the confines of this model, which is normally too idealized for the study of real auctions. In the next appendix, we will review the theoretical advances in several directions, often with an eye towards applying the results to our understanding of eBay, as well as other real-world auctions.

B.8 Questions

1. Prove that equation B.2 is sufficient, as well as necessary, for optimality.

2. Is there always a well-defined entry value v_* for any auction in class $\mathcal{A}_{rs}$?

3. Consider first-price auctions where the distribution of values is iid and uniform, the value of the object to the seller is zero, and the seller's reserve is chosen optimally. Find the equilibrium bidding strategy and expected revenue for n bidders, thus generalizing equation B.21.

How does the advantage of choosing a seller's reserve b_0, as compared with allowing all positive bids, diminish as the number of bidders grows?

4. Show that the expected value of the marginal revenue, equation B.12, for any distribution F, is zero.

5. Here's a suggestion from Case (1979):

> An envelope containing a particular bidder's sealed offer would include a promise to pay one sum of money if his were the only bid received, another if just two bids were received, ..., and a last if ten or more bids were forthcoming. Then each would be protected, in part, from the submission of bids by unexpected rivals, and less deterred from aggressive action. This proposal, like Vickrey's, would appear to be advantageous to buyers and sellers alike.

Case argues that this format would reduce risk, and that "reduced risk means more aggressive bidding and consequently higher sales prices." Discuss this proposal.

6. The specter of an unbounded equilibrium bidding function in the sad-loser auction can be dispelled by requiring the winner to pay some percentage, say $\alpha < 1$, of her bid. Show that if we modify the sad-loser auction rules in this way, the resulting equilibrium bidding function is no longer unbounded on $[0, 1]$, the support of the bidders' value distribution.

7. Consider the sad-loser auction where, instead of setting a reserve, the seller charges buyers wishing to bid a fixed entry fee c, as in Riley and Samuelson (1981). What is the optimal choice for c in the example in section B.4.1? How is the equilibrium bidding function changed, if at all? Check the expected revenue using the equilibrium bidding function.

8. Generalize the Santa Claus auction to n bidders by deriving the appropriate seller's payment and showing that truthful bidding is an equilibrium.

9. In this appendix we used five different auction forms in $\mathcal{A}_{rs}$ as examples for the case when values are uniformly distributed and there are two bidders: the first-price, second-price, sad-loser, Santa Claus, and all-pay auctions. Check in each case, using the bidding function as a function of v_*, that the expected revenue is the same function of v_* that we found in the second-price case, equation B.23: $R(v_*) = v_*^2 - (4/3)v_*^3 + 1/3$. Notice that $R(v_*)$ is maximized at $v_* = 1/2$, that $R(0) < R(1/2)$, and that $R(1) = 0$, as expected. Then check that the general result in equation B.11, which uses the marginal revenue, yields the same $R(v_*)$.

10. Is the California auction, our idealized abstraction of eBay, in Riley and Samuelson's class of auctions, $\mathcal{A}_{rs}$?

Myerson's Optimal Mechanisms

C.1 Directions

THE THEORY up to this point takes the bidders' values to be private, independent, and identically distributed. The main results center around the wide class studied by Riley and Samuelson (1981), which includes the English, Vickrey, and first-price auctions, and any of these auctions with the same entry value has exactly the same expected revenue. Despite this remarkable unification, the guidance it provides in selecting reserves, and the insight gained into bidding strategies, this theory remains unsatisfying—especially from the point of view of the seller who wants to choose an auction form to suit a particular set of circumstances. After all our work, it is something of an embarrassment to arrive at the conclusion that there is nothing to distinguish any of the four standard auction forms as far as expected revenue is concerned. The bland conclusion of revenue equivalence is especially troubling in light of the fact that the English ascending auction has been the clear preference of all the large, traditional auction houses for centuries, and the fact that its internet counterpart, the California auction and its eBay instantiation, is now the mechanism of choice in the electronic auction arena.

The natural response is to develop more sophisticated models to reflect the complexities of real auction behavior that we observed in chapter 3. Where in the theory is the idea that different bidders can have different value distributions for the same item? Where is the fact that bidders are often uncertain about their values? Or that the values might be statistically correlated with each other, and hence that bidders can acquire useful information by observing their rivals' bids? How about bidding wars? As mentioned at the end of the previous appendix, since the early 1980s auction theorists have aimed at expanding the lean Riley and Samuelson model to include more realistic and general pictures of what bidders know about their values and how they behave strategically. Their work has yielded some important insights into how to design auctions (and more general selling mechanisms), and how bidders should or might behave in different settings.

Roughly, these research directions can be divided into two broad branches, accommodating *interdependent values* and *asymmetric bidders*. Next, we will review, briefly, most of the important results in the case of interdependent values, most of which are valid only for symmetric bidders. We will then devote the remainder of this appendix to a more detailed survey of the theory for asymmetric bidders with independently distributed private values.

C.2 Interdependent Values

Up to now, in our discussion of theory, we have assumed that bidders always know their values with certainty, but an important accommodation of the theory to reality is the modeling of situations where they don't. The way this is usually done is to assume that bidders have information about their values that is to some extent uncertain, in the form of *signals* s_i, which are, in general, random variables. The actual values to bidders—which determine their payoffs—is then taken to be some function

$$v_i = \varphi_i(s_1, s_2, \ldots, s_n), \tag{C.1}$$

where we assume that the function φ_i is nondecreasing in all its variables, and strictly increasing in s_i, the signal most relevant to bidder i.[1] Also, as usual, we assume that the functions φ_i are smooth enough for any manipulations that are needed.

In general, the signals s_i are statistically interdependent, which then makes the values interdependent through the functions φ_i. One of the key contributions of Milgrom and Weber (1982)[2] is adding the further

---

[1] We follow Krishna's (2002) formulation here, which is bit more streamlined than Milgrom and Weber's (1982) original presentation.

[2] It is fair to say that the four papers, Vickrey (1961), Riley and Samuelson (1981), Myerson (1981), and Milgrom and Weber (1982), are the cornerstones of auction theory.

assumption that the signals are *affiliated*. This has a definition that is technical and not particularly transparent. Roughly, it means that if one signal is high, the other signals are likely to be high also. Since each value function φ_i is increasing in the signal s_i, this means that, intuitively, a bidder who attaches a relatively high value to an item can reasonably infer that other bidders do also. Milgrom and Weber (1982, p. 1099) use the example of the auction sale of a painting: "a bidder who finds a painting very beautiful will expect others to admire it, too."

The affiliated model in equation C.1 is broad enough to cover most standard situations that auction theorists like to think about. First, it is easy to see that the independently distributed private-value model is included; just let $v_i = \varphi_i(s_1, s_2, \ldots, s_n) = s_i$, where the s_i are independent random variables, so that the value of the ith bidder is just her signal, which she knows with certainty. Notice that if the signals in this case are *not* independently distributed, bidders will still have private values, but these private values will in general be statistically correlated.

The *common-value* (or *mineral-rights*) model is one where the value of the item for sale is the same to all the bidders (but unknown to any of them before the end of the sale), say V. This case, too, is included in the affiliated-values model; just let $v_i = \varphi_i(s_1, s_2, \ldots, s_n) = V$ for all i. It is usually assumed that, given the common V, the signals s_i are independently distributed. In the simplest kind of common-value model, the s_i are taken to be $V + \delta_i$, where the δ_i are iid random variables.

The results in Milgrom and Weber (1982) that are derived for the general affiliated model seem very satisfying at first, because they distinguish among the four standard forms on the basis of revenue. In general, if values are affiliated in a nontrivial way, then the expected revenues in the four main auction forms are ranked as

$$\text{English} > \text{Second-Price} > \text{First-Price} \equiv \text{Dutch}.$$

Milgrom and Weber cite Cassady (1967, p. 66) for some verification that this result is consistent with practice, at least as it was in 1967:

> Empirical evidence reveals that, of the three principal types of auctions, the English is by far the most common. An estimated 75%, or even more, of all the auctions in the world are conducted on the

ascending-bid basis. Second in popularity is undoubtedly the Dutch auction, with its heavy reliance on electronic mechanisms.

First- and second-price sealed-bid auctions are not included in Cassady's appraisal of the principal auction types, which makes sense in pre-internet days. We should note, however, that Milgrom and Weber's English auction is actually what we call the "Japanese button auction," described in section 1.4.

Milgrom and Weber (1982) also consider the situation when the seller has a private source of information (such as expert knowledge or an independent appraisal), positively affiliated with the bidders' signals, and asks himself how revenue would be affected if he revealed some or all of this information publicly. The seller has a very wide choice of policies, including reporting all his information, reporting none of his information, reporting only the most favorable information, or releasing a noisy version of his private information. The result is that in first- and second-price auctions, as well as in the English auction, full disclosure maximizes price.

This result is paraphrased as "Honesty is the best policy" by Milgrom and Weber (1982, p. 1096), and it is often cited this way. But, as usual, it is very important that we understand the assumptions used to arrive at this celebrated and perhaps counterintuitive result. First, we must assume that any information provided by the seller is *credible*—there must be good incentives for the seller not to lie, such as concern for his reputation and repeat business. The seller must earn the trust of the buyers. Second—and these are common assumptions in much of game theory—we must assume that the seller has committed in advance to a policy which determines exactly how he is going to report his private information, and, further, that *this policy is known to the buyers*. In other words, the seller can choose just how much of his private information he releases and under what circumstances, but his policy must be public, and he cannot choose to lie. We should also not forget that, as usual in auction theory, the formulation assumes that the probability distributions of the bidders' signals are common knowledge. These are very strong assumptions, and the general result, while sometimes invoked slavishly, should be applied with caution in the world of real auctions, including eBay.

Milgrom and Weber introduce a powerful idea to explain both the revenue-ranking results and the recommendation to reveal private information, called the *linkage principle*. The basic argument can be summarized as follows.[3] Consider the expected price paid by the winner when her signal is x but she bids as if her value is z, denoted by $W(z, x)$.[4] The main result hinges on the relative value of what I'll call the *linkage*:

$$L(x) = \left. \frac{\partial W(z, x)}{\partial x} \right|_{z=x}, \tag{C.2}$$

the sensitivity of the expected price paid by the winner with respect to variations in her received signal when her bid is held fixed. It then turns out that two auction mechanisms with symmetric and increasing equilibria, and with $W(0, 0) = 0$, are revenue-ranked by their linkages. That is, the mechanism with the higher linkage has the higher revenue.

In a first-price auction, the winner pays her bid, and the linkage is zero, directly from the definition, equation C.2. But in a second-price auction, the amount paid, the second price, is uncertain and is statistically linked through the affiliated signals to bidder 1's signal, so in general $L > 0$, and the expected revenue is higher.

The same intuition works for ranking the revenue in English auctions relative to second-price auctions when signals are affiliated. In a second-price auction, the price paid by the winner (say bidder 1) is linked to the signal of only one other bidder, the second-highest bidder (say bidder 2). But in an English auction, the price paid by bidder 1 is linked to the signals of bidders 3 through n as well. When signals are affiliated, therefore, the public revelation of information during the course of the English auction increases the linkage, and therefore increases the expected revenue relative to the Vickrey auction. The argument that the seller will, in general, increase his revenue by revealing his affiliated information about the item is similar.

As satisfying as these conclusions are for interdependent values, most of them fail to carry over when bidders are asymmetric. As Krishna

---

[3] We follow Krishna (2002) here.

[4] This version assumes that the winner is the only bidder who pays a positive amount. See Krishna (2002) for a version of the linkage principle when the winner is not the only bidder who parts with cash.

(2002, p. 111) puts it in his understated way, this failure of the results for interdependent values to generalize "strikes a discordant note." It is not just that the more general theoretical results are not yet available. They are false. Krishna continues, "Much of the theory developed in the symmetric case is fragile and does not extend to situations in which bidders are asymmetric." This is especially disappointing because it is difficult to live with the assumption that bidders (and their information) are symmetric, especially in the rough-and-tumble world of eBay. Partly for this reason, and also because the techniques in Milgrom and Weber (1982) are more complicated than our usual freshman calculus standard, we will not cover their results in more detail, but will concentrate on the asymmetric, independent values case.

However, before we leave the interdependent values case, there is the one outstanding result of Engelbrecht-Wiggans et al. (1983) that is mentioned in chapter 3, for the asymmetric-bidder, common-value, first-price case when one bidder is perfectly informed, and the others are not informed at all. The result is very satisfying: in the equilibrium described, the informed bidder bids exactly as if the other bidders also had private values in a first-price auction, but the other bidders' equilibrium is a randomized strategy, a so-called *mixed* equilibrium. And as mentioned in section 3.3, in equilibrium, the informed bidder earns an expected surplus that is positive, while the other bidders earn zero—a striking demonstration of the value of information.

C.3 Asymmetric Bidders

Myerson (1981) is a cornucopia of ideas for extending our understanding of auctions beyond the limits of the four standard auction forms, and, as mentioned before, is more general and more mathematically sophisticated than the down-to-earth paper of Riley and Samuelson (1981). As we'll see in this appendix, Myerson, in pursuing the goal of maximizing revenue, introduces several new ideas that play a central role in today's thinking about selling mechanisms, especially the *revelation principle*. One important message that emerges from Myerson (1981) is that maximizing revenue for asymmetric bidders means going beyond ordinary auctions, and requiring information about bidders' value distributions that is ordinarily not available to the seller. But the ideas are very useful, nevertheless, and we will describe them in some detail, as well as a very pretty and well-known application by Bulow and Klemperer (1996). We will assume independent private values for the remainder of this appendix.

C.4 Efficiency

Given the work we've already done in appendix B, the extension from symmetric to asymmetric bidders is straightforward, but we first need to examine an assumption in the setup that will prove critical when we allow asymmetric bidders. Recall that in the symmetric case, Riley and Samuelson's starting point is the expected surplus of a typical bidder if she bids as if her valuation is z, given that her true valuation is v_1, equation B.1. To calculate this, we needed the probability that the bidder wins the auction. At this point, we used a part of the definition of the class A_{rs} that may seem quite innocuous: namely, that the bidder who submits the highest bid wins the auction. Since we also assumed that the equilibrium bidding function is increasing, and since all the bidders in the symmetric case adopt this same bidding function, it follows that the bidder with the highest value always wins the auction. This allowed us to pin down the probability that a typical bidder wins to $F(z)^{n-1}$ (in the symmetric case), and the derivation of the optimal auction continued on track.

The property that the bidder with the highest value always wins is very important in some situations, and prompts the following definition:

DEFINITION (Efficiency, strict) A selling mechanism of any sort is called *efficient* if an object always ends up in the hands of the participant (possibly including the seller) who values it the most. $\square$

Optimal first- or second-price auctions with a reserve provide simple examples of auctions that are not, strictly speaking, efficient, even in the symmetric case. We saw in section B.3 that in such auctions the seller sets the reserve to be strictly positive, even when his valuation for the item is zero. Therefore, when the highest bid is less than the reserve price, the seller retains the item, despite the fact that there is a bidder who values the item more than he does. This is a missed opportunity for mutually beneficial trade, but is offset on the average by increased revenue to the seller because prices are increased when sales do take place.

I would argue, however, that including the seller as a participant when defining efficiency is a bit contrived. Usually, efficiency is an important consideration only when high-value public resources are sold, most notably radio spectrum, Treasury securities, or offshore oil and gas leases. In these contexts, achieving auction efficiency is often thought of as maximizing "social welfare." But in such situations, it hardly seems fair to consider an allocation to be inefficient if an item goes unsold when a bidder values it more than the government, because there is a good possibility that it will be offered for sale again at a later time. The question of commitment on the part of the seller to withhold an item from future sale creeps into the strategic framework, especially when reserves are used. The possibility of future sale may reduce present demand, and, as we've mentioned in regard to eBay, future negotiation may take place (illegitimately) outside the original auction venue.[5] In any event, the real focus of efficiency is the possibility of misallocation to buyers, and I will therefore, for our purposes anyway, redefine efficiency to exclude cases when an object is not sold:

DEFINITION (Efficiency, loose) A selling mechanism of any sort is called *efficient* if, when an object is sold, it is always bought by the bidder who values it the most. □

This redefinition allows us to regard all the optimal auctions in Riley and Samuelson's class (where bidders are symmetric) as efficient. It is also true that with this notion of efficiency, second-price auctions remain efficient in the asymmetric case, as long as the bidder's values are private—that is, as long as each bidder knows her value with certainty. This is because bidding truthfully in second-price auctions remains a dominant strategy in the asymmetric case, all bidders have the same bidding strategy, and the bidder with the highest value wins.

---

[5] For some discussion of this issue, see Krishna (2002, pp. 27–28).

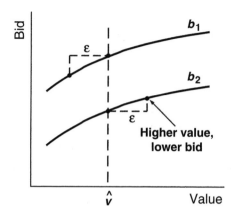

Figure C.1 Illustrating inefficiency in a first-price auction when bidders have differing value distributions.

In first-price auctions with asymmetric bidders, however, the situation is quite different; inefficiency can arise very naturally. To see this, consider a typical situation in a first-price auction when two bidders have different value distributions, and hence, in general, different equilibrium bidding functions, say $b_1(v)$ and $b_2(v)$ (see fig. C.1).[6] Choose a value $\hat{v}$ where the bidding functions differ. Say, without loss of generality, that $b_2(\hat{v}) < b_1(\hat{v})$, and suppose bidder 1 happens to draw the value $\hat{v} - \epsilon$ and bidder 2 the value $\hat{v} + \epsilon$. For sufficiently small ϵ, b_2's bid, $b_2(\hat{v} + \epsilon)$, is below b_1's bid, $b_1(\hat{v} - \epsilon)$, even though his value is above that of bidder 1. This shows that an inefficient outcome can arise in this generic situation with positive probability.

We conclude that if we plan to extend our work on optimal auctions to the case of asymmetric bidder valuations, we must throw efficiency overboard. This hardly seems a tragedy on eBay, or, in fact, in any sale of a private good, where the question of social welfare is much less compelling than in the sale of a public good.

Large-scale auctions of public goods, where efficiency is a key criterion, almost always deal with the sale of many items at once (*multi-unit auctions*, which we don't consider in this book), and often with values that are interdependent. For example, two oil leases that are geographically contiguous may have values that are uncertain but highly

---

[6] This argument is from Krishna (2002, p. 54).

correlated. See Morgan (2001) for a survey of how inefficiencies can arise in multi-unit auctions, and ways they can be avoided. For some detailed history and entertaining discussion of recent work on designing government auctions, see Ausubel and Cramton (1998) and Milgrom (2004), which describe the design of U.S. Treasury security auctions, and FCC auctions of radio spectrum. In general, the area of multi-unit auctions is less highly developed than that for single-item auctions, and can become very intricate when buyers place special values on certain bundles of items.

C.5 Myerson's Optimal Mechanism in the Asymmetric-Bidder Case

We now continue with the program of generalizing Riley and Samuelson's optimal auctions to the asymmetric bidder case. We can no longer say that the bidder with the highest value necessarily wins, and we can no longer claim, therefore, that a bid corresponding to value z wins with probability $F(z)^{n-1}$. Instead, we will designate who wins the auction with an arbitrary function, $\mathbf{Q}$, called the *allocation function*, or *allocation rule*, which we are free to choose. Similarly, we will describe the payments when the sale is over with the arbitrary function $\mathbf{P}$, as we did when analyzing Riley and Samuelson's class.

To be more specific, the allocation function will have n components, $Q_1, Q_2, \ldots, Q_n$, where Q_i is the probability that bidder i wins the auction. Moreover, each of these components Q_i is a function of the n values of the bidders, $v_1, v_2, \ldots, v_n$. To make the notation concise, we use boldface for vectors, and write $\mathbf{Q}(\mathbf{v})$ to indicate the vector of allocation values $Q_i(\mathbf{v})$ as a function of the vector of all the bidder valuations. Similarly, the vector of expected payments as a function of the value vector is written $\mathbf{P}(\mathbf{v})$. Notice that we have shifted attention away from *bids*, and we concentrate on *values*. We'll see shortly how we can get away with this important change in viewpoint.

It's easy to check that this notation takes care of the auctions in Riley and Samuelson's class $\mathcal{A}_{rs}$ in a straightforward way. All these auctions are efficient, so the function $\mathbf{Q}(\mathbf{v})$ simply finds the largest component in the value vector $\mathbf{v}$, and if this component is v_i, it assigns the value one to $Q_i(\mathbf{v})$, and assigns the value zero to $Q_j(\mathbf{v})$ when $j \neq i$. That is, bidder i wins the auction with probability one. The payment rule, on the other hand, must be tailored to the auction. In the first-price auction, for example, the function $\mathbf{P}(\mathbf{v})$ assigns the value $b(v_i)$ to $P_i(\mathbf{v})$, and the value zero to $P_j(\mathbf{v})$ when $j \neq i$, where i is the winning bidder and b is the equilibrium bidding function in the first-price auction. In the second-price auction, $\mathbf{P}(\mathbf{v})$ assigns the second-highest value to $P_i(\mathbf{v})$, and zero to the others, and so on.

The pair $(\mathbf{Q}, \mathbf{P})$ is called a *direct mechanism.* It sets the rules and enforces them. Notice that in addition to being an executive with police power, a direct mechanism is very well informed and very clever. It requires that bidders report their values, and it knows how to compute their equilibrium bidding strategies.

Consider instead an ordinary auction. It also sets the rules and enforces them, but, in contrast to the direct mechanism, it receives *bids*, not values, and determines the outcome of the auction on the basis of those bids. It is easy to see that any such bid-taking auction house can be replaced for theoretical purposes, assuming that bidders are using equilibrium bidding strategies, by a direct mechanism. Whatever bid calculations would be used by the bidders can simply be performed *for them* by the direct mechanism, and bidders are asked only to report their actual values to the direct mechanism.

The idea of an "ordinary auction" can be enlarged to include any set of rules for negotiation, no matter how complicated, by defining the set of allowable bids appropriately. For example, in multistage negotiations, each bidder can have lists of bidding functions, each of which is invoked at a given stage in a way that depends on what happens in previous stages. We call any such conceivable method for selling an item a *selling mechanism,* or, interchangeably, when we want to emphasize the generality, a *negotiation.* And exactly the same observation holds for selling mechanisms: there is always a direct mechanism that can do the work of finding the equilibrium bids, if it is given the values of the bidders.

But we must ask the key question: Why should the bidders report their true values to a direct mechanism? They are free to lie, and will do so if it is in their interest. The answer is that if they do lie about their values, the resulting calculated bids will be different from their equilibrium bids, and by definition there is certainly no incentive to have this happen. In other words, lying to the direct mechanism is equivalent to making a mistake when following one's bidding strategy in the original selling mechanism.

The general situation when there is no incentive to lie is important enough to prompt some terminology:

DEFINITION When agents who participate in any mechanism have no incentive to lie, we say that the mechanism is *incentive compatible*. □

The observation that any negotiation to sell an item can be replaced by the conceptually much simpler direct mechanism is due to Myerson (1981), and, in retrospect, seems very straightforward. In fact, without seeing it put to good use, it may seem trivial. But we *will* put it to good use, and, far from being trivial, it gives us a new way to think about mechanisms that are more general than auctions, because it abstracts away from particular bidding functions. The celebrated result can be summarized (somewhat informally) as:

RESULT 4 (The revelation principle) In so far as equilibrium behavior is concerned, any negotiation can be replaced by an incentive-compatible direct mechanism. □

We can now go back to Riley and Samuelson's own bit of abstracting away, and look for the direct mechanism with the highest revenue when bidders are asymmetric. Thanks to the revelation principle, we can restrict our attention to direct mechanisms with no fear of missing some complicated scheme with correspondingly complicated bidding functions. All we need is the pair $(\mathbf{Q}, \mathbf{P})$ that determines a direct mechanism.

Our starting point is the expected surplus of a typical bidder, say bidder i, if she reports that her value is z when it is actually v_i. As we discussed above, in the asymmetric case, it is no longer necessarily true that the bidder with the highest value wins. Therefore, the old expression for the surplus (eq. B.1),

$$v_i F(z)^{n-1} - P(z), \qquad (C.3)$$

is obsolete. We need to replace $F(z)^{n-1}$ by the probability that i wins the auction, and $P(z)$ by the expected payment if she wins. The probability that i wins the auction can be expressed in terms of $\mathbf{Q}(\mathbf{v})$ by taking the expectation over all the values except v_i. With apologies, I need to introduce one more bit of notation, which is, however, standard in auction theory, and very useful. Denote by $\mathbf{v}_{-i}$ the vector $\mathbf{v}$ with the ith value omitted. The allocation function when bidder i reports the value z instead of v_i can then be written $\mathbf{Q}(z, \mathbf{v}_{-i})$. We now can carry out the averaging we need to get the probability that i wins as a function of z only:

$$Q_i(z) = \int_{\mathbf{V}_{-i}} Q_i(z, \mathbf{v}_{-i}) \, d\mathbf{F}(\mathbf{v}_{-i}), \qquad (C.4)$$

where $\mathbf{V}_{-i}$ is the space of all v's except v_i, and $\mathbf{F}(\mathbf{v}_{-i})$ is the corresponding distribution.

Notice that $Q_i(z)$ in equation C.4 is a scalar function of the scalar variable z, the function we're after, the allocation function analogous to the probability of winning in the symmetric case, $F(z)^{n-1}$. We can also derive the corresponding expected payment from bidder i if she bids z using exactly the same notation,

$$P_i(z) = \int_{\mathbf{V}_{-i}} P_i(z, \mathbf{v}_{-i}) \, d\mathbf{F}(\mathbf{v}_{-i}). \qquad (C.5)$$

I should stress that all this maneuvering was just notational. Our immediate goal has been no more ambitious than to rewrite equation C.3 in terms of the more general allocation and payment functions $Q_i(z)$ and $P_i(z)$ of the direct mechanism. We're there. This expected surplus, as a function of the reported value z, is just

$$S_i(z) = v_i Q_i(z) - P_i(z), \qquad (C.6)$$

where the subscripts i of $Q_i(z)$ and $P_i(z)$ reflect the fact that the bidders are no longer symmetric, and hence these functions vary in general from bidder to bidder.

C.5.1 Interlude: Revenue Equivalence Revisited in the Asymmetric-Bidder case

Before we concentrate on an optimal selling mechanism in the asymmetric case, we return for a moment to the correspondingly more general version of revenue equivalence. The more general setting forces us to step even farther away from the details than we have before, and, remarkably, the proof of revenue equivalence becomes even easier.[7]

Suppose, as above, that bidder i reports her value to be z when it is really v_i. Differentiate equation C.6 with respect to z and impose the condition that this must be zero when the reported value z is equal to the true value v_i, reflecting the fact that bidding truthfully is equilibrium behavior in a direct mechanism. This yields

$$v_i Q_i'(v_i) - P_i'(v_i) = 0. \tag{C.7}$$

On the other hand, the total derivative of equation C.6 with respect to v_i when $z = v_i$ is

$$S_i'(v_i) = v_i Q_i'(v_i) + Q_i(v_i) - P_i'(v_i). \tag{C.8}$$

Using equation C.7 in this gives us the astonishingly simple relation

$$S_i'(v_i) = Q_i(v_i). \tag{C.9}$$

Integrating, we get the following explicit expression for the expected surplus as a function of valuation:

$$S_i(v_i) = S_i(0) + \int_0^{v_i} Q_i(x)\,dx. \tag{C.10}$$

The expected surplus of bidder i is just $v_i Q_i(v_i) - P_i(v_i)$, so we can put this in terms of expected payments:

$$P_i(v_i) = P_i(0) + v_i Q_i(v_i) - \int_0^{v_i} Q_i(x)\,dx. \tag{C.11}$$

Voilà! The expected payment of every bidder depends only on the allocation function, so all selling mechanisms with the same allocations result in the same revenue to the seller. There we have revenue equivalence in this more general setting.

[7] This proof is due to Myerson (1981), but I've sidestepped some technicalities and, as usual, stuck to freshman calculus. Klemperer (1999) and Krishna (2002) provide other variations.

C.5.2 *The Optimal Allocation Rule*

We can now carry Riley and Samuelson's program forward in exactly the same way as in the symmetric case.[8] The same manipulations, starting with equation C.7, lead to the following expression for the expected payment of bidder i, analogous to equation B.11, but now individualized to bidder i in the asymmetric case (see question 1):

$$E[P_i(\mathbf{v})] = P_i(0) + \int_{\mathbf{v}} MR_i(v_i)Q_i(\mathbf{v}) \, d\mathbf{F}(\mathbf{v}), \qquad \text{(C.12)}$$

where the marginal revenue is now specific to bidder i,

$$MR(v_i) = v_i - \frac{1 - F_i(v_i)}{f_i(v_i)}. \qquad \text{(C.13)}$$

There is one small difference here, in the way we treat the boundary conditions. Instead of using the entry value v_*, where the expected payment is zero, we average from the minimum bid of zero and use the expected payment $P_i(0)$ explicitly for each bidder. We'll see shortly that reserves are handled in this framework in a different and more elegant way than in the symmetric case.

The total expected revenue to the seller is simply the sum of the contributions from all the bidders, or

$$R_m = \sum_i P_i(0) + \int_{\mathbf{v}} \sum_i MR_i(v_i)Q_i(\mathbf{v}) \, d\mathbf{F}(\mathbf{v}), \qquad \text{(C.14)}$$

where we use R_m for Myerson's revenue, in the asymmetric case, in place of R_{rs} for Riley and Samuelson's revenue.

I now want to argue that in an optimal auction, one that maximizes revenue, the payments $P_i(0)$ are all zero. To see this, recall from equation C.10 that the expected surplus when the item has value v is an increasing function of v. Thus, $S_i(0)$ is the lowest possible value that $S_i(v)$ can take on. Furthermore, the surplus to a bidder with value zero is just $S_i(0) = -P_i(0)$, and it is therefore in the interest of the seller to

---

[8] We also use the paper by Bulow and Roberts (1989), which played an important role in interpreting the Myerson results in graphical terms, and relating optimal auctions to monopoly theory.

have $S_i(0)$ as small as possible. But no bidder will agree to participate in an auction when she is required to pay more than zero for an item that is worth nothing to her.[9] So the seller can do no better than to arrange the sale in the optimal case so that $P_i(0) = -S_i(0) = 0$.[10]

The expected revenue can therefore be written, finally, as

$$R_m = \int_{\mathbf{V}} \sum_i MR_i(v_i)Q_i(\mathbf{v}) \, d\mathbf{F}(\mathbf{v}). \tag{C.15}$$

Equation C.15 is the heart of the matter. First, it shows us that the expected revenue depends only on the allocation rule $\mathbf{Q}$ of the direct mechanism, and not on the payment rule $\mathbf{P}$. But it tells us much more than that; it tells us how to select an allocation rule that maximizes seller revenue. The idea is to use the allocation rule $\mathbf{Q}$ to select the term in the summation that contributes the most to the overall integral. This is easy: we need only look at the maximum value of the $MR_i(v_i)$, $i = 1, \ldots, n$, which occurs, say at i^*, and observe whether or not the corresponding $MR_{i^*}(v_{i^*})$ is positive. If it is, we set $Q_{i^*}(\mathbf{v}) = 1$, and all the other components $Q_i(\mathbf{v})$ to zero. If, on the other hand, the maximum value of the $MR_i(v_i)$, $i = 1, \ldots, n$, is less than zero (as usual, ignore ties), the seller should hold on to the item, there is no allocation, and we set all the $Q_i(\mathbf{v}) = 0$.

To summarize, if

$$\max_i\{MR_i\} > 0, \tag{C.16}$$

the item is awarded to the bidder with the highest MR. If, on the other hand,

$$\max_i\{MR_i\} \le 0, \tag{C.17}$$

the item is retained by the seller.

Figure C.2 shows a graphical representation of this allocation process when there are two bidders (Bulow and Roberts, 1989). For simplicity, assume for now that value distributions are uniform on intervals $[a, b]$,

[9] The constraint that agents will participate only if their expected surplus is non-negative is sometimes called a *participation constraint*. Agents who behave in this way are called *individually rational*.

[10] We will see shortly that this is possible. See question 2.

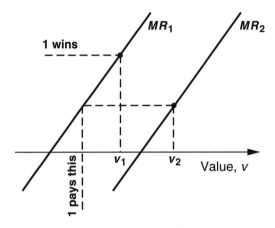

Figure C.2 The determination of winner and payment in an optimal auction, using Myerson's result for asymmetric bidder distributions. There are two bidders with uniform distributions on different intervals.

which means that

$$f = 1/(b - a), \qquad a \le v \le b,$$
$$F = (v - a)/(b - a), \qquad a \le v \le b, \tag{C.18}$$

and

$$MR(v) = 2v - b. \tag{C.19}$$

Thus, each bidder is represented by an ascending straight line of the form $2v - b_i$. When the bidders draw random values of v_1 and v_2, the winner is determined by the higher of $MR_1(v_1)$ and $MR_2(v_2)$, provided the higher of the two is greater than zero. Otherwise, the seller keeps the item. Notice that the lowest possible value that can result in bidder i winning the item varies from bidder to bidder; in effect, the seller has tailored a different reserve for each bidder—specifically the value for which $MR_i(v) = 0$. In this example, when values are distributed uniformly on intervals, each bidder's reserve is the intercept $v_i = b_i/2$. It is reassuring that this is consistent with the optimal reserve in the special case when the bidders are symmetric with values uniform on the unit interval, when the optimal reserve is 1/2, as we saw in appendix B.

The intercepts and values in figure C.2 were chosen to illustrate the fact that, in general, this mechanism can be inefficient. Bidder 1's value v_1 is below v_2, but bidder 1 wins. This comes as no shock, we are already reconciled to the fact that optimality of revenue must come at this price.

We still have some work remaining to complete the specification of Myerson's direct mechanism. In particular, we need to specify the payment rule, and then we need to verify that the proposed payment rule, together with the allocation rule, provide bidders with the incentives to report their values truthfully—that the mechanism is incentive compatible.

C.5.3 The Payment Rule

Myerson's mechanism must reduce to a Riley and Samuelson auction that is truthful in the special case when bidders are symmetric, and this observation gives us a strong clue that the appropriate payment mechanism must be something like the one in a conventional second-price auction. In fact, when bidders are symmetric, all their marginal revenue curves coincide, and the winner pays the lowest she can while still winning, just the second price, reflecting the dynamics of the English auction. This generalizes naturally to the following payment rule **P**: If bidder i wins the item, she pays the lowest she can while still having the highest marginal revenue. Figure C.2 shows the situation. Imagine bidder 1's value v_1 sliding left until $MR_1(v_1)$ just wins; her payment is indicated.

It is now easy to verify that with this payment rule, there is an incentive for bidders to report their values truthfully. The argument is Vickrey's, once again. If bidder 1 were to report a value slightly above v_1, say $v_1 + \epsilon$, it would introduce the possibility that another bid could land between v_1 and $v_1 + \epsilon$, in which case bidder 1 might pay more then her value, and incur a loss. If another bid does not happen to land in this interval, the resulting payment is the same, so the slightly higher bid can only hurt bidder 1. The argument against underreporting is similar. If bidder 1 reports a value below v_1, she might miss an opportunity for surplus, but can never gain, so we can conclude that the Myerson mechanism with this payment rule is incentive compatible.

C.5.4 *A Wrinkle*

The construction of an optimal mechanism just concluded uses the fact that every marginal revenue is an increasing function of v (see question 3), in which case we call the corresponding distribution $F(v)$ *regular*. Many common distributions, such as the uniform one in this section, are regular, but some are not (see question 4). Fortunately, Myerson (1981) was able to extend the construction of the optimal mechanism to nonregular distributions, but we won't go into the process here.

C.5.5 *Is This Practical?*

We ought to consider whether this optimal mechanism could be made to work in practice. Suppose first we use the usual indirect bid-taking mechanism. As a first requirement, the value distributions of the bidders must be common knowledge to the bidders—but this is a standard assumption if we expect bidders to find equilibrium behavior. Also, the seller needs to know the bidders' value distributions, so he can calculate the winner's payment. Then we require that the bidders go along with the prescription: they must submit bids $MR_i(v_i)$, accept the outcome that the highest MR wins the auction, and, further, accept the winning price as determined by the second-highest MR. Alternatively, if we use the (theoretically equivalent) direct mechanism, we require perhaps even more of the bidders: they must agree to submit their true values, and to accept the fact that the bidder with the highest reported value does not always win the auction.

All this is a tall order. To be more realistic, we should retreat to the position that we can't really expect bidders and sellers to know value distributions, or to act on the information in such sophisticated ways—even allowing for the fact that equilibrium behavior can, sometimes, be learned by trial and error. What we can take away from the theory, though, is guidance and insight. In the next two sections we describe a beautiful example of how the mathematical constructs we've been working with, which may at times seem far removed from the everyday decisions we might face in buying and selling in auctions, can nevertheless give us very useful advice.

C.6 Optimal Riley and Samuelson Auctions
Are Optimal Mechanisms

We can now put together a short chain of results to show that when bidders' values are symmetrically distributed, independent, and private, an auction with an optimally chosen reserve—in other words an optimal auction in Riley and Samuelson's class $\mathcal{A}_{rs}$—is at least as good as any mechanism whatsoever for selling an object. Such general mechanisms include any sort of negotiations or bargaining, and this is therefore a very strong statement.

The reasoning is actually very direct. First, the revelation principle allows us to restrict attention to direct mechanisms. Second, we know that all direct mechanisms with the same allocation rule have the same revenue (eq. C.15). Third, since the marginal revenues are increasing functions of value (here we use the regularity assumption), an optimal mechanism allocates the item to the bidder with the highest value, as does every auction in $\mathcal{A}_{rs}$. Therefore, all the optimal auctions in $\mathcal{A}_{rs}$ are optimal mechanisms. To summarize:

RESULT 5 Assuming that the underlying value distribution is regular, any optimal auction in Riley and Samuelson's class $\mathcal{A}_{rs}$ is an optimal selling mechanism. □

C.7 Auctions vs. Negotiations

In a famous paper, Bulow and Klemperer (1996) propose a comparison between the following two ways to sell an item. We assume that the item has zero value to the seller.

Sale 1 First, there is only one buyer, her value is uniformly distributed on [0, 1], and the seller is free to choose any selling mechanism at all.

Sale 2 Second, there are two buyers, with iid values, also uniformly distributed on [0, 1], and the seller is constrained to run a standard auction with no reserve.[11]

---

[11] No-reserve auctions are sometimes called *absolute* auctions.

Which situation yields the most revenue to the seller? We can work this out easily. In Sale 1, we know that the optimal mechanism is also an optimal auction in Riley and Samuelson's class, and that the optimal reserve is given by the point at which the marginal revenue becomes zero. The marginal revenue in the uniform case is $MR(v) = 2v - 1$, so, as we've seen before, the optimal reserve is $v_* = 1/2$. We can then use equation B.11 to find the expected revenue.[12] There is only one bidder, and the integral works out to be 1/4. In Sale 2, equation B.11 can now be used with two bidders and no reserve; the integral works out to be 1/3.

So the no-reserve auction with two bidders yields more expected revenue than the optimal auction with only one bidder. Furthermore, as we noted in section C.6, this optimal auction is the best of all possible negotiations. The extra bidder in a no-reserve auction is worth more to the seller than the advantage of using the best of all possible negotiating strategies with one buyer.

It turns out that this result is not just a fluke in this special case, but holds when we compare n against $n + 1$ bidders for any n, at least with the assumption that their values are iid, private, and have a regular distribution. We prove this next. It takes a few steps, but isn't difficult.

Consider first Sale 1 with n bidders. Since we assume that the common distribution is regular, the expected revenue for an optimal mechanism is, by the derivation in section C.5, the expected value of the maximum of the $MR(v)$'s, provided this maximum is nonnegative. We can write this as

$$R_1 = E[\max\{MR(v_1), \ldots, MR(v_n), 0\}]. \qquad (C.20)$$

Similarly, the expected revenue in the no-reserve auction with n bidders is

$$R_2 = E[\max\{MR(v_1), \ldots, MR(v_n), MR(v_{n+1})\}]. \qquad (C.21)$$

The only difference between the two expressions is that we have zero in R_1 where we have $MR(v_{n+1})$ in R_2. Our claim is that the expectation of the second is greater than or equal to the expectation of the first.

---

[12] It might be good review to use the more general equation C.14. In this case the allocation function $Q_1(\mathbf{v})$ is just 0 when $v_1 < v_2$ and 1 when $v_1 \geq v_2$, and similarly for $Q_2(\mathbf{v})$.

To see why this is true, consider first the expectation of $MR(v)$. This is just the expected revenue in a no-reserve auction with only one bidder, which must be zero, because the bidder can always win the object by bidding zero (see question 7). We therefore have the expectation of the maximum of $n + 1$ random variables, the first n of which are the same, and the $(n + 1)$st of which is zero in R_1, and a zero-mean random variable in R_2.

Break the rest of the argument into two cases:

CASE 1 Consider all the realizations of values where

$$T_n = \max\{MR(v_1), \ldots, MR(v_n)\} \geq 0. \qquad (\text{C.22})$$

Then

$$R_2 - R_1 = E[\max\{T_n, MR(v_{n+1})\}] - E[\max\{T_n, 0\}]$$

$$= E[\max\{T_n, MR(v_{n+1})\}] - E[T_n]$$

$$\geq 0, \qquad (\text{C.23})$$

since the maximum can only increase the result. $\qquad \square$

CASE 2 Now suppose that

$$T_n = \max\{MR(v_1), \ldots, MR(v_n)\} < 0. \qquad (\text{C.24})$$

Then

$$R_2 - R_1 = E[\max\{T_n, MR(v_{n+1})\}] - E[\max\{T_n, 0\}]$$

$$= E[\max\{T_n, MR(v_{n+1})\}] - 0$$

$$\geq E[MR(v_{n+1})] = 0, \qquad (\text{C.25})$$

since, again, the maximum can only increase the result. $\qquad \square$

We can summarize the conclusion informally as:

RESULT 6 A *no-reserve* auction in Riley and Samuelson class $\mathcal{A}_{rs}$ with $n + 1$ bidders will yield at least as much revenue in expectation as any negotiation with n bidders.[13] $\qquad \square$

---

[13] Besides proving Result 6, Bulow and Klemperer (1996) also provide generalizations in the direction of affiliated values, but not in the direction of asymmetrical bidders.

This conclusion gives us a big hint about how best to sell, at least to the extent that we are willing to go along with the underlying assumptions. If we swallow the argument whole, the benefits seem quite spectacular. Instead of fussing over the optimal setting of a reserve, or, more generally, deciding on the best of all possible negotiating schemes—perhaps of nightmarish complexity—we adopt the quiet alternative of a no-reserve auction in any of the standard formats. And we devote all our energy to attracting more bidders. The news is too good to be true, of course, and our usual skepticism about the model assumptions must nag us with the usual worries: bidders are asymmetric, their values are neither private nor independent, and they don't necessarily follow equilibrium behavior even if they know it.

C.8 Summary

We have concluded our brief survey of the main results, the pearls, the plums—what economists call the "received theory." This theory tells us a great deal when we can assume that values are independently distributed and private: We know how to sell an item in a way that maximizes revenue. In the symmetric bidder case we accomplish this using any standard auction with an appropriately chosen reserve. In the asymmetric case, we need a more general mechanism, one that uses marginal revenues. We need to sacrifice efficiency to achieve revenue maximization, but we are rewarded with a more general version of revenue equivalence. In some special situations, we can even claim that auctions are the best of all negotiating mechanisms.

On the other hand, when bidders are, quite reasonably, unsure of their values, or when values are not statistically independent, many of these results become shaky, if not invalid. But the ideas are beautiful and suggestive; they give us tools, a grammar, to help us think about auctions.

Theory is not much good without empirical confirmation, to which we turn next.

C.9 Questions

1. Fill in the steps leading from equation C.6 to equation C.12. Hint: We already have an integration over $\mathbf{V}_{-i}$ built in to $Q_i(z)$. The integration to average the payment over v_i extends the integration to the entire space of values $\mathbf{V}$.

2. Check that the payment rule in Myerson's optimal mechanism results in $P_i(0) = 0$ for any bidder i. We argued that the seller wants to arrange this so as to maximize revenue.

3. At what points in the construction of Myerson's optimal mechanism with asymmetric bidders did we rely on the assumption that the marginal revenues were increasing?

4. Construct an example of a value distribution that corresponds to a marginal revenue that is not increasing.

5. What is the marginal revenue corresponding to the exponential distribution, $F(v) = 1 - e^{-\lambda v}$?

6. Check the expected revenue calculations for the examples of Sale 1 and Sale 2 (with one and two bidders) in section C.7. What is the expected revenue with one bidder and no reserve?

7. In section C.7 we argued that the expected value of $MR(v)$ is zero because it is the expected revenue in a standard no-reserve auction with only one bidder. Show the same thing algebraically.

Laboratory Evidence: A Summary

D.1 Introduction

There are three main kinds of empirical evidence for how people behave in auctions:

- *Laboratory experiments*: Collection from artificial auctions, devised for the purpose, with recruited subjects;
- *Field observations*: Passive data collection from real auctions;
- *Field experiments*: Collection from real auctions initiated by the observer.

All this work is relatively new, especially that in the second and third categories, which has become possible on a reasonably large scale only with the arrival of internet. But the first kind of work, in the "laboratory," is by far the most mature, and this appendix is devoted to summarizing its current generally accepted results. I'll try to stick to conclusions that can be drawn safely at this time, and be conservative about what I consider an established experimental fact.

Because of the control over the experimental conditions, laboratory settings can give us some important insights into how auction theory, and economic theory in general, works—and doesn't work. Many theoretical results have such special setups that they are almost impossible to test in real auctions. On the other hand, the work in categories 2 and 3, while less controllable, is more directly relevant to the aim of this book. It is usually tied to real internet auctions with deadlines, and an uncertain number of diverse bidders. So when I've been aware of relevant work in these latter two categories, which is usually very recent, I've either described it in the main text, or at least mentioned it there.

D.2 Laboratory Experiments

Experimental work in auctions started in the early 1980s, when several groups began testing the implications of the newly developed theory in controlled laboratory settings. Typically, these experiments are conducted with volunteer student subjects or captive classes, but sometimes with experienced professional bidders, either with modest amounts of real money, or with fictitious currency redeemable at the end of the experiment. Almost always, subjects are granted a budget with which to participate, and stand to gain a positive surplus, on the average, by participating. University experiments that in the long run extract money from students would not go over well with the administration, not to mention the students, but there are occasions when taking money from a subject is necessary to make a point, as we will see when we come to experiments with the common-value model.[1]

Any time we discuss experiments in economics, the following nagging question arises: Do people behave the same way in the real world as they do under controlled laboratory conditions? In the real world they are bidding on items of some importance to themselves, often spending significant sums, and participating on their own initiative. In the laboratory, subjects are usually spending relatively small amounts of money, and not their own money at that, so we might expect them to take more risks. Perhaps the caged animal behaves differently in the wild.

Vernon Smith, a pioneer in the field of experimental economics, gives a name to the hypothesis that people behave the same way in the laboratory as they do in the field: he calls the principle *parallelism* (1982). Whenever conclusions from the field clash with those from the laboratory, it is always necessary to consider as an explanation the possibility that parallelism has failed. Katok and Kwasnica (2002), for example, raise this possibility in their study of the effect of clock speed in Dutch auctions, which we discuss in section 6.5.1.

We conclude this appendix with a summary of those results of laboratory experiments that seem clear from the literature and are

---

[1] We might argue that a subject who is relieved of money in such a classroom experiment is amply compensated by the bonus education, but the wise instructor will see to it that any profit is fed back to the class in a more tangible form as well, such as pizza.

generally accepted—first for the independent private-value model, and then for the common-value model.

D.3 Experimental Results for the IPV Model

The literature reporting the results of laboratory experiments with private-value auctions is a bit hazardous to summarize, mainly because the field is relatively new, and some experiments have simply not yet been run, or have been run only once or twice. Furthermore, some reported results conflict with others. For example, the very first[2] published experiment with independent private values, Coppinger, Smith, and Titus (1980), produced results consistent with revenue equivalence between second-price and English auctions, confirming Vickrey's theoretical prediction. The paper itself, however, describes its work as "preliminary," and, in fact, later work leads to the general conclusion that prices in the second-price auction are higher, as we will see below. When I compiled this section, therefore, I found myself surrounded by stacks of papers, at times befuddled. My solution was to be very conservative about drawing conclusions when there was any doubt at all. This sorting-out-on-the-floor process also explains why you will find this section more peppered with citations and footnotes than usual.

I also worry about whether subjects across experiments have the same background and level of experience. People continually learn strategies for bidding in auctions (as in all games), and illustrating this is one of the points of running experiments in class. On eBay the "newbie" is a recognizable type, with a low feedback total, and a propensity for engaging in early, incremental bidding and climactic wars. The behavior of a scarred veteran is likely to be quite different.

To continue with general caveats, it is critically important that experiments be repeated with exactly the same instructions to the participants and rules, and not all published reports make those details clear. A particularly alarming example of a variation in protocol that could lead to confusion is pointed out by Kagel (1995, p. 511).

---

[2] According to Davis and Holt (1993).

The question is how subjects bid in sealed-bid second-price auctions, and in particular, whether they follow their dominant (truthful) strategy. Cox, Roberson, and Smith (1982) point out that prices in the second-price auction converge to truthful values from below, but it turns out on careful reading that subjects in the experiment were prohibited by the rules from bidding above their values.[3]

Kagel (1995, chapter 7) has given us a careful and extensive survey of the experimental literature as of the mid-1990s, and I relied on that source in trying to sort out the published results in laboratory auctions, in this section as well as the next (for common-value auctions).[4]

The conclusions fall into two categories: those that establish the relative sizes of the revenues in two auction forms (so-called "revenue ranking"), and those that establish the size of revenue relative to that predicted by Nash equilibrium behavior (so-called "point predictions"). A good place to start is with the clearest and most generally accepted result, a ranking comparing first-price and Dutch:

- *Revenue equivalence between first-price and Dutch auctions in the independent private-value case fails, with prices in first-price exceeding those in Dutch (First-Price > Dutch).*

The result is reported in the first paper on laboratory auctions with independently distributed, private values, Coppinger et al. (1980), and has been confirmed by several subsequent papers.[5]

This verified and least controversial fact of experimental auction theory is very difficult to explain, because, as we discussed in chapter 1, the first-price and Dutch auctions are not only revenue equivalent, but

[3] Cox et al. (1982, pp. 19–20) did this for a reason: they wanted to design their experiments so that the range of possible price outcomes in the Dutch and second-price auctions was the same. Actually, their Dutch experiment started a few ticks above the highest possible valuation. I'll cite Cox et al. (1982) below, but not when second-price auctions are involved.

[4] Also useful is the comprehensive Davis and Holt (1993), which treats all of experimental economics, and has a half-chapter on experimental auctions. It also includes a good discussion of experimental design and statistical analysis, with further references. Both these sources just missed the arrival of internet auctions, and with that the exciting new work using field data.

[5] For example, Cox et al. (1982); Cox, Smith, and Walker (1983, 1988); and Dyer, Kagel, and Levin (1989b).

strategically equivalent. But our job in this appendix is to set down the more or less established results of laboratory experimentation, and we will leave discussion of these questions to the main text.

Not only are prices in first-price auctions higher than those of Dutch, but

- *Bidding in first-price auctions is above the Nash equilibrium (First-Price > Nash).*

Kagel (1995) includes two plots from Dyer et al. (1989b) that show this very clearly, both for 3 bidders and 6 bidders. Furthermore, the plots go on for 20 consecutive auction periods, which shows that the bidders do not learn the Nash equilibrium, even when given many opportunities. I should point out that I refer here to the Nash equilibrium assuming that bidders are *risk neutral.* I prefer to think of risk aversion as one way of explaining this deviation, rather than defining the equilibrium itself.

On the other hand, it seems uncertain whether bidding in Dutch auctions is consistently above the Nash equilibrium. Kagel (1995) cites some evidence to this effect in Cox et al. (1982), for more than 3 bidders, but *not* for 3 bidders. I'll be conservative, and pass on this question.

The evidence is good[6] that revenue equivalence of English and second-price auctions also breaks down:

- *Bidding in second-price auctions is above that in English auctions (Second-Price > English).*

But bidding in English auctions does converge quickly to truthful bidding (which is, of course, also the Nash equilibrium):

- *Bidding in English auctions approaches truthful bidding with learning (English → Nash),*

where I use "→" to indicate that some learning still seems to be necessary, even though we might think that remaining silent when the bidding has exceeded one's value would be the most natural thing in the world.

---

[6] See Kagel et al. (1987) and Kagel and Levin (1993).

We have left to consider the relative ranking between second-price and first-price auctions, and this question doesn't seem to be settled with any certainty at this point. Kagel and Levin (1993) report that in their experiments the average revenues "were significantly greater" in first-price auctions than in second-price auctions for 5 bidders, but not for 10 bidders. Again, I'll pass on this question, although Lucking-Reiley (1999, footnote, p. 1066) does conclude in his summary of the literature that "First-price auctions consistently earn higher revenues than do second-price auctions."

To collect the firmly established experimental facts about average prices in independent private-value auctions, based on the work to date:

Second-Price > English → Nash

First-Price > Dutch

First-Price > Nash (Risk Neutral)

From the beginning, and through the 1980s and 1990s, auction experiments in the laboratory have focused on the most fundamental theory for the four standard auction forms. The majority of experiments have tested, first, the classic pair of theoretical revenue equivalences, and second, the bidding levels in the case of independent, private values. This is not hard to understand. The revenue equivalence of first-price and Dutch auctions is based on the very strong principle of strategic equivalence, and that between second-price and English auctions is based on the principle of dominant strategy (at least for the Japanese button version of the English auction). The theoretical prediction of absolute bidding levels in first-price and Dutch auctions is based on the idea that bidders find and play Nash equilibria. Here we have experimental testing of the most basic building blocks of the theory, and the finding of some significant violations as well as confirmations. Serious work—with implications for all of economics.

D.4 Experimental Results for the Common-Value Model

The experimental picture is much simpler for the common-value model than for the independent private-value model. Almost all the laboratory experiments deal in one way or another with the winner's curse, and the verdict is clear: The winner's curse is real and persistent. In fact, it was recognized and understood from empirical evidence by 1971, when Capen, Clapp, and Campbell published their remarkable study of auctions in government Outer Continental Shelf (OCS) lease auctions, for offshore drilling rights. The general phenomenon was treated theoretically even earlier by Robert Wilson in 1969.

Again, Kagel (1995) provides an excellent survey of the experimental results. He describes a representative study in the paper of Kagel, Levin, Battalio, and Meyer (1989), which reports the results of a study of profits in first-price common-value auctions. Although the theoretical expected profits at (risk-neutral) Nash equilibrium were positive in these experiments, inexperienced subjects realized positive profits in only 17% of the auction periods. He summarizes the results in several papers quite forcibly (p. 540): "The winner's curse for inexperienced bidders is a genuinely pervasive problem, which has been reported under a variety of treatment conditions (Kagel et al., 1989; Lind and Plott, 1991) and for different subject populations, including professional bidders from the commercial construction industry (Dyer, Kagel, and Levin 1989a)."

Kagel and Levin (1986) report results for experienced bidders— bidders who have participated in previous similar experiments. *With three or four bidders*, the profits are now positive, but still below the theoretical prediction for equilibrium behavior. They also verify the theoretical prediction of Milgrom and Weber (1982) that public information increases revenue, *with three or four bidders*, but again, not as much as predicted by the theoretical equilibrium.

What is most interesting from the behavioral point of view is that with *six or seven bidders*, both weak confirmations of the theory are reversed. That is, with more bidders, bidding becomes more aggressive, and the winner's curse returns. Furthermore, public information *reduced* seller revenue, the opposite of what we would expect from theory. Kagel and Levin attribute this last effect to the fact that the announced public information was the lowest signal value, and that this tends to cause the highest bidder to revise her (overestimated) value downward when the winner's curse is large. Just why experienced subjects return to over-aggressive bidding when the number of rivals increases remains something of a mystery. Kagel and Levin (1986, p. 917) conclude, "Bidders have learned to avoid the winner's curse in small groups out of a trial and error survival process, as opposed to 'understanding' the adverse-selection problem as it applies to new situations."

So Kagel and Levin explain the failures of theory as the number of rivals increases in terms of rational, if insufficiently sophisticated, thinking. But there is an alternative explanation which is based on more emotional factors. We have seen throughout this book that competitive pressure can in many settings lead to bidding wars, price bubbles, and, in general, overbidding with respect to equilibria. It may be that these psychological effects are disproportionately amplified with larger numbers of rivals. Disentangling the rational and emotional forces in human behavior is perhaps the greatest challenge lying ahead in the study of auctions.

REFERENCES

Ashenfelter, O. 1989. How auctions work for wine and art. *Journal of Economic Perspectives*, 3(3):23–36.

Ashenfelter, O., and Graddy, K. 2002. Art auctions: A survey of empirical studies. Center for Economic Policy Research Discussion Paper 3387, London, UK.

Ausubel, L. M., and Cramton, P. 1998. Demand reduction and inefficiency in multi-unit auctions. Working paper, University of Maryland.

Avery, C. 1998. Strategic jump bidding in English auctions. *Review of Economic Studies*, 65:185–210.

Axelrod, R. 1984. *The Evolution of Cooperation*. Basic Books, New York.

Bajari, P., and Hortaçsu, A. 2002. The winner's curse, reserve prices and endogenous entry: Empirical insights from eBay auctions. Working paper, Stanford University and University of Chicago.

Bapna, R., Jank, W., and Shmueli, G. 2004. Consumer surplus in on line auctions. Working paper, Department of Operations and Information Management, University of Connecticut School of Business, Storrs, CT.

Bauwens, L., and Ginsburgh, V. 2000. Art experts and auctions: Are pre-sale estimates unbiased and fully informative? *Recherches Economiques du Louvain*, 66(1):131–144.

Beggs, A., and Graddy, K. 1997. Declining values and the afternoon effect: Evidence from art auctions. *RAND Journal of Economics*, 28(3):544–565.

Boyd, J. 2001. Virtual orality: How eBay controls auctions without an auctioneer's voice. *American Speech*, 76(3):286–300.

Bulow, J., and Klemperer, P. 1994. Rational frenzies and crashes. *Journal Political Economy*, 102(1):1–23.

Bulow, J., and Klemperer, P. 1996. Auctions versus negotiations. *American Economic Review*, 86(1):180–194.

Bulow, J., and Roberts, J. 1989. The simple economics of optimal auctions. *Journal of Political Economy*, 97(5):1060–1090.

Caginalp, G., and Balenovich, D. 1993. Market oscillations induced by the competition between value-based and trend-based investment strategies. Economic Science Association Fall Meeting, Tucson, AZ.

Capen, E. C., Clapp, R. V., and Campbell, W. M. 1971. Competitive bidding in high-risk situations. *Journal of Petroleum Technology*, 32:641–653.

Case, J. H. 1979. *Economics and the Competitive Process.* New York University Press, New York.

Cassady, R. 1967. *Auctions and Auctioneering.* University of California Press, Berkeley. Reprinted by the University of California Press, July 1980.

Chanel, O., Gérard-Varet, L.-A., and Vincent, S. 1996. Auction theory and practice: Evidence from a market for jewellry. In V. Ginsburgh and P.-M. Menger, editors, *Economics of the Arts: Selected Essays.* Elsevier, Amsterdam.

Chippindale, C., and Gill, W. J. 2001. On-line auctions: A new venue for the antiquities market. *Culture without Context,* Newsletter of the Illicit Antiquities Research Centre, Cambridge University, UK, issue 9, http://www.mcdonald.cam.ac.uk/IARC/cwoc/issue9/internet.htm.

Coppinger, V. M., Smith, V. L., and Titus, J. A. 1980. Incentives and behavior in English, Dutch, and sealed-bid auctions. *Economic Inquiry,* 18:1–22.

Cox, J. C., Roberson, B., and Smith, V. L. 1982. Theory and behavior of single object auctions. In V. Smith, editor, *Research in Experimental Economics,* vol. 2, pp. 1–43. JAI Press, Greenwich, CT.

Cox, J. C., Smith, V. L., and Walker, J. M. 1983. A test that discriminates between two models of the Dutch-first non-isomorphism. *Journal of Economic Behavior and Organization,* 4(2–3):205–219.

Cox, J. C., Smith, V. L., and Walker, J. M. 1988. Theory and individual behavior of first-price auctions. *Journal of Risk and Uncertainty,* 1:61–99.

Cramér, H. 1946. *Mathematical Methods of Statistics.* Princeton University Press, Princeton, NJ.

Davis, D. D., and Holt, C. A. 1993. *Experimental Economics.* Princeton University Press, Princeton, NJ.

Dyer, D., Kagel, J. H., and Levin, D. 1989a. A comparison of naive and experienced bidders in common value offer auctions: A laboratory analysis. *Economic Journal,* 99:108–115.

Dyer, D., Kagel, J. H., and Levin, D. 1989b. Resolving uncertainty about the number of bidders in independent private-value auctions: An experimental analysis. *RAND Journal of Economics,* 20:268–279.

Engelbrecht-Wiggans, R., Milgrom, P. R., and Weber, R. J. 1983. Competitive bidding and proprietary information. *Journal of Mathematical Economics,* 11:161–169.

Forsythe, R., Isaac, R. M., and Palfrey, T. R. 1989. Theories and tests of "blind bidding" in sealed-bid auctions. *RAND Journal of Economics,* 20(2).

Foster, K. R., Wenseleers, T., and Ratnieks, F.L.W. 2001. Spite: Hamilton's unproven theory. *Annales Zoologici Fennici,* 38:229–238.

Gadagkar, R. 1993. Can animals be spiteful? *Trends in Ecology and Evolution*, 8:232–234. See also L. Keller, M. Milinski, M. Frischknecht, N. Perrin, H. Richner, and F. Tripet, Spiteful animals still to be discovered, ibid., 9:103, and reply.

Gibbon, E. 1776. *The Decline and Fall of the Roman Empire*, vol. 1. Modern Library, New York, no date. Originally published 1776–88.

Gintis, H. 2000. *Game Theory Evolving*. Princeton University Press, Princeton, NJ.

Graham, D. A., and Marshall, R. C. 1987. Collusive bidding behavior at single-object second price and English auctions. *Journal of Political Economy*, 95(6):1217–1239.

Graham, D. A., Marshall, R. C., and Richard, J.-F. 1990. Phantom bidding against heterogeneous bidders. *Economics Letters*, 32:13–17.

Hamilton, W. D. 1970. Selfish and spiteful behaviour in an evolutionary model. *Nature*, 228:1218–1220.

Hill, G. F. 1924. *Becker, the Counterfeiter*. Spink and Son, Ltd., London. Two volumes, 1924–25.

Holt, C. A., and Sherman, R. 2000. Risk aversion and the winner's curse. Working paper, University of Virginia, Charlottesville, VA.

Hossain, T., and Morgan, R. J. 2003. Test of the revenue equivalence theorem using field experiments on eBay. Working paper, Haas School of Business and Department of Economics, University of California at Berkeley, http://faculty.haas.berkeley.edu/rjmorgan/.

Izmalkov, S. 2004. Shill bidding and optimal auctions. Working paper, Department of Economics, MIT, Cambridge, MA.

Kagel, J. H. 1995. Auctions: A survey of experimental research. In J. Kagel and A. Roth, editors, *The Handbook of Experimental Economics*. Princeton University Press, Princeton, NJ.

Kagel, J. H., Harstad, R. M., and Levin, D. 1987. Information impact and allocation rules in auctions with affiliated private values: A laboratory study. *Econometrica*, 55:1275–1304.

Kagel, J. H., and Levin, D. 1986. The winner's curse and public information in common value auctions. *American Economic Review*, 76:894–920. See also comment on this paper by J. C. Cox, S. H. Dinkin, and V. L. Smith, *American Economic Review* 89 (1999):319–324; and the reply by C. M. Campbell, J. H. Kagel, and D. Levin, 89 (1999): 324–334.

Kagel, J. H., and Levin, D. 1993. Independent private value auctions: Bidder behavior in first-, second-, and third-price auctions with varying numbers of bidders. *Economic Journal*, 103:868–879.

Kagel, J. H., Levin, D., Battalio, R., and Meyer, D. J. 1989. First-price common value auctions: Bidder behavior and the winner's curse. *Economic Inquiry*, 27:241–258.

Kahneman, D., Knetsch, J. L., and Thaler, R. H. 1990. Experimental tests of the endowment effect and the coase theorem. *Journal of Political Economy*, 98(6):1325–1348.

Kahneman, D., and Tversky, A. 1979. Prospect theory; An analysis of decision under risk. *Econometrica*, 47:263–291.

Katkar, R., and Lucking-Reiley, D. 2000. Public versus secret reserve prices in eBay auctions: Results from a Pokémon field experiment. Working paper, Department of Economics, Vanderbilt University, http://eller.arizona.edu/~reiley/cv.html.

Katok, E., and Kwasnica, A. M. 2002. Time is money: The effect of clock speed on seller's revenue in Dutch auctions. Working paper, MS&IS Department, Pennsylvania State University, University Park, PA, http://lema.smeal.psu.edu/kwasnica/.

Kauffman, R. J., and Wood, C. A. 2003. Running up the bid: Detecting, predicting, and preventing reserve price shilling in online auctions. In *Proceedings of the 5th International Conference on Electronic Commerce, ACM International Conference Proceeding Series*, vol. 50, pp. 259–265, Pittsburgh, PA. ACM Press, New York.

Kells, L. M. 1954. *Elementary Differential Equations*. McGraw-Hill, New York. Fourth edition.

Keynes, J. M. 1936. *The General Theory of Employment, Interest, and Money*. Harcourt, Brace & World, New York, 1964.

Klawans, Z. H. 1977. *Imitations and Inventions of Roman Coins: Renaissance Medals of Julius Caesar and the Roman Empire*. Society for International Numismatics, Santa Monica, CA.

Klemperer, P. 1999. Auction theory: A guide to the literature. *Journal of Economic Surveys*, 13(3):227–286.

Knetsch, J. L., and Sinden, J. A. 1984. Willingness to pay and compensation demanded: Experimental evidence of an unexpected disparity in measures of value. *Quarterly Journal of Economics*, 99(3):507–521.

Krishna, V. 2002. *Auction Theory*. Academic Press, San Diego.

Levin, D., and Smith, J. L. 1996. Optimal reservation prices in auctions. *Economic Journal*, 106:1271–1283.

Lind, B., and Plott, C. R. 1991. The winner's curse: Experiments with buyers and with sellers. *American Economic Review*, 81:335–346.

List, J. A., and Lucking-Reiley, D. 2000. Demand reduction in multiunit auctions: Evidence from a sportscard field experiment. *The American Economic Review*, 90(4):961–972.

List, J. A., and Lucking-Reiley, D. 2002. The effects of seed money and refunds on charitable giving: Experimental evidence from a university capital campaign. *Journal of Political Economy*, 110(1):215–233.

Lucking-Reiley, D. 1999. Using field experiments to test equivalence between auction formats: Magic on the internet. *American Economic Review*, 89(5):1063–1080.

Lucking-Reiley, D. 2000a. Field experiments on the effects of reserve prices on the internet: More Magic on the internet. Working paper, Department of Economics, Vanderbilt University, http://eller.arizona.edu/~reiley/cv.html.

Lucking-Reiley, D. 2000b. Vickrey auctions in practice: From 19th century philately to 21st century e-commerce. *Journal of Economic Perspectives*, 14(3):183–192.

Lucking-Reiley, D., Bryan, D., Prasad, N., and Reeves, D. 2000. Pennies from eBay: the determinants of price in online auctions. Working paper, Economic and Business Administration, Vanderbilt University, Paper 00–w03.

Mackay, C. 1841. *Extraordinary Popular Delusions and the Madness of Crowds.* Noonday Press, Farrar, Straus and Giroux, New York, 1970.

Marks, L. 1998. *Between Silk and Cyanide: A Codemaker's War, 1941–1945.* Free Press, New York.

McMillan, J. 1992. *Games, Strategies, and Managers.* Oxford University Press, New York, NY.

Mei, J., and Moses, M. 2004. Vested interest and biased price estimates: Evidence from an auction market. *Journal of Finance.* Forthcoming.

Milgrom, P. R. 2004. *Putting Auction Theory to Work.* Cambridge University Press, Cambridge, UK.

Milgrom, P. R., and Weber, R. J. 1982. A theory of auctions and competitive bidding. *Econometrica*, 50:1089–1122.

Mizuta, H., and Steiglitz, K. 2000. Agent-based simulation of dynamic online auctions. In *Proc. Winter Simulation Conference*, Orlando, FL.

Morgan, R. J. 2001. Efficiency in auctions: Theory and practice. *Journal of International Money and Finance*, 20:809–838.

Morgan, R. J., and Steiglitz, K. 2003. Pairwise competition and the replicator equation. *Bulletin of Mathematical Biology*, 65:1163–1172.

Morgan, R. J., Steiglitz, K., and Reis, G. 2003. The spite motive and equilibrium behavior in auctions. *Contributions to Economic Analysis and Policy*, 2(1). http://www.bepress.com/bejeap/contributions/vol2/iss1/art5.

Myerson, R. B. 1981. Optimal auction design. *Mathematics of Operations Research*, 6:58–73.

Nagel, R. 1995. Unraveling in guessing games: An experimental study. *American Economic Review*, 85:1313–1326.

Nash, J. F. 1950. The bargaining problem. *Econometrica*, 18:155–162.

Ockenfels, A., and Roth, A. E. 2006. Late and multiple bidding in second price internet auctions: Theory and evidence concerning different rules for ending an auction. *Games and Economic Behaviour*, 55:297–320.

Porter, D. P., and Smith, V. L. 1994. Futures contracting and dividend uncertainty in experimental asset markets. Social Science working paper, California Institute of Technology.

Porter, D. P., and Smith, V. L. 2003. Stock market bubbles in the laboratory. *Journal of Behavioral Finance*, 4(1):7–20. Reprinted from *Applied Mathematical Finance*, 1(2):111–127, Dec. 1994.

Rasmusen, E. 2006. Strategic implications of uncertainty over one's own private value in auctions. Working paper, Indiana University, http://www.rasmusen.org/papers/auction.pdf.

Resnick, P., Zeckhauser, R., Friedman, E., and Kuwabara, K. 2000. Reputation systems. *Communications of the ACM*, 43(12).

Rheims, M. 1961. *The Strange Life of Objects: 35 Centuries of Art Collecting*. Atheneum Publishers, New York. (Translated from the French by D. Pryce-Jones).

Richardson, A. 1992. An econometric analysis of the auction market for impressionist and modern pictures, 1980–1991. Senior thesis, Department of Economics, Princeton University.

Riley, J. G., and Samuelson, W. F. 1981. Optimal auctions. *American Economic Review*, 71:381–392.

Robinson, F. S. 1992. *Confessions of a Numismatic Fanatic*. Clio's Cabinet, Lodi, WI.

Roth, A. E., and Ockenfels, A. 2002. Last-minute bidding and the rules for ending second-price auctions: Evidence from eBay and Amazon auctions on the internet. *American Economic Review*, 92(4).

Rothkopf, M. H., and Harstad, R. M. 1995. Two models of bid-taker cheating in Vickrey auctions. *Journal of Business*, 68(2):257–267.

Rothkopf, M. H., Teisberg, T. J., and Kahn, E. P. 1990. Why are Vickrey auctions rare? *Journal of Political Economy*, 98:94–109.

Sanfey, A. G., Rilling, J. K., Aronson, J. A., Nystrom, L. E., and Cohen, J. D. 2003. The neural basis of economic decision-making in the Ultimatum Game. *Science*, 300:1755–1758.

Schmidt, U., and Zank, H. 2002. What is loss aversion? Working paper, Lehrstuhl für Finanzmarkttheorie, Universität, Hannover, Germany; and School of Economic Studies, University of Manchester, UK.

Shmueli, G., and Jank, W. 2004. Visualizing online auctions. *Journal of Computational and Graphical Statistics*. Forthcoming; available at http://www.rhsmith.umd.edu/ceme/statistics/AuctionDisplays.pdf.

Smith, A. 1776. *Inquiry into the Nature and Causes of the Wealth of Nations*. Knopf, New York, (1991 edition).

Smith, V. L. 1982. Microeconomic systems as an experimental science. *American Economic Review*, 72:923–955.

Smith, V. L., Suchanek, G. L., and Williams, A. A. 1988. Bubbles, crashes, and endogenous expectations in experimental spot asset markets. *Econometrica*, 56(5):1119–1151.

Steiglitz, K., Honig, M. L., and Cohen, L. M. 1996. A computational market model based on individual action. In S. Clearwater, editor, *Market-Based Control: A Paradigm for Distributed Resource Allocation*. World Scientific, Hong Kong.

Steiglitz, K., and Shapiro, D. 1998. Simulating the madness of crowds: Price bubbles in an auction-mediated robot market. *Computational Economics*, 12:35–59.

Stiglitz, J. E. 1990. Introduction to Symposium on bubbles. *Journal of Economic Perspectives*, 4(2):13–18. (The entire number of this volume is devoted to papers on bubbles.)

Thaler, R. H. 1985. Mental accounting and consumer choice. *Marketing Science*, 4:199–214.

Thaler, R. H. 1994. *The Winner's Curse*. Princeton University Press, Princeton, NJ.

Thaler, R. H. 2000. From Homo economicus to Homo sapiens. *Journal of Economic Perspectives*, 14(1):133–141.

Tversky, A., and Kahneman, D. 1991. Loss aversion in riskless choice: A reference-dependent model. *Quarterly Journal of Economics*, 106:1039–1061.

Vickrey, W. 1961. Counterspeculation, auctions, and competitive sealed tenders. *Journal of Finance*, 16:8–37.

Vincent, D. R. 1995. Bidding off the wall: Why reserve prices may be kept secret. *Journal of Economic Theory*, 65:575–584.

Whittle, P. 1992. *Probability via Expectation.* Springer-Verlag, New York.

Wilcox, R. T. 2000. Experts and amateurs: The role of experience in internet auctions. *Marketing Letters,* 11(4):363–374.

Wilson, R. B. 1969. Competitive bidding with disparate information. *Management Science,* 15(7):446–448.

Youssefmir, M., Huberman, B. A., and Hogg, T. 1994. Bubbles and market crashes. Dynamics of Computation Group, Xerox Palo Alto Research Center, Palo Alto, CA.

INDEX

Aalsmeer flower market, 19
absolute auction, 249
affiliated values. *See* values, affiliated
all-pay auction, 203–205, 222–223
allocation rule, 239;
    optimal, 244–247
Amazon auctions, 28–29;
    deadline extension, 28–29
Antinous, 79, 81
Aronson, J. A., 176, 269
artifacts (ancient), 53, 166–168
Ashenfelter, O., 22, 80–81, 84, 86–88, 90,
    95, 161, 263
Atlantic City, N. J. (auctions in), 157
Ausubel, L. M., 239, 263
Avery, C., 50, 263
Axelrod, R., 44, 165, 263

Babylon, auctions in, 5
Baertlein, L., 49
Bajari, P., 100, 106, 176, 263
Balenovich, D., 146, 263
Bapna, R., 97, 263
Battalio, R., 260, 266
Bauwens, L., 88, 263
Beauty Contest (Keynes), 148–149
Becker, C. W., 171
Bedford, E., 159
Beethoven, L. van, 1–2
Beggs, A., 87, 263
Berk, H. J., 56
Best Offer (on eBay), 23
bid shading. *See* shading
bidder rings, 158–161
bidders:
    asymmetric, 235–236
    asymmetrically informed, 41

symmetric, 68
symmetrically informed, 41
bidding histories:
    bidding war, 36–37
    early bidder, 38–39
    searching up, 54–55
    shill, 152–153
    sniping, 34–36
    start and end clustering, 34–36
bidding war, 36–37, 43, 140
bids:
    book, 7, 16
    from the chandelier, 22, 90
    off the wall, 22, 90
    phantom, 22, 90
Bloemenveiling Aalsmeer. *See* Aalsmeer
    flower market
Bluck, J., 9
Bogucki, P., 167
bots. *See* robot bidding programs
bounded rationality, 148
Boyd, J., 22, 263
Bryan, D., 58, 63, 138, 165, 267
bubbles. *See* price bubbles
Bulow, J., 50, 73, 104, 106, 201, 211, 236,
    244–245, 249, 251, 263
burned items, 80
buy-it-now option (on eBay),
    56–57
BVA. *See* Aalsmeer flower market

Caginalp, G., 146, 263
California auction, 25–28
Campbell, C. M., 265
Campbell, W. M., 260, 263
Capen, E. C., 260, 263
Case, J. H., 228, 264

Reiley, D. *See* Lucking-Reiley, D.
Reis, G., 27, 132–134, 268
replicas. *See* fakes
reproductions. *See* fakes
reserve, 79–80;
 in first-price auction, 91–92, 213–214
 in second-price auction, 90–91,
 215–216
 open, 52, 90–95
 open vs. secret, 99–100
 optimal, 92–93, 211–213
 secret, 53–56, 88–90, 161
Resnick, P., 165, 268
revelation principle, 239–241
revenue, 29, 73–74;
 in Riley and Samuelson's class,
 208–211
 marginal, 211
 of first-price auction, 191–192,
 197–198
 of second-price auction, 188–189
 ranking, 76–77, 121–124, 224–227,
 232–235, 257–259
revenue equivalence, 73, 84, 180–183,
 190–192, 200–202, 211, 242–243;
 failure of, 137–138, 256–259
 test of, 120–125, 256–259
reverse auction, 2
Rheims, M., 138, 268
Richard, J.-F., 155, 265
Richardson, A., 87, 268
Riley and Samuelson's class, 207–208
Riley, J. G., 51, 91, 101, 123, 179–180,
 205, 207–231, 235–237, 239, 241, 244,
 247, 249–251, 268
Rilling, J. K., 176, 269
rings. *See* bidder rings
risk aversion, 126–130, 224–227;
 constant-absolute, 128
 constant-relative, 128
 measurement of, 128–130
Roberson, B., 257–258, 264
Roberts, J., 201, 211, 244–245, 263

Robinson, F. S., 47, 61, 82, 98, 268
robot bidding programs, 177
Rome, auctions in ancient, 5
Roth, A. E., 29, 32, 36, 43–45, 47, 51,
 56, 268
Rothkopf, M. H., 21–22, 268
Rowlandson, T., 9
running, 22

sad-loser auction, 217–219, 228
Samuelson, W. F., 51, 91, 101, 123,
 179–180, 205, 207–231, 235–237, 239,
 241, 244, 247, 249–251, 268
Sanfey, A. G., 176, 269
Santa Claus auction, 219–222, 228
SBNE. *See* equilibrium, symmetric
 Bayesian Nash
Schmidt, U., 127, 269
screenscrapers. *See* programming projects
sealed-bid auction, 3, 7, 14
Sear, D., 172
second-price auction, 14, 25–26;
 differences from eBay, 30–32
 equilibrium, 215–216
 overbidding in, 256–259
 reserve in, 90–91, 215–216
Seinfeld, 10, 18
shading, 66–73, 189
shadowing, 42, 164
Shapiro, D., 146–147, 269
Sherman, R., 120, 128–130, 134, 148, 265
shill bidding, 22, 54, 90, 150–158;
 theory of, 155–156
shipping costs (on eBay), 60, 123–125
Shmueli, G., 62, 97, 263, 269
simulation, 144–147, 176
sincere bidding. *See* truthful bidding
Sinden, J. A., 46, 61, 266
single auction, 1
Slaveys (fakes), 170
Smith, A., 1, 269
Smith, J. L., 94–95, 106, 266